OTHER TITLES IN THE SERIES

Alternative Kilns
Ian Gregory

Ceramics with Mixed Media
Joy Bosworth

Ceramics and Print
Paul Scott

Coiling
Michael Hardy

Colouring Clay
Jo Connell

Crystalline Glazes
Diane Creber

The Electric Kiln
Harry Fraser

Glazes Cone 6
Michael Bailey

Handbuilding
Michael Hardy

Impressed and Incised Ceramics
Coll Minogue

Kiln Building
Ian Gregory

Large-scale Ceramics
Jim Robison

Lettering on Ceramics
Mary White

Oriental Glazes
Michael Bailey

Paper Clay
Rosette Gault

Porcelain
Jack Doherty

Raku
John Mathieson

Resist and Masking Techniques
Peter Beard

Setting Up a Pottery Workshop
Alistair Young

Single Firing
Fran Tristram

Slipcasting
Sasha Wardell

Stoneware
Richard Dewar

Soda Glazing
Ruthanne Tudball

Throwing Pots
Phil Rogers

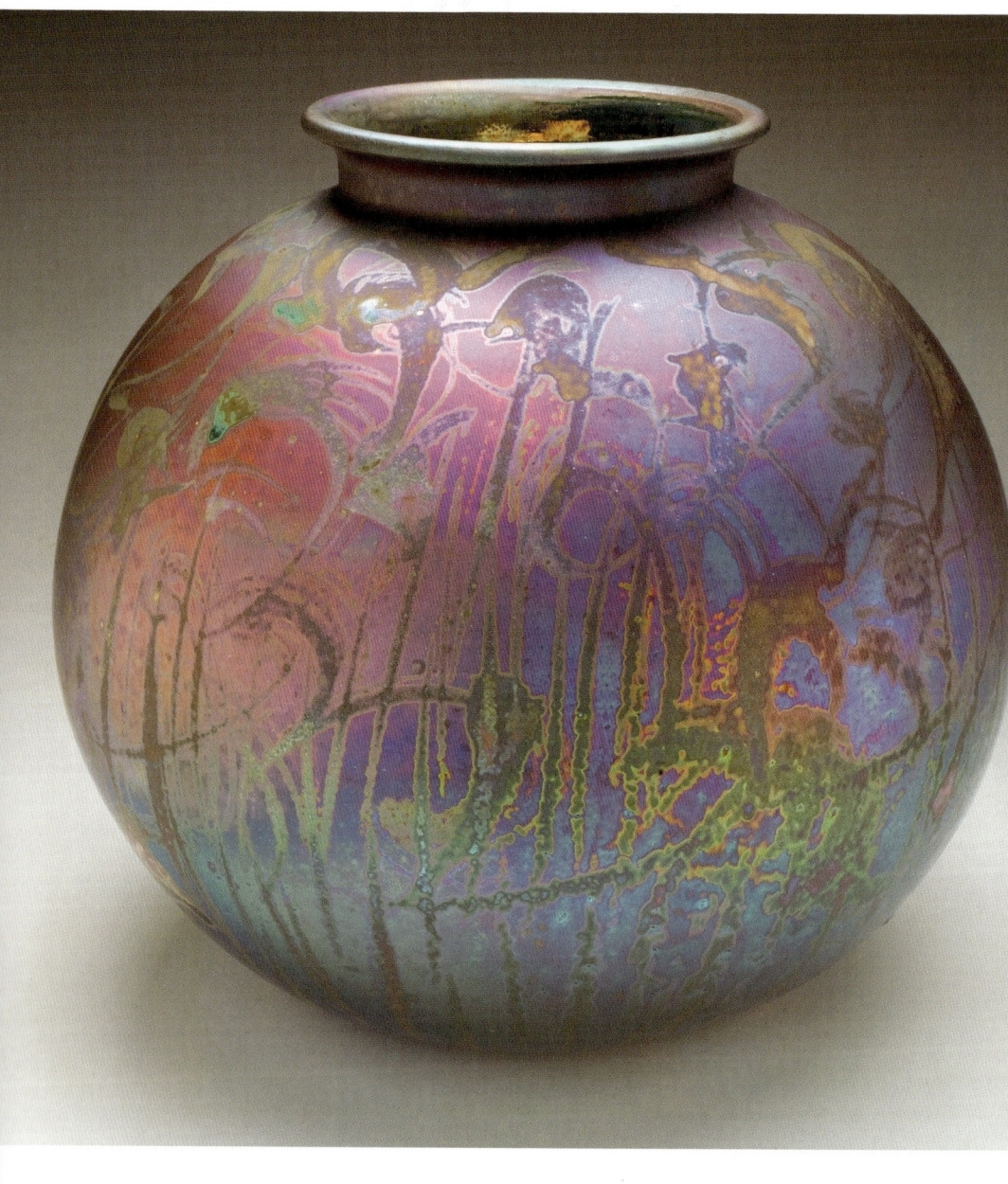

LUSTRE

Greg Daly

H E R B E R T   P R E S S
LONDON • OXFORD • NEW YORK • NEW DELHI • SYDNEY

Dedication

For John and Helen Daly

FRONTISPIECE Lustre-glazed vase with silver and copper decoration by Greg Daly, 2010. Ht: 28cm (11in.), dia: 29cm (11¼in.). *Photo by Stuart Hay.*

HERBERT PRESS
Bloomsbury Publishing Plc
50 Bedford Square, London, WC1B 3DP, UK
Bloomsbury Publishing Ireland Limited,
29 Earlsfort Terrace, Dublin 2, D02 AY28,
Ireland

BLOOMSBURY, HERBERT PRESS and the
Herbert Press logo are trademarks of
Bloomsbury Publishing Plc

First published in Great Britain in 2012
This edition published in 2018

A catalogue record for this book is available from
the British Library
Library of Congress Cataloguing-in-Publication
data has been applied for

ISBN: 978-1-9122-1765-6

6 8 10 9 7 5

Typeset in 10 on 12.5pt Photina MT
Book design by Susan McIntyre
Cover design by Sutchinda Thompson

Printed and bound in India by Replika Press

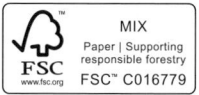

MIX
Paper | Supporting
responsible forestry
FSC™ C016779

To find out more about our authors and books
visit www.bloomsbury.com and sign up for our
newsletters
For product safety related questions contact
productsafety@bloomsbury.com

Cover image: Lustre-glazed bowl with silver
decoration by Greg Daly, 2010. Ht: 20cm (8in.),
dia: 28cm (11in.)

Contents

Introduction 7

1 Lustre: A brief history 11

2 Pigment lustres 29
  - Introduction 29
  - Developing glaze for lustre pigments 30
  - Mixing and applying a line blend 34
  - Glaze bases for lustre 40
  - Pigments 40
  - Mixing of the pigments 41
  - Colour blend for lustre pigments 47
  - Firing 50
  - Kiln types 53
  - Cycling of reduction for pigment lustres 57

3 Lustre glazes 65
  - Introduction 65
  - Mixing the tests 66
  - Process 68
  - Firing of lustre glazes 84

4 Resin lustre 95
  - Introduction 95
  - Making resin lustre 96
  - Application of resin lustre 108
  - Resist decoration methods 113
  - Firing 118

5 Fuming 123
  - Introduction 123
  - Fuming salts 123
  - Testing and firing 128
  - Fuming resin lustres 133

Bibliography 137
Chemical supplies 139
Orton cones 141
Temperature conversion chart 142
Analysis of frits used 142
Index 143

Acknowledgements

I would like to firstly thank all the lustre potters over the last 900 years or so for their passion, the work that they left us to enjoy and learn from, and their technical developments in the different forms of lustre. It is truly an amazing body of work.

To my family for their support, and sufferance in the testing and writing of this book, thank you. To my son John, for his help and attention for the photography. To Helen, my daughter, for her support too.

To the many potters who freely supplied images and knowledge of their techniques and approach, thank you. The National Gallery of Victoria and the Victoria and Albert Museum for their resources of lustreware.

To Alison Stace and Julian Beecroft for their patience in the editing of this book, thank you.

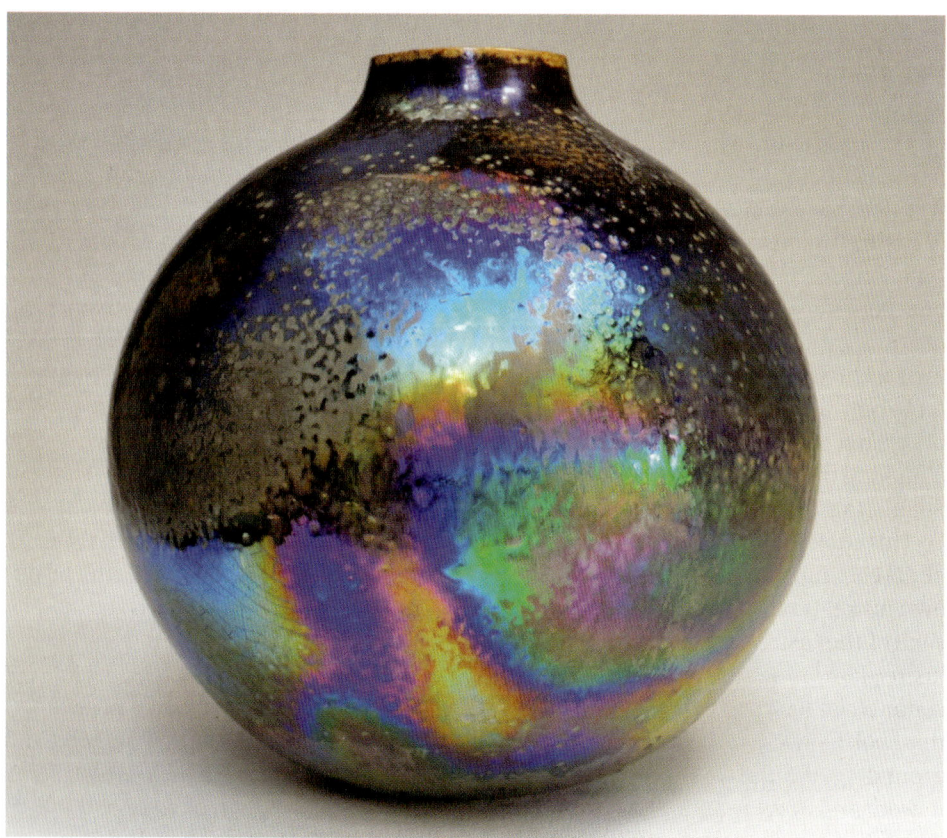

Fumed lustre-glazed vase by Greg Daly, 2010. Lustre glaze LG5. Ht: 38cm (15in.), dia: 35.5cm (14in.). *Photo by Greg Daly.*

Introduction

The history of lustre goes back over 1000 years, it has always drawn potters to its secrets, and drawn people to its ability to trap and reflect light in golds, reds and a rainbow of colours creating wares of magnificent beauty. The alchemy of lustre to change copper and silver into gold has been always been an allure for potters. In the beginning it was closely connected with alchemy, truly being able to turn copper into gold. Today lustre is still connected to science; you will find many papers by scientists on the internet on lustre and nano-particles and nano-technology, more in fact than papers by potters on the use of lustre. The history of the subject is very well documented in numerous texts but there has been very little over the centuries on how to create the actual lustre; it was knowledge that was passed on to only a few. Unlike other techniques of ceramic decoration it was made in just a handful of centres in the Middle East, Spain, Italy and a few other countries.

This book is about the adventure of developing, mixing and firing your own lustre. It will take you through each of the lustre techniques: pigment, lustre glaze/ in-glaze lustre, resinate/ commercial lustre and fuming. What this book focuses on is giving you a basic grounding of information from which to work and develop your choice of lustre. With each form of lustre we will use a simple base to begin. Going back to the basic make-up of each lustre, and understanding the variables that create each lustre, will give you the confidence to explore further.

Lustres in all forms are easily achieved, but there are many variables that change the final outcome. By learning how to begin you will be able to experiment further and develop your range by adding and controlling your own variations. The four main lustre techniques have their own characteristics and can be used in conjunction with each other to create further effects.

There is no hierarchy in lustre, as each technique has its own unique character. You may know some of them by different names, but this will be discussed as we go along.

I have used just two readily obtainable frits as the bases for the glazes. But, as you will see, you can use this same method with any of the frits/ fluxes available to you. The bottom line is that there is no secret knowledge; all that matters is learning how to read results and developing those that work well, in order to know the parameters within which you get good results. Observation is the key.

There are many pigment recipes for pigment lustres for which trying to acquire some of the materials can be very frustrating. However, it is also not necessary. We are going to keep it simple, as well as discussing what some of these components may or may not do in the mix.

Glaze is for me a journey, but lustre is a real adventure! Complete with highs and lows filled with excitement, challenges, mysteries, alchemy, discoveries and dazzling results. You will develop a high regard and respect for the lustre potters of the past. Lustre was 'high tech' in those days. Knowledge being passed on was very valuable, especially as there were no suppliers to purchase their silver nitrate and other materials from!

Throughout the text I will constantly make reference to health and safety. There are a number of materials that will be used which are poisonous, corrosive and very dangerous to your health and need to be handled with respect and care. Most are water-soluble and can be taken in through the skin; chlorides when heated give off chlorine gas. You will need masks that comply with the different environments you will find yourself in. Vapour masks, dust masks, latex gloves and face shields may be required, depending on what area you are researching. You need to take these health and safety precautions seriously.

OK, let these adventures begin.

All photos are by Greg Daly unless otherwise stated.

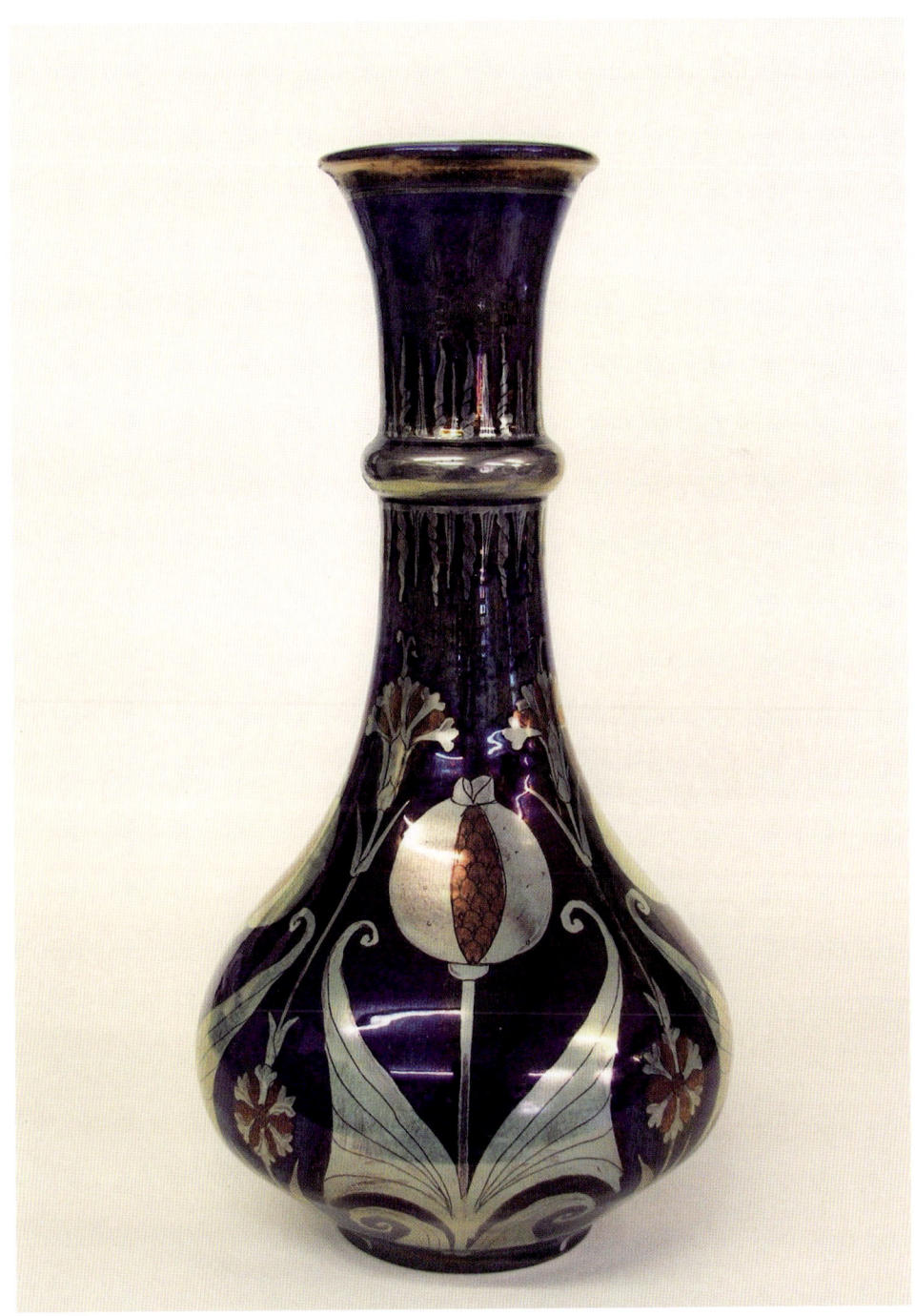

Tall vase by Jonathan Chiswell-Jones, Pomegranate and Dianthus pattern; copper and mixed
lustre. Transparent lead bisilicate and calcium borate frit glaze over ground of copper and cobalt.
Photo by Kerry Bosworth.

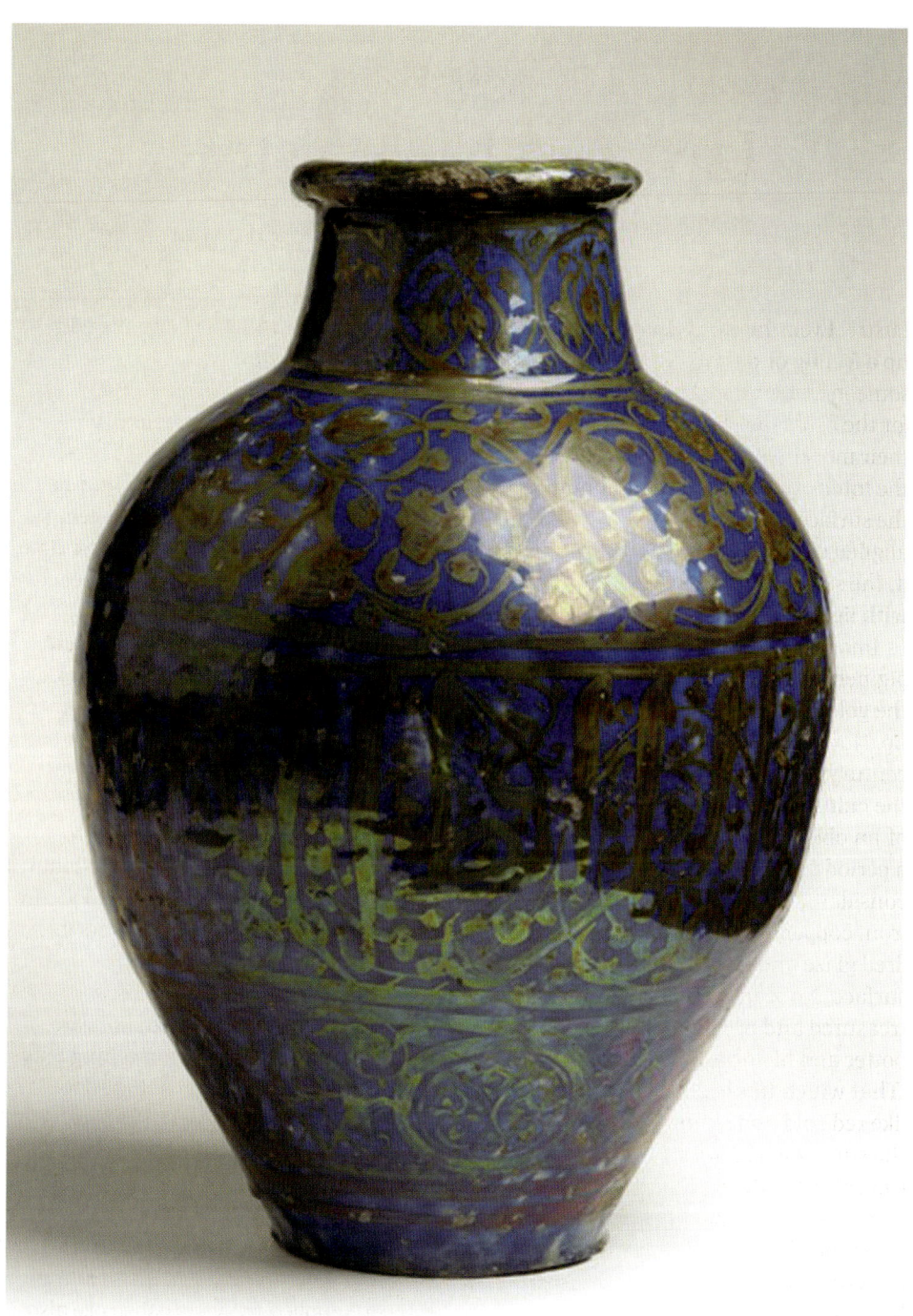

Fig. H1: Jar painted in silver lustre over a cobalt-blue glaze, Syria (probably Damascus), 1300–1400. Collection: V&A. *Photo © V&A Images/ Victoria and Albert Museum, London.*

Chapter 1

Lustre: A brief history

Lustre. Even the word itself conjures up a feeling of desire. Watch the eyes of someone when they behold a lustre pot for the first time. Listen to them, watch their movements: they are entranced by the intensity of the light as it illuminates the surface. In a dim room, if you are aligned correctly, when the light strikes it, the surface of the piece will explode with light and colour.

Imagine a potter rubbing away the pigment and revealing for the first time the golden lustre surface, suddenly lit up. Now take that potter back to the 9th century, where gold was so important to the cultural status, even the sacredness, of an object. Remember that this was a period in time when alchemy was considered science. Clay mixed with iron, copper and mercury, applied to a fired glaze and re-fired, created a gold surface. No wonder such a secret was treasured and prized. The medieval potter and historian Abu'l Qasim said, 'That which has been evenly fired reflects like red gold and shines like the light of the sun.' (*Ceramics from Islamic Lands* by Oliver Watson).

It is only now, with the development of nanotechnology, that the internal structure and complexity of the lustre layer can be fully understood and appreciated. Today all around us there is reflection. Skyscrapers with their gold-tinted windows reflect the sun,

intensifying sunrises and sunsets with a lustrous glow that would have been probably unimaginable and quite possibly vulgar to Abu'l Qasim. We live in a different time and aesthetics, one whose chief characteristic may be sensory overload. Nevertheless, seeing a lustre pot catch the light for the first time can still be a transcendental experience.

Back in the 9th century metal, glass and ceramics were breaking new technological ground. The three subjects also have a relationship with each other, in that they all relate to heating and changing the raw material into a new and usable material: copper and tin into bronze; sand and soda/lead into glass; and clay into a durable functional material. The science of the day, alchemy, was looking for existential answers in these changed material states.

In earlier times a lot of secrecy surrounded the making of lustreware, which, unlike today, was something only the rich could afford. It is not hard to see why. It was expensive to produce. A potter had to make the silver compound from silver and copper coins, design the kiln, and learn how to fire it — a few degrees one way or the other would result in no lustre. The thickness of the pigment applied with a brushstroke also needed to be correct (something that was only learnt with experience), as well as the composition of the base glaze, so there were a lot of elements to get right. So, after spending so much time and money on getting all of this right, why would you go and give away your hard-earned skill and knowledge, along with the marketplace you have created? If you were able to produce something that no one else could, and kept production small, you could control the market and make money. You will find the same story throughout history, with fabric dyes and metals, and today with software and computer chips. It's why the patenting process was devised.

Shrouded in secrecy, the lustreware vessels, whose glistening surfaces were achieved by transforming silver and copper into shimmering gold, must have seemed like the magical outcome of a mystical, alchemical process. It is no wonder that the knowledge of it was so closely guarded. Indeed, there were times when such expertise was nearly lost altogether, with only a few centres sustaining the practice. Nevertheless, there continued to be outstanding individuals who left their mark on the development of lustreware, such as Mastro Giorgio of Gubbio in the 16th century.

It was during this period, in 1558, that Cipriano Piccolpasso, a celebrated painter of majolica, wrote about the making of Italian lustreware, along with kiln plans and pigment recipes, the first written account of the lustre process in 400 years. From this seminal work, *The Three Books of the Potter's Art*, we can see that the principles underlying the making of pigment lustre today are the same as those that existed in the past. Of course, no matter how much help we get from modern technology in analysing how those pieces were made, there will always be gaps in our knowledge, but ready access to materials and kilns (not to mention the development of temperature controllers) makes the modern-day process easier than it has ever been.

Now with knowledge exchange being freer than at any point in history, lustre has been discovered afresh. William De Morgan, artistic polymath and one of the prime movers of the Arts and Crafts Movement, noted that knowledge of lustre was rediscovered again and again. His French contemporary Clément Massier's methods were said to be very demanding and intuitive and as he was very secretive, only a few who worked with him – such as Jacques Sicard, hired in 1901 to produce a line of iridescent art pottery – made lustre for anyone else. Sicard went to the USA to work for the Weller company. Most lustre potters feel that their intuition is the most important factor in making and firing lustre, though this is also underpinned by experimentation.

The lustre technique can be expensive and difficult, and needs perseverance. Early lustre makers tried to keep variables to a minimum, using one glaze and one or two pigments. Potters today want to explore the variables, opening up ever greater possibilities. But the lustre process, no matter how apparently simple you make it, requires patience as well as experience. The rewards, in my opinion, are unequalled.

In 1962, when Alan Caiger-Smith began to experiment with lustre there were three books available, two in English and one in Spanish. Each contained a few basic facts, which he found he was able to build on. He has written that he felt it was like a detective story, a mystery in which each piece of information helps to solve the puzzle, in this case of pigment lustre. His book *Lustre Pottery* stands out for the attention it gives to the history of lustre and the approach taken by various makers over the centuries.

What I find interesting is that of the articles and research papers being published today, more are being written by scientists than by potters. One area that interests those researchers is how lustre develops in regard to nanotechnology. (Nanotechnology is the study of manipulating matter at an atomic and molecular scale. The build-up of metal particles interacting with the glaze, creating a thin metal layer occurs at a nanostructural level. The interest is in how the lustre layer is built and constructed, and in the molecular changes it undergoes.)

The first lustre was produced in Egypt in the 6th or 7th century AD. Silver and copper were painted onto the surface of the glass and reheated in a reducing flame in order to reduce the metals back to yellow and/or red (see fig. H2).

The first pigment lustres came out of Egypt and were developed to decorate glass lamps, as being transparent the lustre colour shone when illuminated and enhanced the decoration. Lustre on pottery is said to have begun in Iraq in the early 9th century, and early fragments have been found in Samarra in Mesopotamia (now modern Iraq) and Fustat, the first Arab capital of Egypt, now part of old Cairo.

Then sometime between 856 and 863AD the Aghlabid Emir Abu Ahmand summoned a potter from Bagdad to make lustre tiles for the great mosque at Kairouan, establishing the tradition of lustre manufacture at Ifriqiya (Tunisia).

This bowl (see p.15) is made from

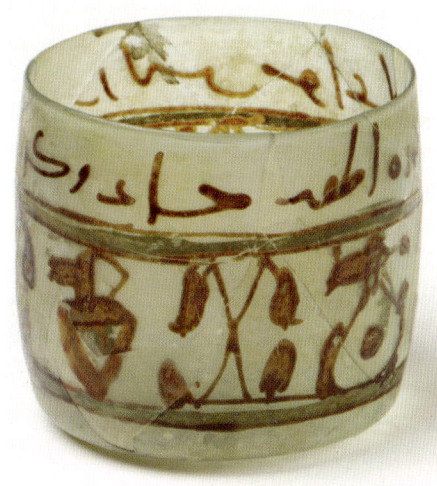

Photo © V&A
Images/ Victoria and Albert Museum, London

fritware (also called stone paste and quartz paste), an artificial ceramic body developed by Middle Eastern potters around the middle of the 11th century to imitate the hard, bright white body of imported Chinese porcelains. The main ingredient in fritware was fine quartz powder made by grinding sand or pebbles. Small quantities of white clay and a glassy substance known as frit were added to the quartz powder – the clay to give plasticity, the frit to fuse the body after firing. In the 12th and early 13th centuries, fritware was used in Kashan and other pottery centres in Iran. The decoration of this bowl was painted using silver lustre.

By about 1000AD, lustre potters are said to have emigrated from the city of Basra, in modern-day southern Iraq, and moved to workshops in Fustat, Egypt, then under the rule of the Fatimids. Fatimid dynasty lustres brought a new level of diversity to the prevailing pottery styles. Fatimid pottery was made from a coarser clay than was available to the Basra potters, and decorative techniques on the surfaces of the vessels reflect a much higher quality than the clay or glazes to which they were applied. The decoration of Fatimid lustres also shows a great deal of variation within a wide variety of styles, motifs and approaches, including royal hunting scenes, wrestlers, birds and gazelles; the artwork has a sustained informal naturalism.

In about the mid-11th century, the colours used in Fatimid pots became warmer, with golden, orange and red-gold lustres becoming dominant. Previously, lustre colours had been mainly greens, browns, dark crimson and yellows.

The main source of copper and silver for pigments was coins of the day, heated and soaked in acids then mixed with an iron-bearing clay, before being calcined and reground. Trace metals in the coins, such as tin, zinc and lead, would also have an effect on the final colour.

The use of acetic acid in alchemy extends back as far as the 3rd century BC, when the Greek philosopher Theophrastus described how vinegar acted on metals to produce pigments that were useful in art, including white lead (lead carbonate) and verdigris, a green mixture of copper salts including copper acetate.

During the period between the 11th and 13th centuries lustre work in the Middle East reached a height of magnificence it has rarely attained since. Abu'l Qasim bin Ali bin Muhammed bin Abu Tahir was a historian to the Mongol Court. In his book *The Virtues of Jewels and the Delicacies of Perfume*, he describes for the first time the making of a lustre pigment. Mixing red and yellow, arsenic,

gold, silver and copper; taking this mix and calcining it, then grinding it on a stone for 24 hours and mixing grape juice or vinegar with it; then applying it to a pot and firing in a smoke atmosphere for 72 hours; then washing off the pigment to reveal the surface colour underneath.

But Abu'l Qasim's description of lustreware only goes part of the way towards helping us understand the development of the ancient techniques of lustreware. The successful lustreware process involved painting metals. Copper and silver would be painted onto a glazed, fired vessel, and when fired at low red heat in a smokey atmosphere it produced a lustrous golden shine. After firing, the vivid colours of the glaze sparkled with blue and yellow iridescence. When the potters added lead to the glaze mixture, they produced a metallic gold lustre. The Arabian lustres were fired between 500 and 600°C (932 and 1112°F). These lustres contained vermilion (arsenic), whereas Spanish lustres contained cinnabar (mercuric sulphide). These two ingredients act as a flux to adhere the lustre to the glaze surface at a temperature below that at which the glaze softens. Alan Caiger-Smith refers to these lustres as 'active recipes'.

Lustre technique and knowledge arrived in Moorish Spain in the 12th centuries with the spread of Islam across Northern Africa. Here Hispano-Moresque lustreware developed in Spanish centres such as Calatayud in Andalusia, Malaga in Granada, Manises in Valencia and Muel in Aragon.

Many Moorish potters settled in Manises in the 13th and 14th centuries. The lustre made here was very rich and coppery, with decoration involving cobalt (blue) and copper lustre. However, by the

Fig. H3: Lustre bowl, fritware, Iran (1180–1220). *Photo © V&A Images/ Victoria and Albert Museum, London.*

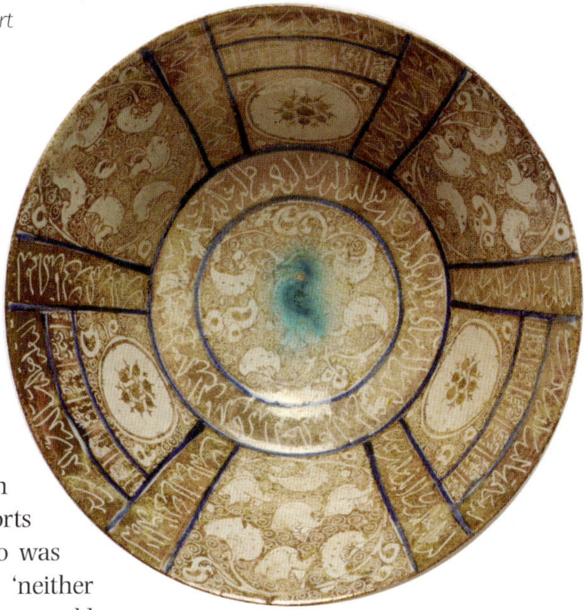

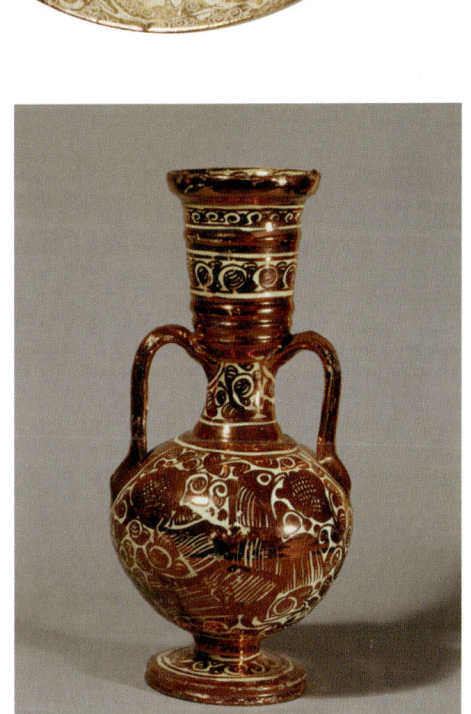

1600s there was a shortage of tin for a white base glaze, and the pale buff clay body that was used instead is what gives this ware its own distinctive character.

Of course, other centres also wanted this knowledge and there is a story of the Conde de Floridablanca in 1785, who sought to encourage the manufacture of lustreware in Madrid. In reaction to these efforts the then mayor of Manises, who was himself a potter, remarked that: 'neither his words nor even the ingredients would be enough to achieve success because of the infinity of small operations which only a skilled master could carry out.' (*Spanish Pottery 1248–1898*, by Anthony Ray).

In the 15th century experiments in lustre were also being carried out in Italy in Gubbio, Faenza, Deruta and Pesaro, and by the early 16th century Deruta and Gubbio in particular had developed their own style and gained much acclaim in the century that followed. Deruta's lustres are a pale gold with blue decoration (a pale gold to Manises's rich copper) which is very fine, as can be seen in Fig. H6, H7 and H8.

Gubbio on the other hand was known for its rich ruby-red lustre. The most famous artist from the city, Mastro Giorgio, took lustre and decoration to a new level of mastery. He developed spectacular rich red lustres, but it was his overall skill in layering of the decoration and different lustres that set him apart. From research carried out in recent

Fig. H4: Vase with copper lustre decoration. Manises, Spain (1625–1700). *Photo © V&A Images/ Victoria and Albert Museum, London.*

15

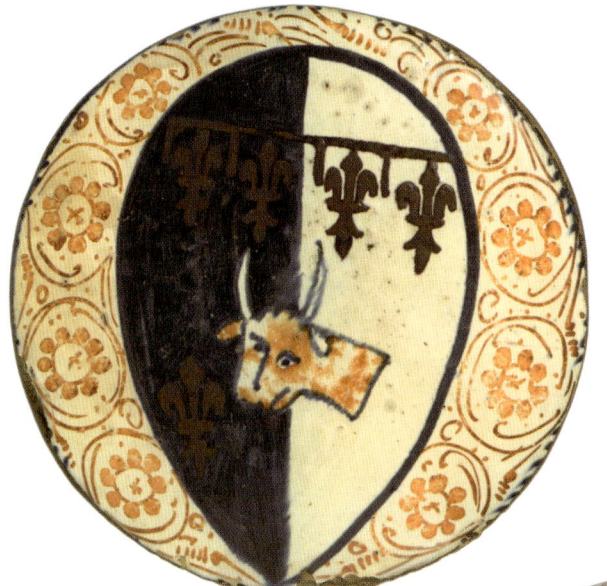

Fig. H5: Plate, tin-glazed earthenware with lustre decoration. Valencia, mid-16th century. Collection of the V&A. *Photo © V&A Images/ Victoria and Albert Museum, London.*

Fig. H6: Dish, Deruta, 1520. Tin-glazed earthenware dish (majolica), painted in cobalt-blue and yellow lustre with a portrait of a lady. Collection of the V&A. *Photo © V&A Images/ Victoria and Albert Museum, London.*

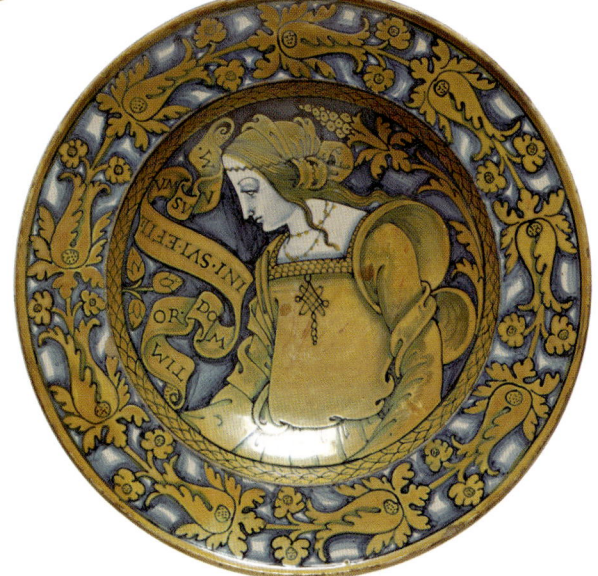

years (see articles p.137–8), it has been found that a clear glaze was laid over a white glaze, which alone can change the colour and quality of the lustre. But on some works the red lustre had been fired first, followed by a silver-gold lustre. The red from copper needs a higher temperature to develop, while the gold from silver a lower temperature (Fig. H7 and H8 are both examples of this).

Lustre reached a high point of development in Europe during the 18th century. But after this heyday comes a period in which the technique dwindles and almost disappears, with production continuing in just a few centres. This

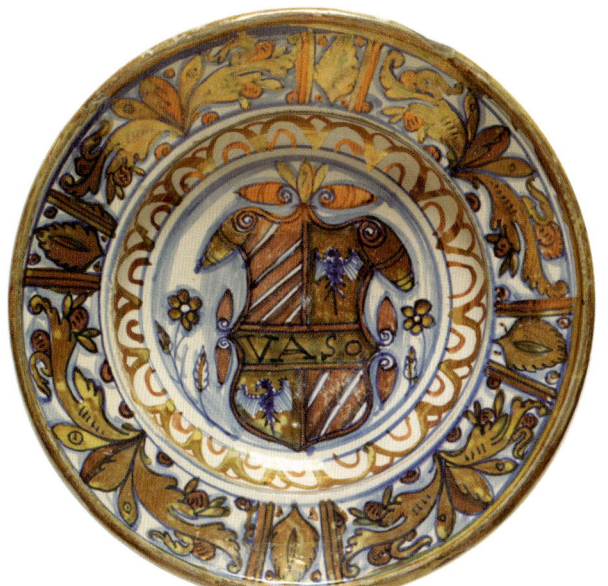

Fig. H7: Dish with, in the middle, a shield with the arms of Montefeltro, probably made in Gubbio, Italy, about 1505. Tin-glazed earthenware. Note the use of both the yellow and red lustre decoration. Collection of the V&A. *Photo © V&A Images/ Victoria and Albert Museum, London.*

Fig. H8: Plate, Mastro Giorgio Gubbio, 1522. Plate bearing a depiction of the Virgin and Child. Collection of the V&A. *Photo © V&A Images/ Victoria and Albert Museum, London.*

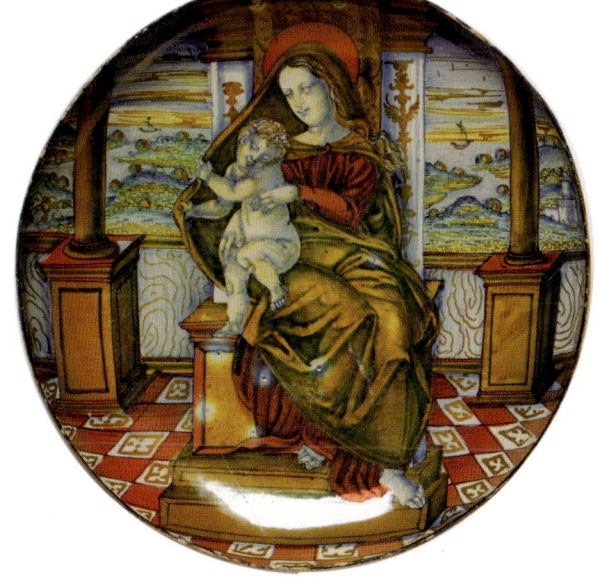

may well have been due to fashion, but the link between generations handing on knowledge was almost cut.

Time passes and by the early 19th century lustre has nearly disappeared. Indeed it isn't until the late 1800s that we see the rediscovery of the technique but with a new and exciting perspective as knowledge of materials and process is rediscovered and explored. Thus Clément Massier in Belle Époque France inspired Zsolnay in Hungary and De Morgan, Pilkington's and Royal Doulton in the UK.

Massier was born into a family of ceramicists and took an interest in the business from an early age. In 1884, after many years of work, study and travel, he relocated his share of the family firm to Golfe-Juan on the Côte D'Azur and began producing Hispano-Moresque-influenced pottery, using silver and copper oxide glazes made iridescent in a smoky kiln. In this he was assisted by the Italian ceramicist Dominique Zumbo (1854–1939), whom he had hired in 1879. Already proficient in the use of metallic oxides, in 1884 Massier produced his first lustre glazes, featuring golden-amber or ruby-red lustre on a cream ground.

During the next two years Massier and Zumbo continued their research, and in 1886 presented multicoloured lustreware at the National Industrial and Fine Arts Exposition in Marseille. The final component for success would arrive in 1887 with the hiring of Lucien Lévy-Dhurmer (1865–1953), whereupon Massier introduced fiery lustre glazes enriched with etching and painting, applying them to forms ranging from thrown to individually hand built to slip-cast vessels. He soon developed a busy factory and a showroom that boasted an elite international clientele.

What for me marks out Massier was that he used not only pigment lustres but lustre glazes too. This opened up a whole new area of surface colour and richness. Then to acid-etch areas back, showing the turquoise glaze underneath, gave a whole new dimension to lustre decoration. In Fig. H9 (and the detail) we see a control of colour and surface unlike pigment lustres that have gone before.

The secrets of lustreware were already being re-explored in the 1850s in Italy and in the 1880s in Spain, generally in relation to copies of historic examples

from the past. In England, William De Morgan duplicated Italian Renaissance lustreware and was successfully followed by the Pilkington firm. By 1900 the Florentine firm of Arte della Ceramica Firenze was creating modern ceramics with iridescent glazes. The Danish potter Herman Kähler of Næstved specialized in richly hued iridescent glazes on zoomorphic vases. The Swedish firm of Rörstrand tried its hand at iridescent wares, as did the Porceleyne Fles pottery in Delft, the Hungarian firm of Zsolnay, and some Austrian potteries. In short, while Massier's glazes were distinctive and extraordinarily successful, they did fit into a larger picture of the revival of lustre pottery. Although we tend to overlook it today, iridescent pottery was universally admired at the turn of the century, its forms and sumptuous colour in harmony, with the Art Nouveau movement.

William De Morgan was a highly inventive man who relished a challenge, be it in engineering, chemistry or design. While imagery and shapes from Persia and elsewhere may have inspired him, he always gave them his own imaginative twist. His particular passion was for Persian colours and lustre glazes and, typically, he set about rediscovering the difficult art of lustre firing for himself. In the following quote De Morgan begins by referring to the 1862 International Exhibition in London (where he had seen lustre work from the Ginori factory at Doccia near Florence and from Carocci at Gubbio), before moving on to the work of Massier at the 1889 Exposition Universelle in Paris:

'In spite of the Doccia and Gubbio reproductions, an impression continued to prevail that the process

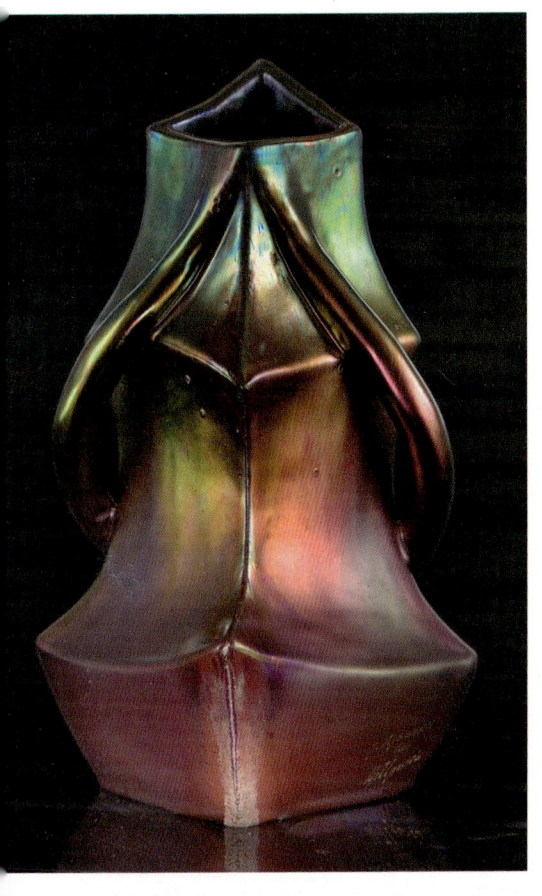

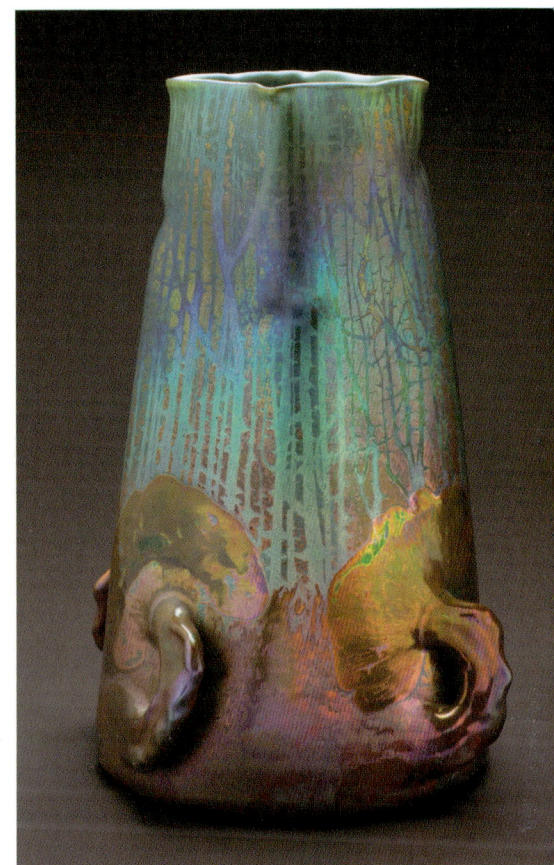

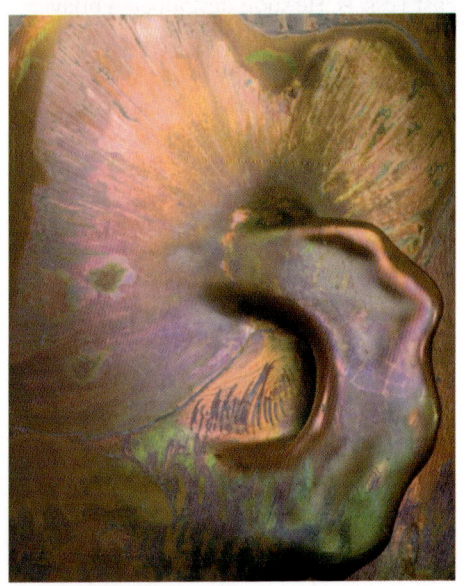

ABOVE LEFT Fig. H10: Jérôme Massier. Handbuilt,
reduced lustre-glaze vase, *c.* 1900, France.
Photo courtesy of Jason Jacques.

ABOVE RIGHT Fig. H9: *Golden Mushroom Vase* by
Clément Massier, France 1900. (Detail, right).
Photo courtesy of Jason Jacques.

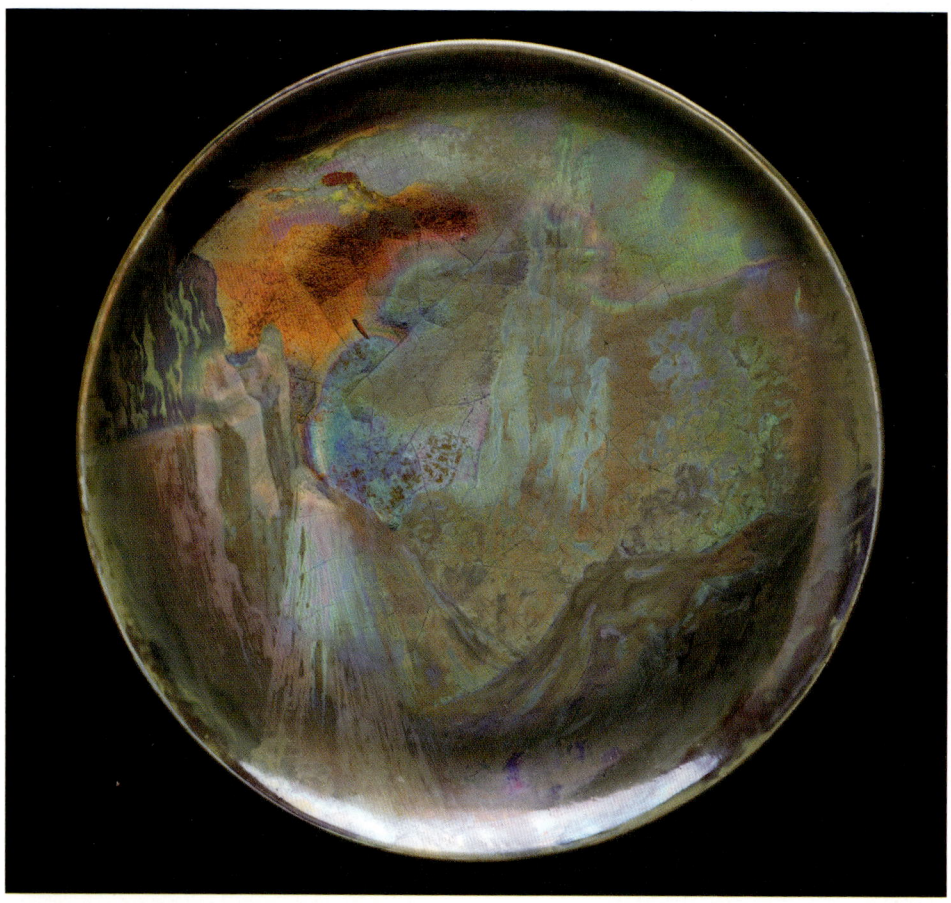

Fig. H11: *Sunset Plate*, by Clément Massier, France 1900. *Photo courtesy of Jason Jacques.*

was a secret. I used to hear it talked about among artists, about twenty-five years ago, as a sort of potter's philospher's stone. My attention was attracted to some very interesting work of Massier, of Cannes, in the last Paris Exhibition, by a newspaper paragraph headed, "Rediscovery of a Lost Art". In fact, rediscovery appears to have dogged the footsteps of the lustres from the beginning. I rediscovered them myself in 1874 or thereabouts. Very likely some others have an earlier record than mine, but the only one I chanced upon when I

was in Staffordshire was that of the late Mr Clement Wedgwood, who showed me a number of experiments which would have been successful if the glaze had been suitable, and a small sample shown me by the late Mr Colin Campbell.'
(From *Leadless Decorative Tiles, Faince and Mosaic*, by William J. Furnival, 1904.)

De Morgan did give lectures on his technique and knowledge of lustre, in his words, 'to save others needless work'. He goes on to say, 'I have, of course, tried endless modifications of the ordinary process, such as using special woods for smoking, sawdust, shavings, paraffin, and other combustibles. Any of these answer the purpose, the application being slightly varied. But nothing material has come of any of these experiments, and the process remains substantially the same as the first.' (*Journal of the Society of Arts*, 24th June 1892).

DeMorgan used kaolin as his carrier, with gum arabic for ease of handling. He fired in a closed muffle kiln, at low red heat with the reducing material in the form of a charge of dry wood, sawdust and woodchips introduced into the muffle at the bottom of the kiln (directly onto the floor of the kiln), with a space left clear under the ware. This was repeated until the draw tests showed the desired surface had been achieved. A muffle kiln is a sealed chamber around which the heat/flame circulates. It is used mainly in the Potteries region for the firing of enamels to low temperatures (see Fig. H12 and H13).

In 1889, while exhibiting in Paris, Vilmos Zsolnay (owner of a successful pottery factory at Pecs, in Hungary) was mesmerized by Massier's 'reflective-metallic' glazes, and soon afterward conducted the first successful experiments in iridescent glazes at the Zsolnay factory. In 1893 ceramic chemist Vinsce Wartha developed a rich red iridescent glaze for Zsolnay, marketed as eosin. The term, named after the Greek goddess Eos, goddess of dawn, was soon to be used to denote the rainbow-hued iridescent finish. Used in combination with etching and gold lustre, it appeared for the first time in the winter of 1899–1900 in Vienna before going on to conquer the spectators at the Exposition Universelle in Paris in 1900 (see Figs H13 and H14).

The secret eosin glaze causes porcelain to appear as if it has an iridescent

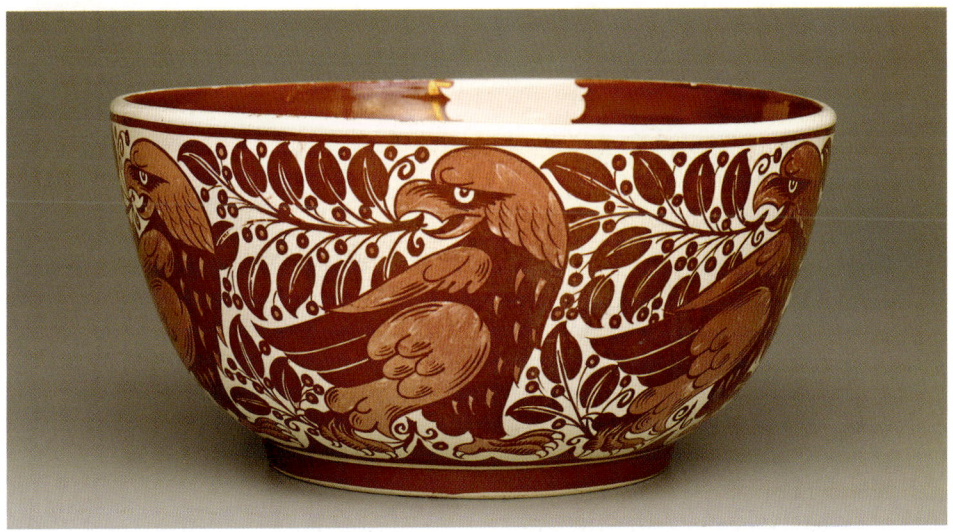

Fig. H12: Copper lustre decorated bowl by William De Morgan & Co. (*c.*1882), England. Earthenware (note the two-tone reds in the lustre). Collection of the National Gallery Of Victoria. *Photo courtesy of the National Gallery Of Victoria (Australia).*

metallic surface in different colours that change with the angle of reflection. Typical colours include shades of green, red, blue and purple.

All forms of lustre have their own character and when compared do have a different feel and quality. The different forms today are pigment lustre (smoked, Arabian), lustre glaze, resinate lustre and fumed lustre.

Resin lustres became a blessing to industry, as they gave repeatable results unlike the more traditional pigment lustres, on the other hand, which needed special knowledge of how to use and fire them, and gave variable results even then. Resin lustres (better known as commercial lustres) were easy to use and needed no special firing techniques, as they are fired in an oxidizing atmosphere and give predictable results.

Resin (commercial) lustre is the most recently developed form of lustre. There is a French patent from 1856, filed by Brianchon, which describes the making of this lustre. But there is also evidence that Wedgwood and other potteries from the Stoke-on-Trent area in the UK were already using this type of lustre (see Chapter 4).

The secret to liquid gold lustre was maintained for many years in the 19th century by the French, until the Duterte brothers working in Paris took out a patent in the mid 19th century. An account of their process was recorded in a book written by Felix Hermann in 1897. To summarise: gold powder was mixed with mercury and oils to create a lustre called burnished or matt gold that needed to be burnished after the firing. This was the most common form of gilding used on wares. Unfortunately, it was very dangerous to the decorators, and many came down with mercury poisoning.

The second lustre technique used by potters was fuming, which was developed initially by glass workers. The iconic Tiffany glass (Fig. H4) is a classic example of what could be achieved in blown and fumed glass in the early 1900s. It is said Tiffany was inspired by Clément Massier's

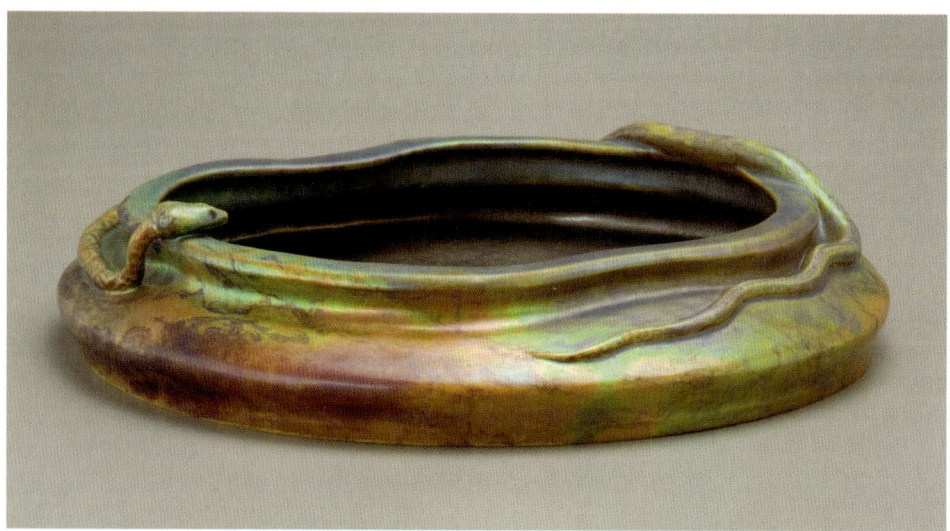

Fig. H13: *Snake Centrepiece*, by Zsolnay c.1900 Hungary. *Photo courtesy of Jason Jacques.*

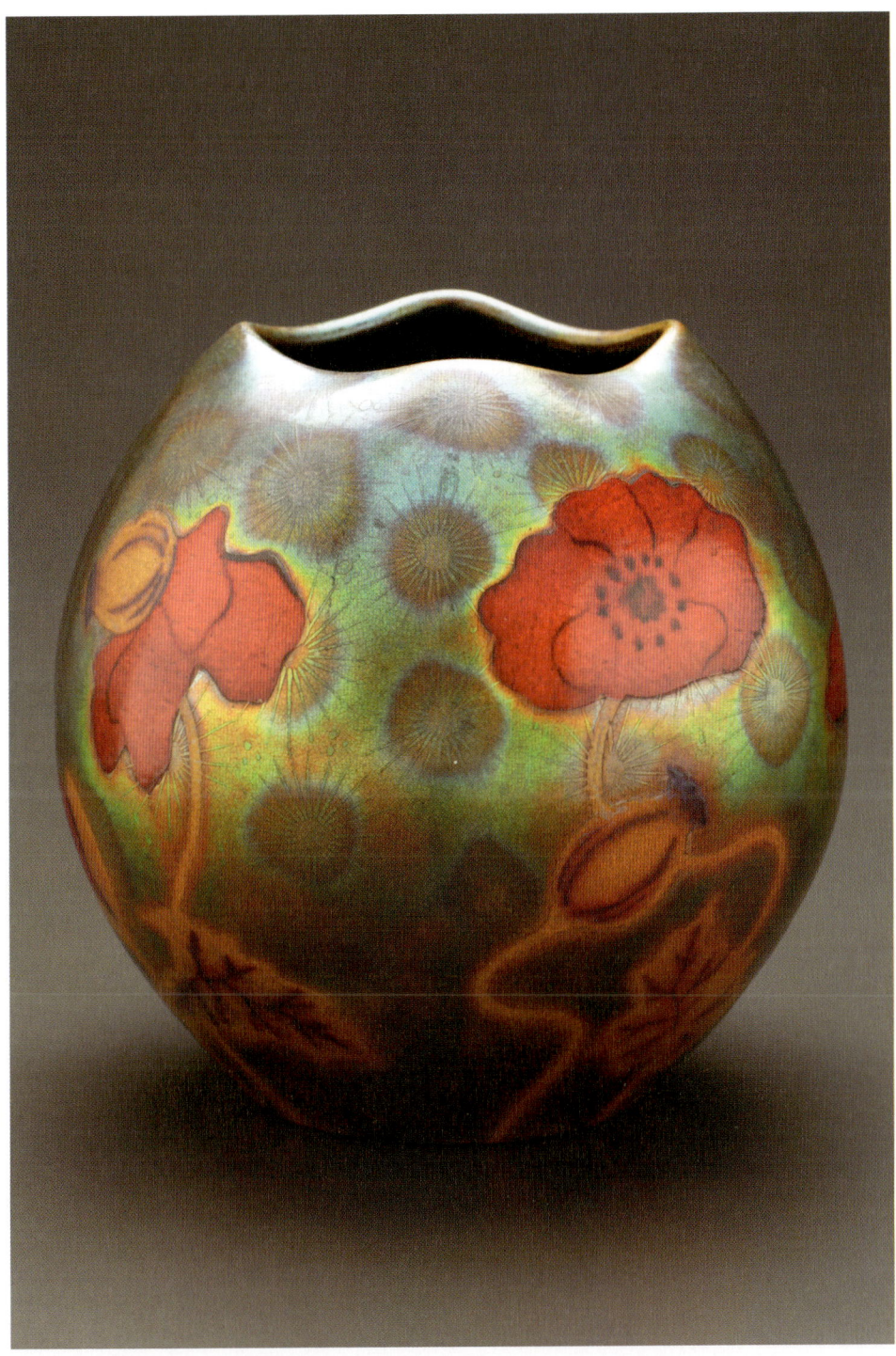

Fig: H14: *Opium* vase by Zsolnay, c.1902 Hungary. *Photo courtesy of Jason Jacques.*

ceramic work, which employed both pigment and lustre glazes (see Figs H10 and 11). To give a brief outline, with fuming, a tube is placed into the spyhole with stannous chloride (other chlorides can be used such as silver, barium or zinc but stannous or tin is the most common) which is then blown into the kiln.

In a book published in 1904, *Leadless Decorative Tiles, Faience and Mosaic*, the author William J. Furnival refers to lustre in the following terms: 'Whatever may be the powers of savants in other realms of art, the ceramicist, at least, is able to mix cunningly devised compounds which yield beautiful iridescent effects when applied to his wares.'

Pilkington's Lancastrian Pottery (1891–1931) was a company made up of multi skilled people. William Burton was a chemist who came from Wedgwood who in 1903 began experimenting with lustre, so that by 1906 production of pigment-based lustreware was awarded a Grand Prize at the Milan Expo. Designers like Walter Crane, (see Figs H16 and H17), Lewis Day and Gordon Forsythe worked with Burton to create the lustreware. Pilkington was also known for other types of ware including aventurine.

William Burton developed a large pallet of lustre colours that was unusual in one workshop. From strong reds, ruby reds, golds, greens, silver with satin surface, iridescent yellows and greys. With many designers and decorators they developed a clear style that

distinguished Pilkington's Lancastrian lustreware from other types.

The discovery and development of resin lustres became a blessing to industry that gave repeatable results, unlike the pigment lustres that needed special knowledge of use and firing, gave variable results even then, and didn't suit industry processes. Resinate lustres, better known as commercial lustres, were easy to use and no special firing techniques were needed as they were (and still are) fired in an oxidizing atmosphere and gave

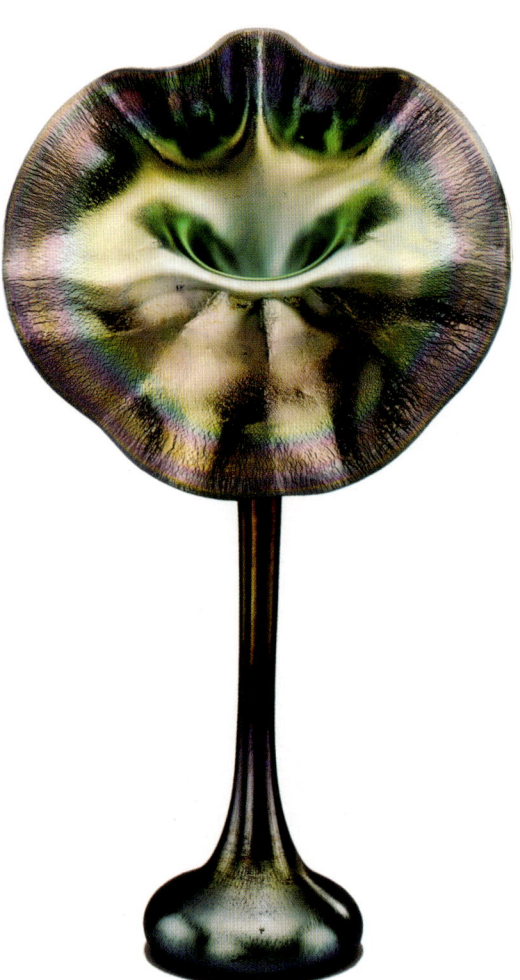

Fig. H15: *Jack-in-the-pulpit Vase*, Louis Tiffany (designer), Tiffany Furnaces, New York (manufacturer). Fumed glass. Ht: 50 cm (19¾ in.). *Photo courtesy of the National Gallery of Victoria, Australia.*

predictable, reliable results. They are still used today in industry.

There are two types of commercial lustre, coloured and colourless. The coloured lustres are from gold, cobalt and platinum, while the colourless are made from bismuth, silver, lead and zinc for example. Sulphates and chlorides (See Chapter 4).

The colours ranged from mother-of-pearl (a colourless lustre) to bismuth, with its iron-gold tone, to uranium a greenish-yellow. One part bismuth lustre mixed with five parts gold lustre gives a copper sheen. Add two parts bismuth and a blue shade can be obtained. Metal oxides were dissolved in acids to obtain nitrate, while acetates of the metals were then dissolved in pine resin, heated and mixed with a suitable solvent, lavender oil being the most commonly used solvent.

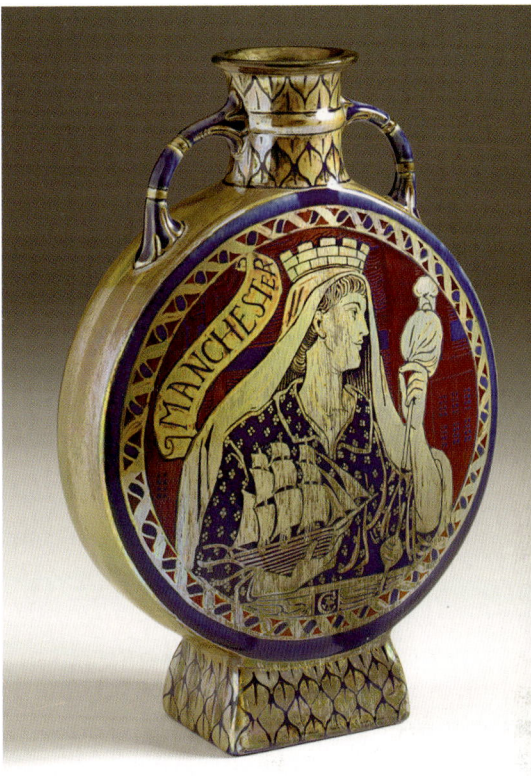

Fig. H16: Pilgrim Flask by Pilkington's Tile & pottery Co., c. 1900. Earthenware (lustre), ht: 38cm (15in.), dia: 28cm (11in.). Walter Crane (designer) and Richard Joyce (decorator). Photo courtesy of the National Gallery Of Victoria, Australia.

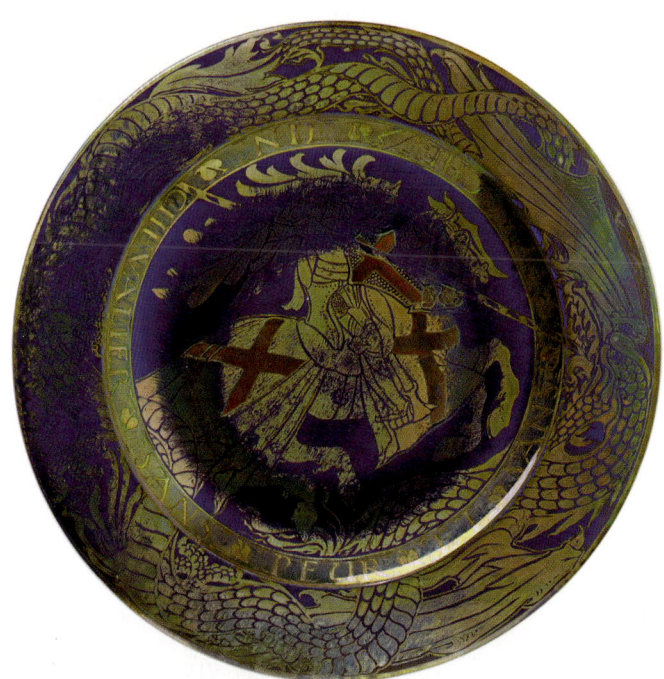

Fig. H17: Charger by Pilkington's Tile & Pottery Co., 1910. Earthenware (lustre), dia: 48.5cm (19in.). Walter Crane (designer), Charles Cundall (decorator). Collection of the National Gallery Of Victoria. *Photo courtesy of the National Gallery Of Victoria, Australia.*

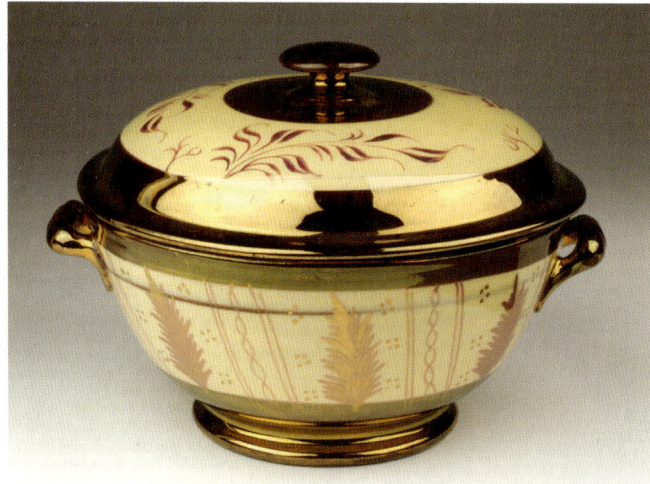

Fig. H18: Covered bowl, Staffordshire, 1830. Lead-glazed earthenware with 'gold' (copper) lustre decoration. Collection of the V&A. *Photo © V&A Images/ Victoria and Albert Museum, London.*

Fig. H19: Earthenware teapot painted in gold-based lustre. Made by A.E Gray & Co Ltd, Stoke-on-Trent, 1937. Collection of the V&A. *Photo © V&A Images/ Victoria and Albert Museum, London.*

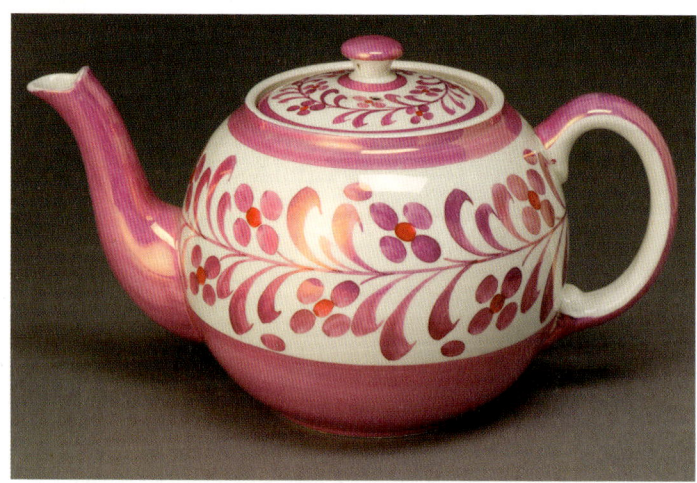

As mentioned at the beginning of this chapter, there has been more written about lustres by scientists and researchers than by potters in the last 10 years. Lustres have come under close scrutiny in both their formation and composition. One of the most interesting findings is the way lustre pigments develop in relationship to the glaze. What has been found is a nano-sized metal/glass composite made of metal (copper and/or silver) nanoparticles embedded in the glassy matrix. What is interesting is that the metal lustre layer doesn't lie on top of the glaze but a fine layer of colourless glaze between 1 and 2 nanometres thick develops over the metal layer. This has an effect on the reflection and refraction of light, helping to develop the iridescence, that special quality that gives lustre life.

The mechanism for the formation of the nanoclusters is still under debate. It is assumed that the formation consists of silver and copper ions penetrating into the glaze. This occurs through an ion exchange between the alkali ions present in the glaze and silver and copper ions present in the mixture of the lustre pigment. (For further research on nanotechnology, see the References.)

Alan Caiger-Smith and Sutton Taylor are two contemporary potters who have revived lustre and pushed the use and understanding of lustre further. Both have exhibited, talked and written on lustre over the years giving guidance to others wanting to take up the challenge through knowledge and recipes. Sutton Taylor is now exploring old tailings (unused and unprocessed materials) from lead and copper mines in his local area, using these raw materials which are rich in metal sources, as a source for pigments, slips and lustre glazes, and opening up new possibilities.

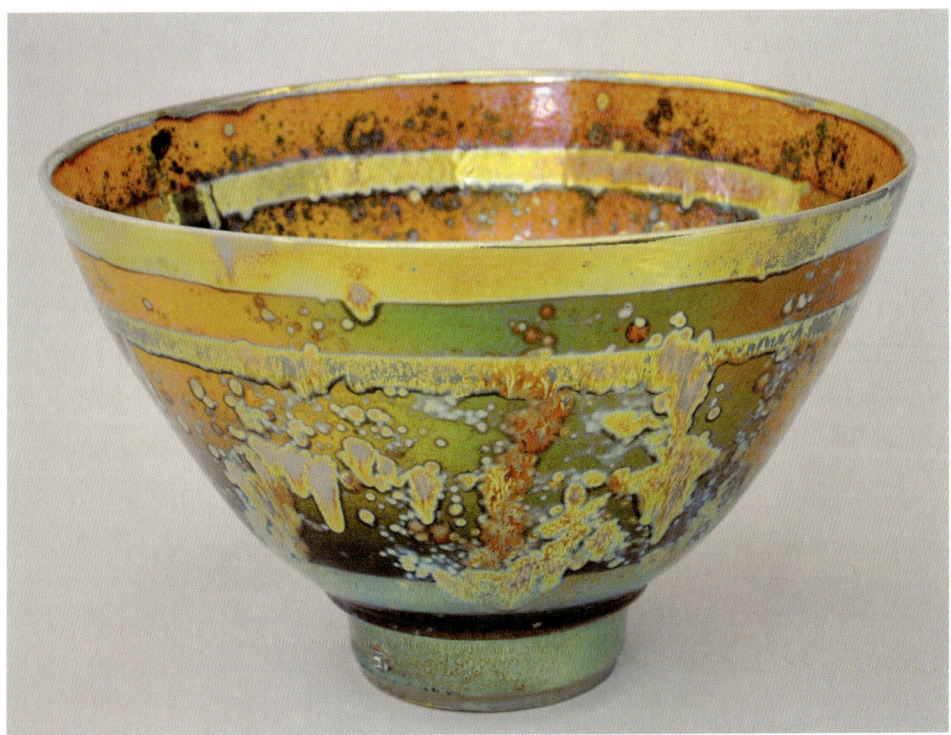

Fig. H20: *Large Elliptical Bowl* by Sutton Taylor, UK,. 20 x 40 cm (8 x 15¾ in.).

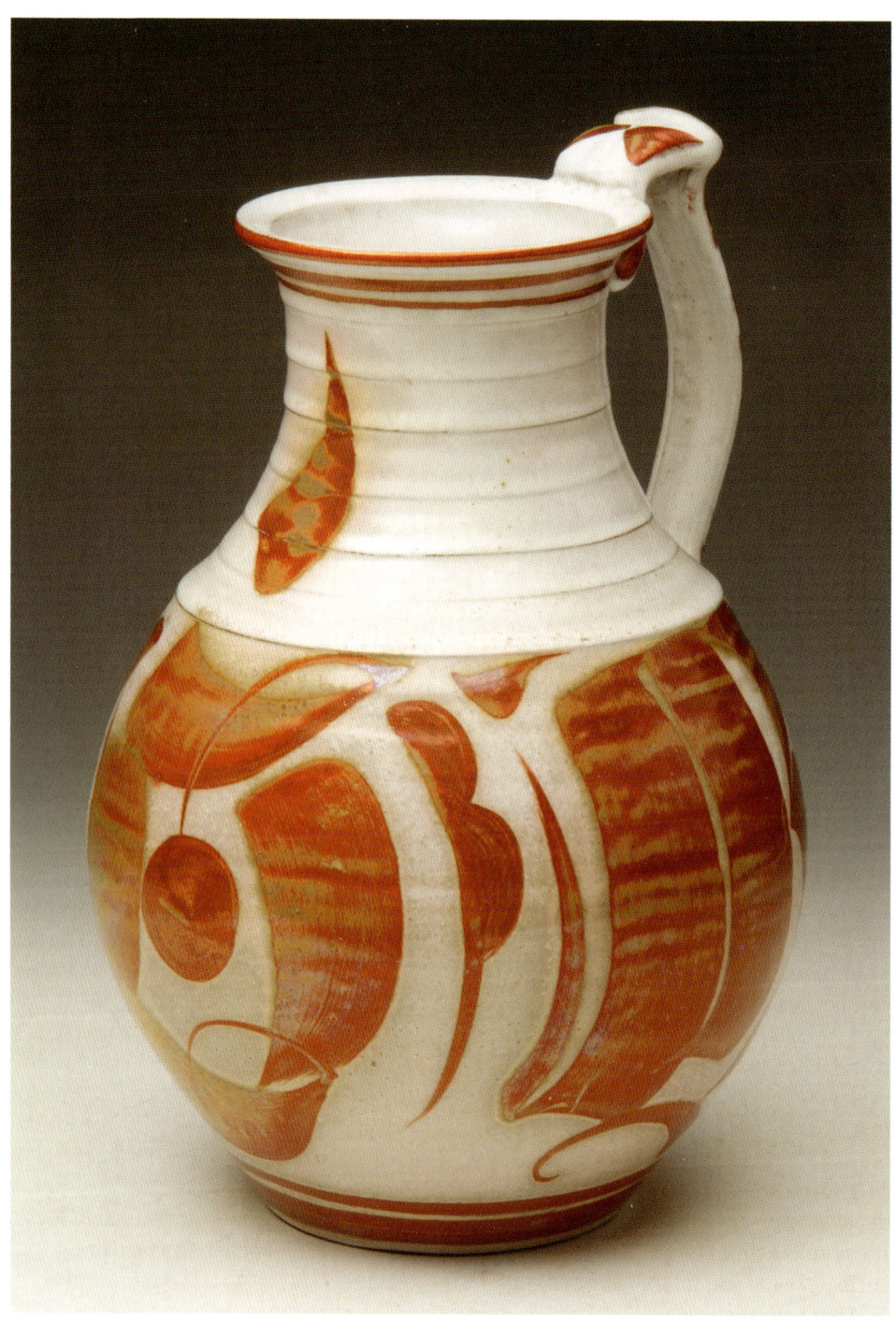

Fig. P1: Lustre pitcher by Alan Caiger-Smith, UK, *c.*1990. Silver/copper pigment on tin glaze. Ht: 25.5cm (10in.). *Photo: Howell Lambert.*

Chapter 2

Pigment lustres

Pigment, Persian, Arabian, smoked and transmutation lustres are different names for the same lustre technique. They began to be used on pottery from the 9th century onwards, beginning in Egypt, having originated for use on glass (see Chapter 1). The overview of this technique is that you take a fired glazed pot – preferably an earthenware glaze traditionally including a percentage of lead. You then apply to the surface of the pot (traditionally a brush was used for the decoration) pigment based on an iron-bearing clay with copper and/or silver added. You then fire the pot to just red-hot (around 630°C/1166°F to start with, see Chapter 4 for more information on firing cycles). The temperature at which reduction begins can be from 600°C/1112°F–650°C/1202°F, although there are occasions where this can be lower or higher (see Chapter 4) and you should heavily reduce the kiln, usually over a number of reduction cycles. Take care not to over-fire the lustre, or the glaze will soften and the pigment will fuse to it. Remove draw rings from the kiln to observe the lustre development. After the firing, wash off the pigment and you will have a lustred surface where you applied the pigment.

That is the technique put simply, but of course it is never quite as simple as that. It isn't difficult either, but you need to take each step in turn. Initially, keep your variables down until you have a feeling for how the processes and variables work together. Developing that feeling for how things work with this and other lustres is important. Yes, at times you have to trust instinct, your gut feeling, watching, learning, observing and removing draw rings, kiln placement, cones, time, flame and smoke – and a very exciting adventure it is. We will begin by going through each of the variables and processes one at a time. Each element that goes into creating the pigment lustre will be considered. By learning to control them, you will begin to feel like an alchemist, as you reap the rewards of creating surfaces that are beloved of both science and the gods.

With pigment lustres there are three main factors that play an important part in the final result – the pigment and base glaze, length of reduction and temperature. All contribute to the final colour from a careful interplay.

The composition of the glaze also has an effect on the outcome of the lustre surface. The higher the optical density of the glaze, the higher the refractive index, giving the glaze brilliance. That is why a lead glaze has a more brilliant surface appearance than one that is alkaline. There are various other factors to consider though, when developing a glaze for lustre.

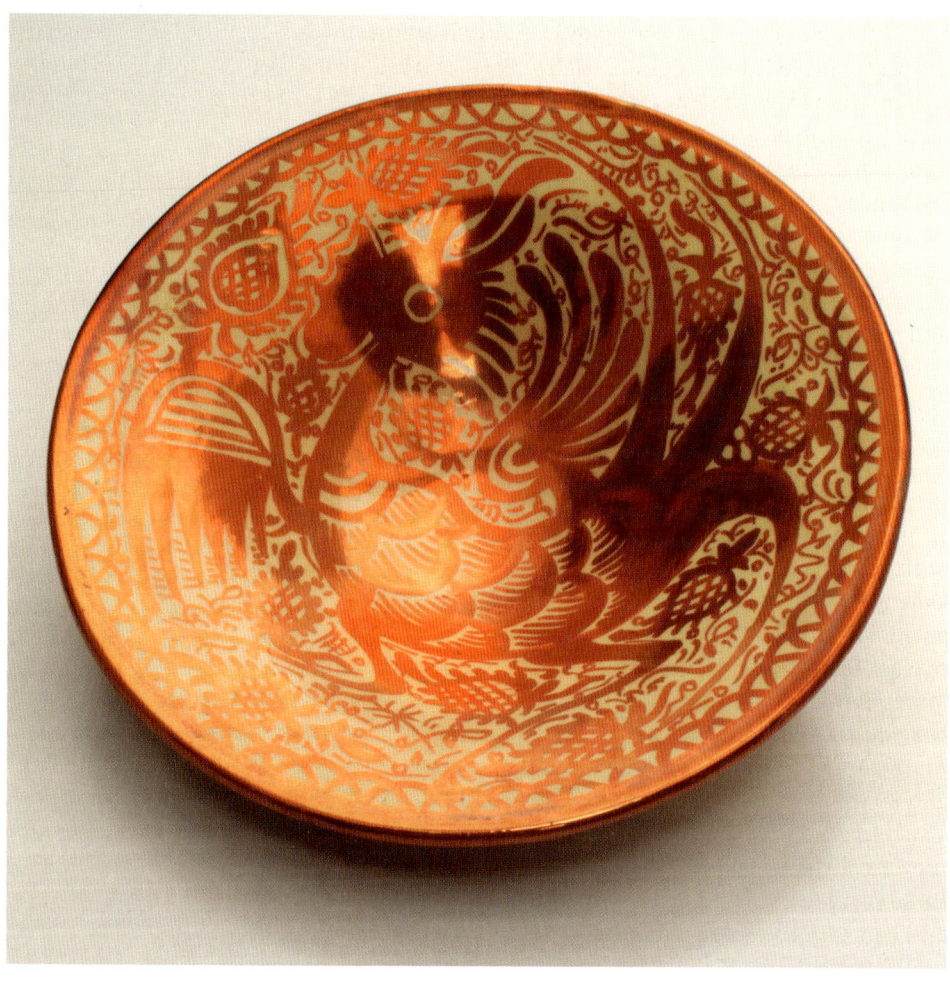

Fig. P2: Copper-pigment lustre-decorated bowl by Gimeko Rios, Manises, Spain, 1988. Dia: 33cm (13in.) *Photo: by Greg Daly.*

Developing glaze for lustre pigments

First you need a base glaze that will accept and develop the lustre from the pigment. You should begin the development of the base glaze using a simple and straightforward series of tests. Alternatively, you can use base glazes developed by other potters as a starting point, though one problem with this can be that the frits used in the making of these glazes can vary slightly from one country to another; if the frit is harder (i.e. it melts at a higher temperature), the lustre may not develop as well or even at all.

If you begin by mixing your own glaze, you will gain a clearer understanding of the glaze and pigment synergy. The base glaze needs to soften at a low temperature, between 600°C (1112°F) and 700°C (1292°F), to allow the development of the metal layer in/onto the glaze. Silver prefers the lower end of this range where copper end of this range where copper reds are best achieved at the higher end. It is more than likely that more than one glaze base will be used from one series of tests to achieve these results. Both a lead and an alkaline glaze are used, based normally on frits. For pigment lustre try a combination of different frits as they will give different results in colour, tone and response from silver and copper. The reason for the use of frits instead of raw fluxes like lead, soda ash and borax, for instance, is that frits are created through a combination of fluxes melted with silica, alumina, calcium etc. into a fluid glass. This is then poured into a water tank, quickly quenching the mix and leaving lumps of the fritted mix to be ground into a fine powder. The two main reasons for this is to render poisonous materials (like lead bi-silicate) non-poisonous, so they can be handled and materials that are water soluble (like soda and borax) into a non-soluble material. The reference to frits in this case, is that they are fluxes used to form the bases of these earthenware glazes. Vary the frit and you vary the outcome.

First select a frit or frits as your base. In these tests I used a soft borosilicate frit (Ferro 3110/ 4110) and lead bisilicate. You can use other frits, of course, but some have a higher temperature for melting and do not easily lend themselves on their own to developing a good base for lustre. A lower-temperature frit will be more useful.

A simple test is to mix up your frits on their own into a paste and apply a pea-sized amount of frit to one end of a tile and fire it standing up or at an angle of 60–90° (preferably on a test shelf). Fire it to 1000°C (1832°F). You will see how the frit has melted and flowed. Low-temperature frits will flow down the tile, where others (higher melting temperature frits) will move only a short way, and still others (the highest-temperature frits) will remain opaque and pea-shaped. This will give you an indication of which frits to use. Choose the more fluid frits; you can then add these to the more refractory frits to create a base glaze.

Using a line blend to arrive at a base glaze is simple and easy to do. For the purposes of this exercise, I have taken a frit line blend using 4 parts of silica and 6 parts of kaolin. You can choose different ratios and materials. I am adding these two materials as they are refractory and the kaolin will help with glaze suspension. If you dry-mix the silica and kaolin first, you only need to weigh one addition. Weigh up silica (40g) and kaolin (60g), place in an airtight container and shake.

Line blend of frit additions of silica 4g, Kaolin 6g each test:

Frit 100	Frit 100	Frit 100	Frit 100	Frit 100	Frit 100
	+ Silica 4 Kaolin 6	+ Silica 4 Kaolin 6 = + Silica 8 Kaolin 12	+ Silica 4 Kaolin 6 = + Silica 12 Kaolin 18	+ Silica 4 Kaolin 6 = + Silica 16 Kaolin 24	+ Silica 4 Kaolin 6 = + Silica 20 Kaolin 30

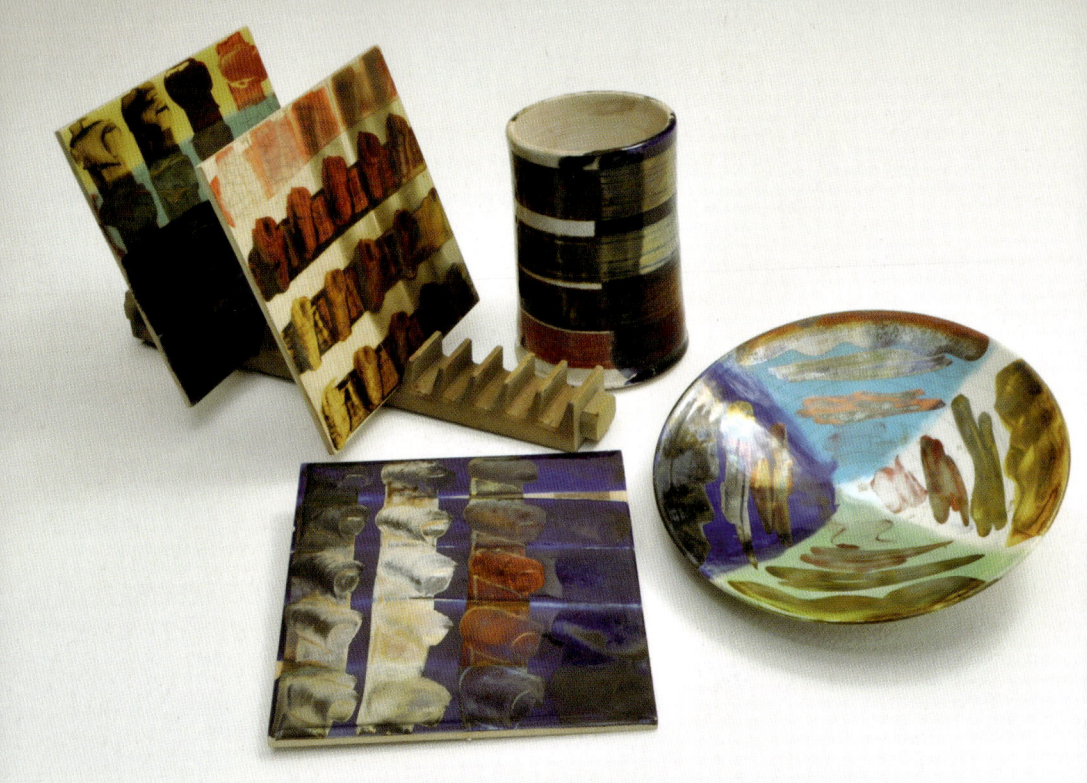

Fig. P3: Different forms for testing glazes and pigments; part of a tile crank used to stand tiles up for firing.

To make testing quick and easy, involving the minimum amount of weighing, you need to consider the following. First, what are you going to test the glazes on? The use of individual tiles for this type of testing isn't the best, as you need to keep all the tests together in the lustre firing. I would suggest 15cm (6in.) square tiles, as the surface is large enough to give good feedback information about glaze and lustre. Commercial bisque tiles are suitable for this testing (you can test a chosen glaze on your clay body for glaze fit later) or else thrown cylinders, bowls or extruded shapes. In any case, a large surface area is required to hold a number of tests for easy comparison. The tiles are fired in a rack in the glaze firing to see if there is any movement and in the lustre firing for better interaction with the reduction atmosphere. (See Fig. P3: bowl, cylinder, and tile in rack.)

Each person has their own way of going about weighing and mixing glazes. If you can do it fast and simply, the process of testing isn't a laboured procedure. For mixing I use either an electric hand food blender for larger mixes over 200g (7oz), or a 2.5–4cm (1–1½in) firm, springy nylon paintbrush (not a soft bristle); the springy bristles will easily break down any lumps. Always add powder to water (as opposed to the other way around) to help prevent lumps. When adding oxides or small amounts of materials to an already mixed glaze, you should also add a small amount of water to the surface. This will be absorbed by the material being added, especially with oxides, and will mix easily with the glaze mixture.

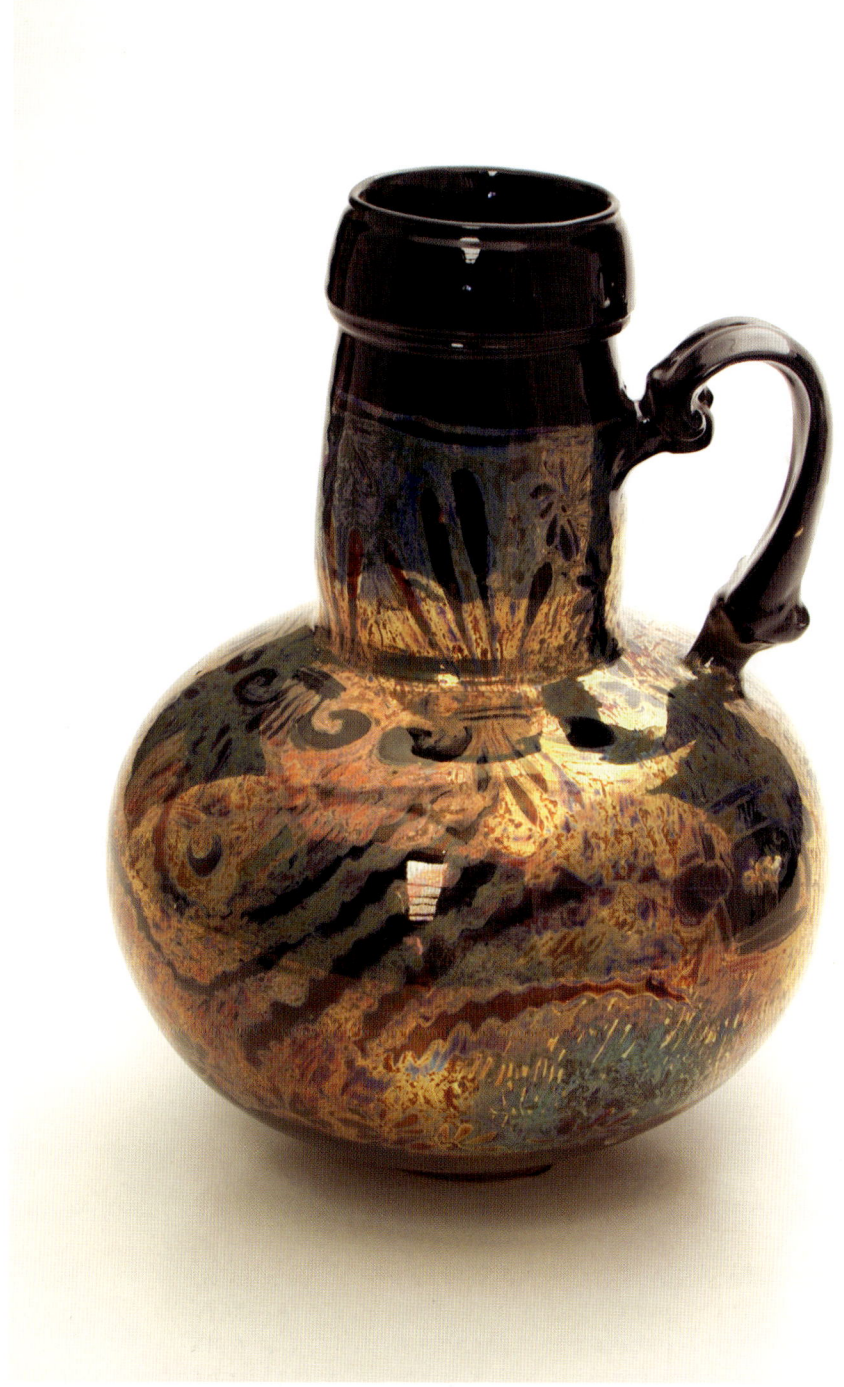

Fig. P4: Lustre-decorated vessel by Alan Peascod (Australia), 1985. Silver/copper pigment lustre over blue earthenware glaze. Ht: 36cm (14¼in.). *Photo by Greg Daly.*

Mixing and applying a line blend

Begin by weighing 100g of frit. Add to water and mix (less water is better, as more can be added later to achieve consistency). The first test will be just frit. In this test there are five glaze tests with four pigments to be tested on each of these five. Divide up your tile (cylinder, bowl) into five equal parts – I use a pencil as it helps with even space application. Mark the base test number on the back. I find full information handy, as then you don't have to keep referring to notebooks. Tiles have a large space on the back to contain all the information, including later lustre firing information. Having mixed up the frit, apply with a 2.5cm (1in) paintbrush. To the frit add 10g of the silica/kaolin mix, then mix well and apply. Repeat this procedure four more times. The final mix will be: frit 100g and silica/kaolin 40g (silica 16g, kaolin 24g). With some frits this last test may produce a satin glaze, but it can still accept a lustre.

You will be correct in thinking that as you are applying glaze to the tile you are decreasing the amount of the mix, which can unbalance the ratios, so the fifth and last test would be more like silica/kaolin 50% and frit 50%, not 40/60%.

It is fine to use this method for small test rings, but in covering a larger area you'll find more variation will occur. You can take this into account later if the tests show promise in lustre response, or to avoid this variable, start off with a larger amount of frit and adjust the additions as necessary. If you double the frit quantity you need to double everything, this uses more materials but means more reliable results. So, for example: Begin with a 200g double-mix frit, then add 20g silica/kaolin.

In Fig. P5, we see this line blend on the two left-hand tiles; the two tiles on the right are the same but with 10g tin oxide added. The two top tiles have been reduced at 650°C (1202°F) with seven cycles of reduction. The two tiles below have been reduced at 700°C (1292°F) with seven cycles. The four pigments used will be discussed later. Each pigment is applied across the five glaze mixes. As can be seen, the results change, in some cases dramatically. The red lustre from copper is enhanced when applied to the glaze with tin. Also to be noted is the red, which develops better at the higher temperature. Resulting base glazes are made with soft sodium borosilicate frit and the mix of silica/kaolin additions of 10g and 20g (silica 10/kaolin 20).

Line blend

Test I	1	2	3	4	5
Frit (soft sodium borosilcate) Ferro Frit No. 3110/4110	100g	100g	100g	100g	100g
Silica/kaolin in the ratio 4:6	0g	10g	20g	30g	40g

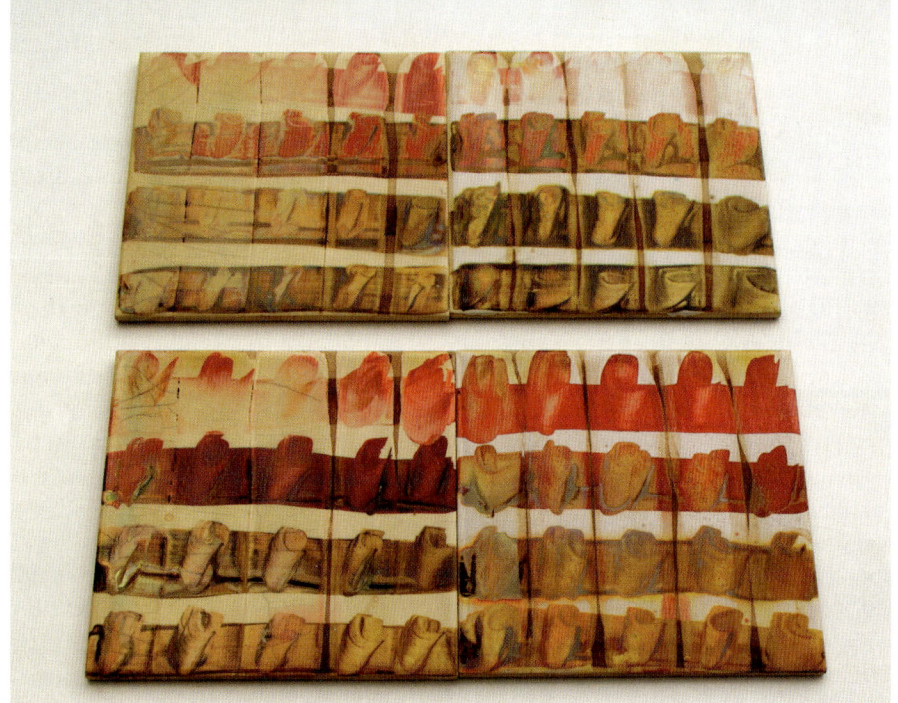

Fig. P5: Soft borosilicate frit line blend with silica and kaolin, with four pigments applied over the fired glaze for their response to the glazes.

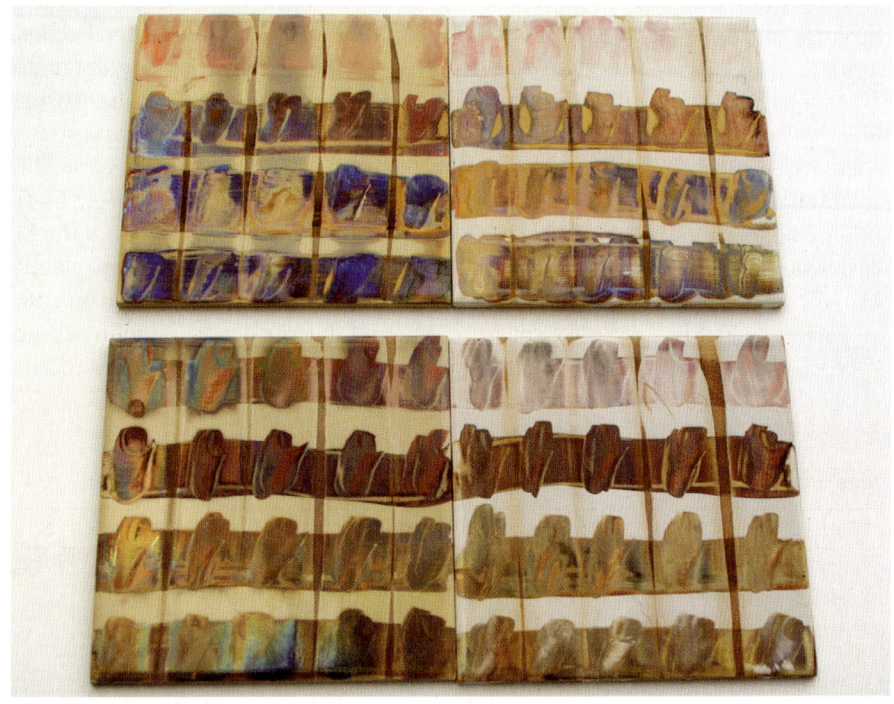

Fig. P6: Lead bisilicate frit line blend with silica and kaolin, with four pigments applied over the fired glaze – showing their response to the glazes.

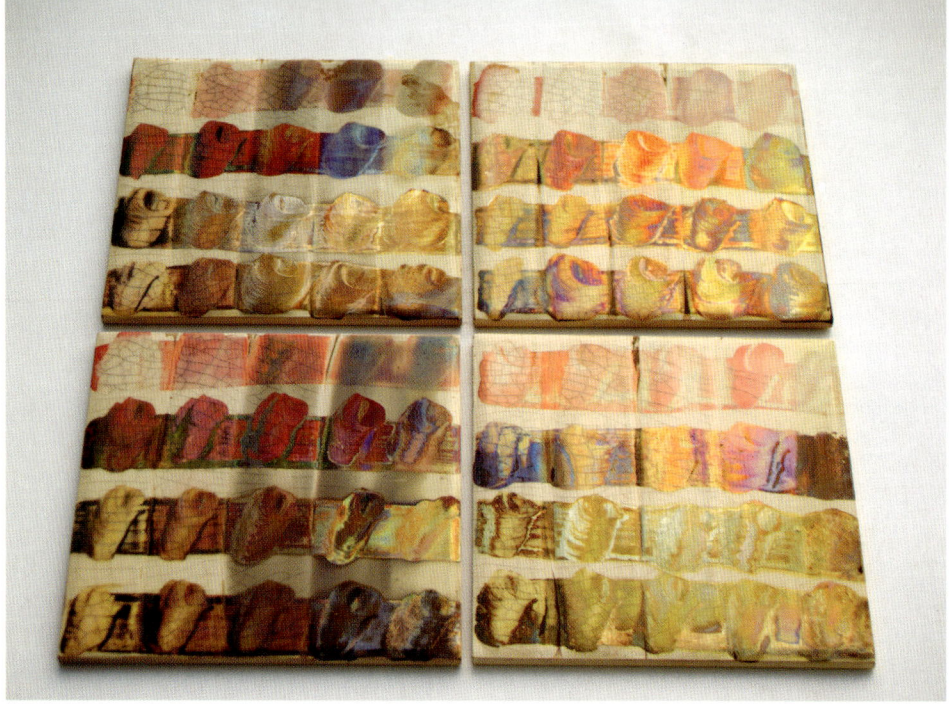

Fig. P7: Soft borosilicate frit line-blended with lead bisilicate, (silica 4, kaolin 6). Four different pigments for lustre response, in four different reduction cycles.

In Fig. P7 we observe what the response is from the pigments with the line blend of the two frits, soft borosilicate and lead bisilicate, but with the 4:6 ratio of silica and kaolin staying constant, and with four different firing cycles and conditions that will be discussed later under reduction and firing cycles. Colour response from the four different pigments can be seen across the tiles as the base flux goes from alkaline to lead. A 50:50 of the two frits gives a base glaze that will produce good lustre surfaces. Note that in the lower left tile,

the lead in the glaze has reduced, creating a greying of the glaze surface stemming from the degree of heavy reduction. It is worth noting that both silver and copper responses are more pronounced in both colour and quality when both frits are in a base glaze. The 50:50 of the two frits is a good starting point for testing. In this series of tests we see the same tile giving 20 separate pieces of feedback information, and each tile was fired in four different reduction cycles, giving 80 pieces of glaze/lustre information in total.

Chart of soft sodium borosilicate frit, line-blended with lead bisilicate for Fig. P7

	Test 1	2	3	4	5
Soft sodium borosilicate Ferro Frit 3110/4110	100	75	50	25	0
Lead bisilicate 0		25	50	75	100
Silica 4 added together = 10 Kaolin 6		10	10	10	10

Note: In some countries the Ferro Frit is 3110 and in others it has the number 4110.

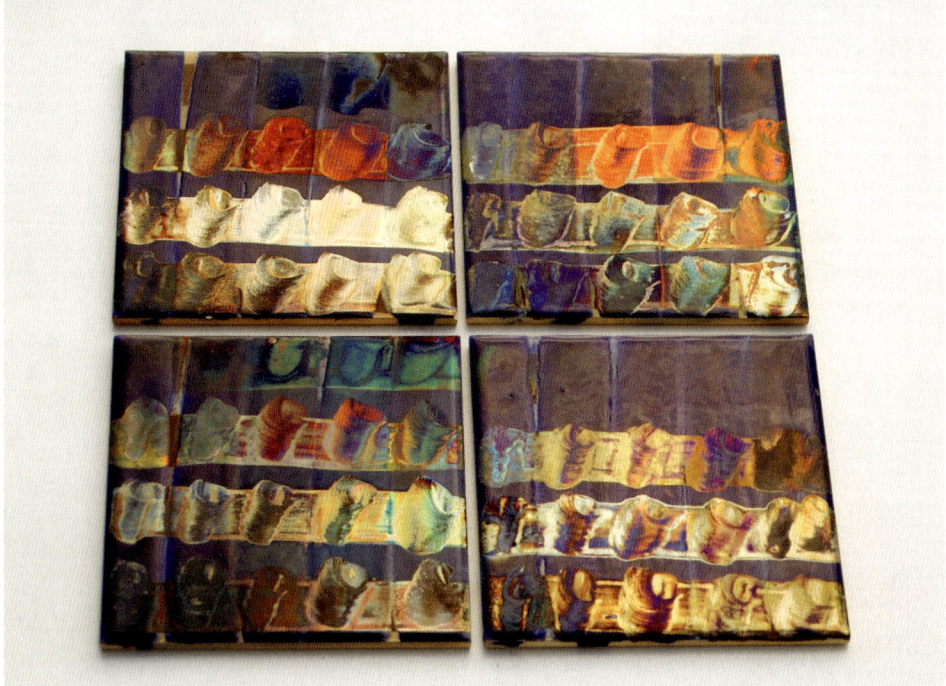

Fig. P7a: The same test as P7 but with 3% cobalt oxide in the line blend.

In this line blend (see p. 36) of a soft sodium borosilicate and lead bisilcate, the silica and kaolin amounts are kept constant. This is a constant through the line blend where the two frits are blended together. The reason for this is to see the pigments develop colour and respond to the different mixes. You start with 100% of the sodium borosilcate, and the fifth test is 100% of the lead bisilcate, with 75/25, 50/50 and 25/75 in between. If there is a noticeable change in colour or response you can then go back and test small division between two tests which show interesting responses. When looking at the tiles in Fig. 6 you will see across the tile a change in colour response from the four pigments. Each tile gives 20 results. Note in the top left tile, second row down, 3 and 4 jump from red to blue; it's the same pigment, but the frit ratio has gone from 50/50 to 25/75.

Reduction cycle information for Fig. P7 and Fig. P7a tests

Gas kiln fired and reduced. Eight cycles (650°C/1202°F). Cone 019 half over.	Electric kiln fired, reduced with gas. Seven cycles (620°C/1148°F). Cone 020 down.
Gas kiln fired and reduced. Seven cycles (620°C/1148°F). Cone 020 down, heavier reduction than firing above.	Electric kiln fired, reduced with coarse sawdust and wood shavings. Seven cycles. (620°C/1148°F).

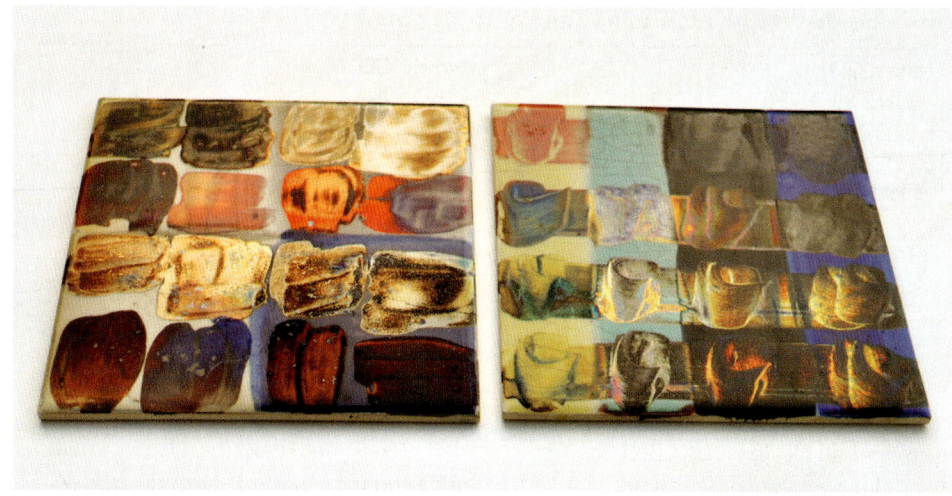

Fig. P8: (Left tile) Four base glazes from line blends; (right tile) metal-oxide additions to the PG2 glaze base.

The left tile in Fig. P8 shows the four base glazes and the four pigments on each glaze (pigment composition will be discussed later). The four base glazes have been selected from three line blend tests found in Figs 5, 6 and 7, with the addition of tin and cobalt. The firing range for these glazes is from 1050°C (1922°F) to 1080°C (1976°C), cones 04–03. Each glaze has the four pigments applied. From this one tile we

have 16 pigment-lustre surfaces with which to explore. The different firing cycles these are fired in will further expand the lustre results.

The base glazes can now be calculated to make the recipe add up to 100. Multiply each material amount by 100 and divide by the total of the materials. The result is the right column (below).

In Fig. P8, the right tile base glaze PG2 has additions of chrome oxide 0.25, copper

From the three line blends, four base recipes were selected

PG1			PG2		
Lead bisilicate	100	83	Soft borosilicate	100	91
Silica	8	7	Silica	4	3.5
Kaolin	12	10	Kaolin	6	5.5
PG 3			**PG 4**		
Soft borosilicate	50	41	Lead bisilicate	100	83
Lead bisilicate	50	41	Silica	8	7
Silica	4	4	Kaolin	12	10
Kaolin	6	5.5	Cobalt oxide	2	2
Tin oxide	10	8.5			

Lustre pigment mixes used on tiles and example pots

Pigment GD1		Pigment GD2	
Burnt umber	25	Burnt umber	25
Silver nitrate	2	Silver nitrate	5
Pigment GD3		**Pigment GD4**	
Burnt umber	25	Burnt umber	25
Silver nitrate	2	Copper carbonate	10
Copper carbonate	5		

oxide 2, with the same pigments across each glaze, giving 16 different responses from this one tile. In Fig. P9, Bob Connery's high-alkaline glaze with chrome, giving a lime-green and copper pigment decoration, is a most effective colour combination.

When applying the same line blend to a number of tiles, work on a mix based on 300–500g. This extra feedback will give you information about the glaze base, the lustre response and the different firing cycles that will affect the outcome. From these tests you will begin to see a picture form as to the controls necessary for lustre development.

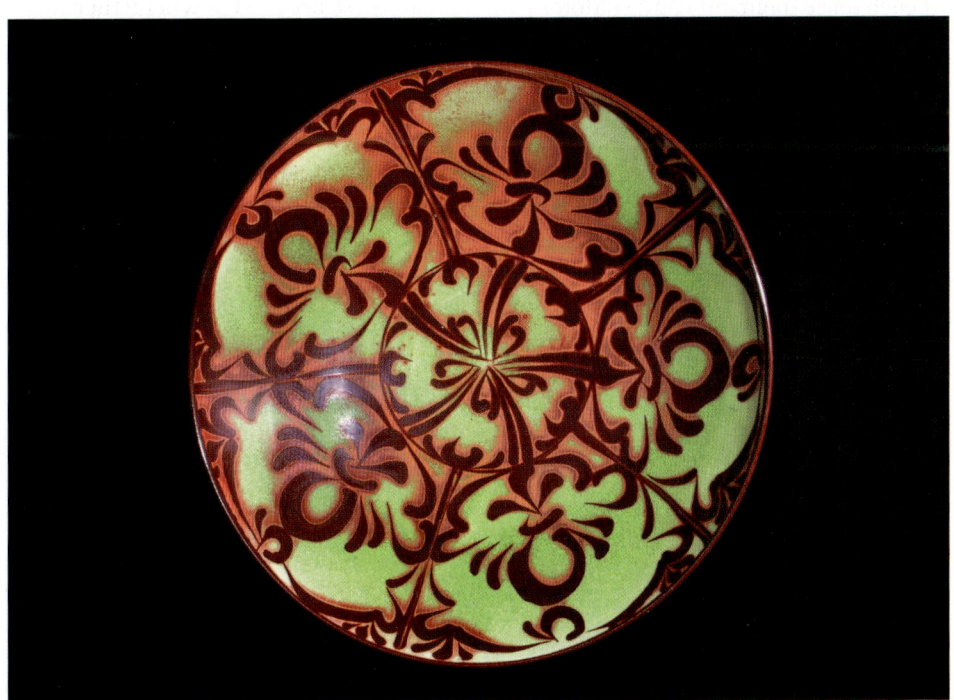

Fig. P9: *Van Lith* by Bob Connery, 2008. Thrown bowl with chrome lime-green alkaline glaze. Copper pigment. Dia: 40cm (15¾in.). *Photo by Jimmy Malecki.*

Glaze bases for lustre

Alan Caiger-Smith

Glaze bases for pigment lustres

Glaze 1

Lead bisilicate frit	35
Calcium borosilicate frit	38
Zinc oxide	5
Silica	3
Kaolin/china clay	2
Zirconium silicate	3
Tin oxide	10

1040°C (1904°F) to 1060°C (1940°F)
For a clear glaze leave out the tin oxide.

Glaze 2

Lead bisilicate	15.8
Calcium- borate frit	61.3
Zinc oxide	4.1
Silica	11.9
Kaolin/china clay	1
Zirconium silicate	5.2
Tin oxide	7.9
Bentonite	0.01

1040°C (1904°F) to 1080°C (1976°F)
Used for the hot parts of a lustre firing, this glaze develops strong reds and silver lustres.

Stan Eley

High alkaline glaze

Soft borosilicate frit (3110/4110)	87
Petalite	11
Bentonite	2

980°C (1796°F) to 1100°C (2030°F)
Copper is added to get turquoise (though it can reduce to red).
Chrome oxide (0.05–0.5g) is added for lime-green.

Greg Daly

Glaze 1

Lead bisilicate frit	75
Soda feldspar	20
Zinc oxide	4
Kaolin/china clay	6

1040°C (1904°F) to 1060°C (1940°F)

Glaze 2

Calcium borate frit (3134/4108)	89
Silica	4.5
Kaolin	6.5
Tin oxide	8
(or Zirconium silicate)	(10)

1060°C (1940°F) to 1100°C (2030°F)

Pigments

For the development of the pigment lustre itself, you will find everyone has their own favourite pigment medium or carrier. By 'medium' I mean what you mix with the silver and copper. Traditionally, burnt umber, burnt sienna, terracotta clay and red ochre were used. Some potters use kaolin. Potters will use a coarser terracotta clay, feeling it is more open to being affected by the reduction, allowing the carbon monoxide to penetrate and reduce the metals. Burnt umber is a high-iron clay which has been calcined and is thus very fine but also open, as it is no longer plastic. Kaolin is used in combination with a red ochre clay. The kaolin primary clay has larger particles to open up the medium and is more refractory than an earthenware red clay. The iron in the clay helps protect the lustre upon cooling, so that it stays reduced.

You can just apply the silver or copper to the surface and achieve a result, but the concentration for the development of lustre is best when these metals are diluted, so the use of a medium makes application of the metals to the surface a lot easier. But how important is the medium used in relation to the outcome of the lustre? In Fig. P8 twelve different clays and materials are tested, 10g of each being mixed with 1g of silver nitrate, and applied to four different base glazes, PGs 1 to 4. As you can see, the result is a variety of surface finishes and colours.

Try different red clay sources to see which works the best. It is surprising that the titanium dioxide gives a definite lustre development; a combination of this and a red clay would be well worth testing. Some potters also add a small amount of tin oxide (2–4%) to the medium. Tin will assist in the reduction of the metals.

Burnt umber was used in the rest of the pigments in this chapter.

Mixing of the pigments

I have mentioned that vinegar has been widely used over the centuries for the mixing of the pigment. As a flocculent it helps to give the clay pigment body, in this case helping the mix to hold onto the pot and not run like a mix of water would do. Vinegar doesn't act as a lubricant; it creates an attraction of the clay particles. In a clay body this translates into a stronger plastic body. Where sodium silicate is a deflocculent the particles are repelled, turning a thick clay paste into a thin slip (casting slip). Vinegar has always been the preferred additive for mixing pigments. It will also dissolve some of the salts to form an acetate that when heated will decompose, giving off carbon dioxide and helping with localized reduction.

CMC medium (Carboxymethyl

Cellulose), glycerine, pine resin & oil CMC medium (Carboxymethyl Cellulose), glycerine, pine resin & oil can be used with success too. They are also organic, and upon firing they carbonize, helping to reduce the pigment. The addition of a small amount of a gum such as gum arabic helps in the decorating, through the flow of the brush, and with handling of the work afterwards. As the gum dries it will act as a gum/ glue that helps prevent smudging of the decoration on the work. Even so, extreme care should be taken when handling the work not to smudge the decoration. If mixed with water your decoration can easily run if too watery, so getting the thickness of the pigment mix right is very important, as different thicknesses of application can result in different colours and effects (and if too thick, results in no lustre, as it acts to block the reduction getting through to the interface of the glaze and pigment).

Note that the pigment in Fig. P10 has been applied with a flat, square, good-quality nylon brush, and deliberately applied with a variation in thickness. This thickness of applied pigment will be important in the outcome of both colour and depth of lustre, so make sure to vary it when doing your tests. How thick should the application be? Well, bearing in mind that if it is too thick you may not see any lustre at all, apply a thick dab to a tile then work it down the tile until it thins out to nothing. Then fire this tile and observe the colour and thickness of application as you wash off the fired clay pigment. You will reveal the lustre that has developed on the surface of the glaze under the pigment.

You can keep the mix in an airtight container, apply some to a glazed tile and use this as your palette, employing

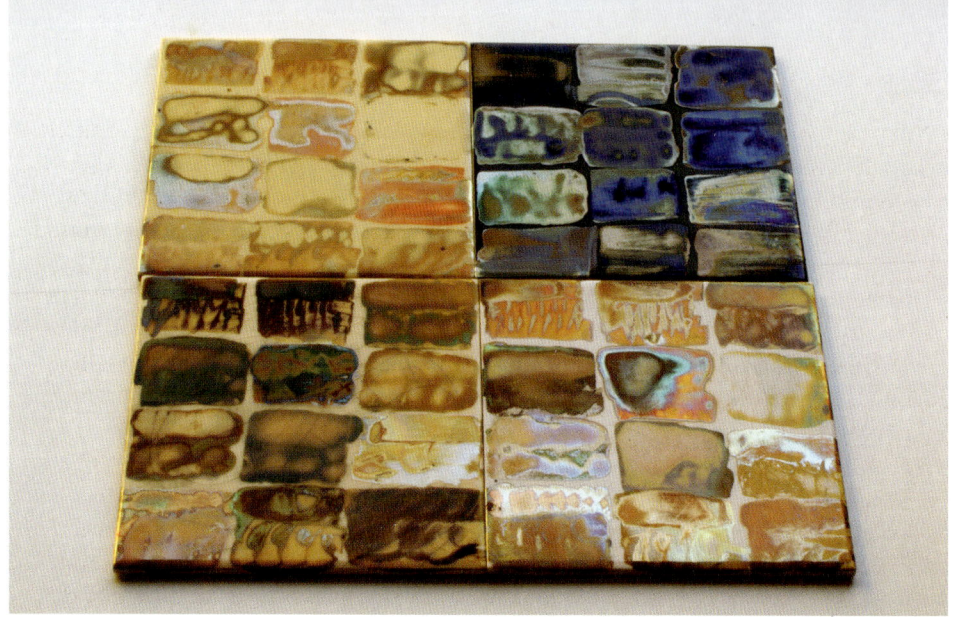

Fig. P10: (Clockwise from top left): Glazes PG1, PG4, PG3 and PG2.

Chart for pigment recipes for Fig. P10

Burnt umber 10g Silver nitrate 1g	Burnt umber 10g Silver nitrate 1g (calcined)	Terracotta 10g Silver nitrate 1g
Red ochre 10g Silver nitrate 1g	Terracotta 10g Silver nitrate 1g (calcined)	Kaolin 10g Silver nitrate 1g
Dirt from outside 10g Silver nitrate 1g	Terracotta 10g Silver nitrate 1g	Yellow iron oxide 10g Silver nitrate 1g
Titanium 10g Silver nitrate 1g	Burnt umber 5g Tin oxide 5g Silver nitrate 1g	Burnt umber 5g Cobalt oxide 5g Silver nitrate 1g

a palette knife to mix and prepare the pigment. The tile gives you an excellent surface on which to work the pigment into the brush so as to get the right quality of application. If it dries out add more vinegar. If you keep it in a plastic container, adding a few ball bearings and shaking before use will help remix the pigment.

The pigment can also be applied by using sponges (stamping), while using coarse and fine brushes will also give different outcomes.

The compositions of individual pigments vary. Alan Caiger-Smith separates pigments into two types – passive and active. The passive pigments can contain clay, red ochre, burnt umber, or kaolin either on their own or sometimes together with a form of copper and silver added. The passive pigments are made up from a choice of terracotta clay, red ochre, burnt umber or kaolin, either individually or in combination, sometimes combined with copper and silver.

Active pigments also contain an active flux such as bismuth, sodium (salt) and potassium (as the addition of a small amount of flux helps with the ion exchange of the metal ion with the glaze interface). Other active fluxes are mercury (vermilion), antimony, arsenic (cinnabar), lead, calcium and zinc in small amounts but as they are highly poisonous, it is strongly recommended that you do not use them at all. It is much safer to stick to bismuth, sodium and potassium.

If these active pigments were used on an earthenware glaze (as they were in Persia, Spain and Italy), the firing was lower than it would be for the passive pigments, usually below 630°C (1166°F). Passive pigments are usually fired in the range between 600°C (1112°F) and 700°C (1292°F) – these are working-guide temperatures. The silver pigments on the whole prefer around 630°C (1166°F) and copper reds develop best at around 700°C (1292°F). I say around these temperatures, as you will find ones that prefer it either hotter or cooler, depending on the particular pigment and the point at which the glaze softens enough to react with the metal in the pigment.

Oxide, carbonate and salts (sulphate, sulphide, chloride, acetate, nitrate, oxalate) of copper and silver can be used in the mix. Copper carbonate and copper sulphate (obtainable from garden centres) are easily come by, so begin with these two for copper. Silver nitrate is the easiest and least expensive of the silver compounds, but it is also corrosive and needs to be handled with extra care. Latex gloves and a face mask should always be used when handling any of the materials. The salts are water-soluble and can easily be taken in through

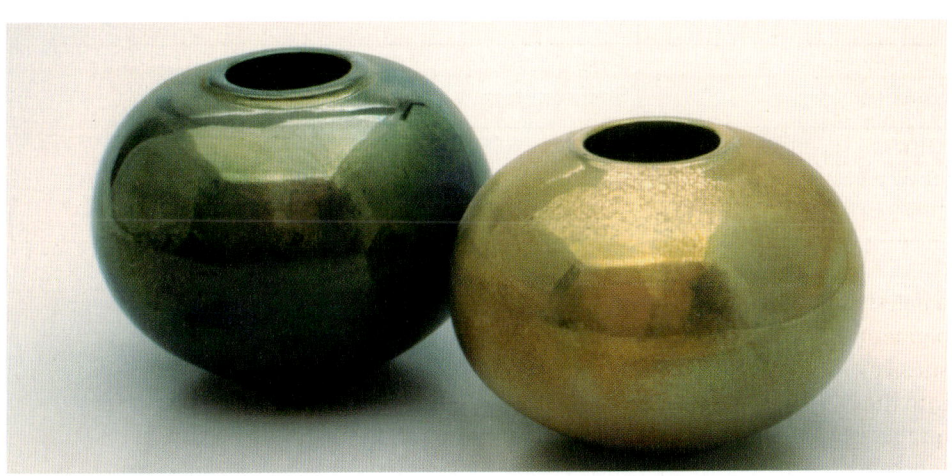

Fig. P11: Two base glazes P4 (blue) and P1 (clear) with GD2 pigment airbrushed over. The control of colour and tone can be carefully achieved with this technique. **You must wear a face mask and rubber gloves, and thoroughly clean your airbrush immediately after use if using silver nitrate in particular.** Spraying of a number of pigments can give interesting colour changes, then the surface can be sgraffittoed back for fine decoration to show the underlying glaze colour.

43

contact with the skin. Silver chloride and silver carbonate are two other silver compounds used.

Copper carbonate can be as much as 70% of the pigment mix, as, being a larger particle, more is needed in the mix than is typical with copper sulphate, which normally makes up between 3 and 15% of the total. Silver ranges between amounts as low as 1% and 5%, though Sutton Taylor has a recipe including as much as 40%. I have already listed four simple pigments that work, and red ochre or a terracotta clay can be exchanged for burnt umber. The following are other pigment recipes:

Passive pigment examples

Orange-gold		Red-gold		Red	
Alan Caiger-Smith		*Alan Caiger-Smith*		*Herbert Sanders*	
Copper nitrate	32	Copper sulphide	19	Burnt umber	68
Silver carbonate	3	Silver carbonate	2	Copper carbonate	30
Red ochre	35	Ferric oxide	16	Bismuth	2
Kaolin	30	Kaolin	63		
(best calcined)		(best calcined)			
Bob Connery		*Bob Connery*		*Herbert Sanders*	
Burnt umber	6	Burnt umber	5	Burnt umber	76
Kaolin	27	Kaolin	30	Bismuth nitrate	8
Molochite	33	Molochite	35	Copper carbonate	8
Copper sulphate	32	Copper carbonate	10	Silver	8
(calcined)		Silver chloride	20		
Bismuth subnitrate	1	(calcined)			
Silver chloride		Bismuth subnitrate	1		
(or carbonate)	1–2	Gum arabic	2		
Gum arabic	2				

Active pigment examples

19th-century Italian recipe		*Herbert Sanders*		*Alan Caiger-Smith*	
Red ochre	43	Yellow ochre	50	Copper carbonate	40
Copper sulphate	43	Copper carbonate	50	Bismuth oxide	20
Silver sulphide	1	Mercury sulphide	1	Kaolin	40
Mercuric sulphide				Gum arabic	2
(very toxic)	3				
				Alan Caiger-Smith	
				Red ochre	9
				Copper sulphide	17
				Silver carbonate	2
				Ferric oxide	15
				Table salt ($NaCl_2$)	57

Alan Caiger-Smith

Red ochre	16
Silver chloride	2
Copper carbonate	2
Tin oxide	2

Red ochre	20
Silver carbonate	2
Copper sulphide	19
Iron oxide	16
Bicarbonate of soda	20

Red ochre	100
Copper carbonate	50
Red ochre	32
Kaolin	8
Silver oxalate	8
Copper sulphide	1

Red ochre	35
Terracotta	30
Silver carbonate	3
Copper nitrate	32

Kaolin	63
Silver carbonate	2
Copper sulphide	19
Iron oxide	16

Sutton Taylor

Kaolin	40
Copper carbonate	40
Bismuth oxide	20

Kaolin	60
Silver nitrate	40

Kaolin	60
Silver nitrate	30
Titanium	30

Spanish Lustres

Terracotta	30
Silver nitrate	8.5
Nickel oxide	62.5

Terracotta	28
Silver nitrate	28
Copper carbonate	5.5
Tin oxide	2.8
Nickel oxide	2.8
*Rochelle salt	33.3

Franchet lustres

Terracotta	70
Silver carbonate	2
Copper carbonate	28

Terracotta	85
Silver carbonate	3
Bismuth nitrate	12
Tin oxide	25

Terracotta	55
Copper sulphide	20
Tin oxide	25

Terracotta	84
Silver carbonate	1
Copper sulphide	5
Bismuth nitrate	10

* Prepare Rochelle salt: 250g of sodium bicarbonate, heat in an oven at 65°C/150°F for around an hour. Increase temperature to 120°C/250°F and hold for an hour. Repeat this rise for 175°C/350°F & 230°C/450°F for an hour each. Remove and allow to cool. Now place 100g of cream of tartar into 150ml of water. The container will need to be twice the size 300ml and able to be heated. Heat the container in a saucepan of water until the water is just simmering. Add half a teaspoon of the sodium carbonate to the beaker and stir. Add more sodium carbonate, until no more bubbles form. Filter the mix through a coffee filter (while hot). Simmer the mix to evaporate half of the water. Cool and leave for several days. Collect the crystals by decanting, and dry on a paper towel. You now have Rochelle salt. In a pigment it is the sodium that helps to activate the lustre.

From these four sources you can see how pigment lustre recipes vary; many are similar but different. You can try out a few of these, but I suggest you select just one or two that are used in each and every firing on your draw rings as reference along with them.

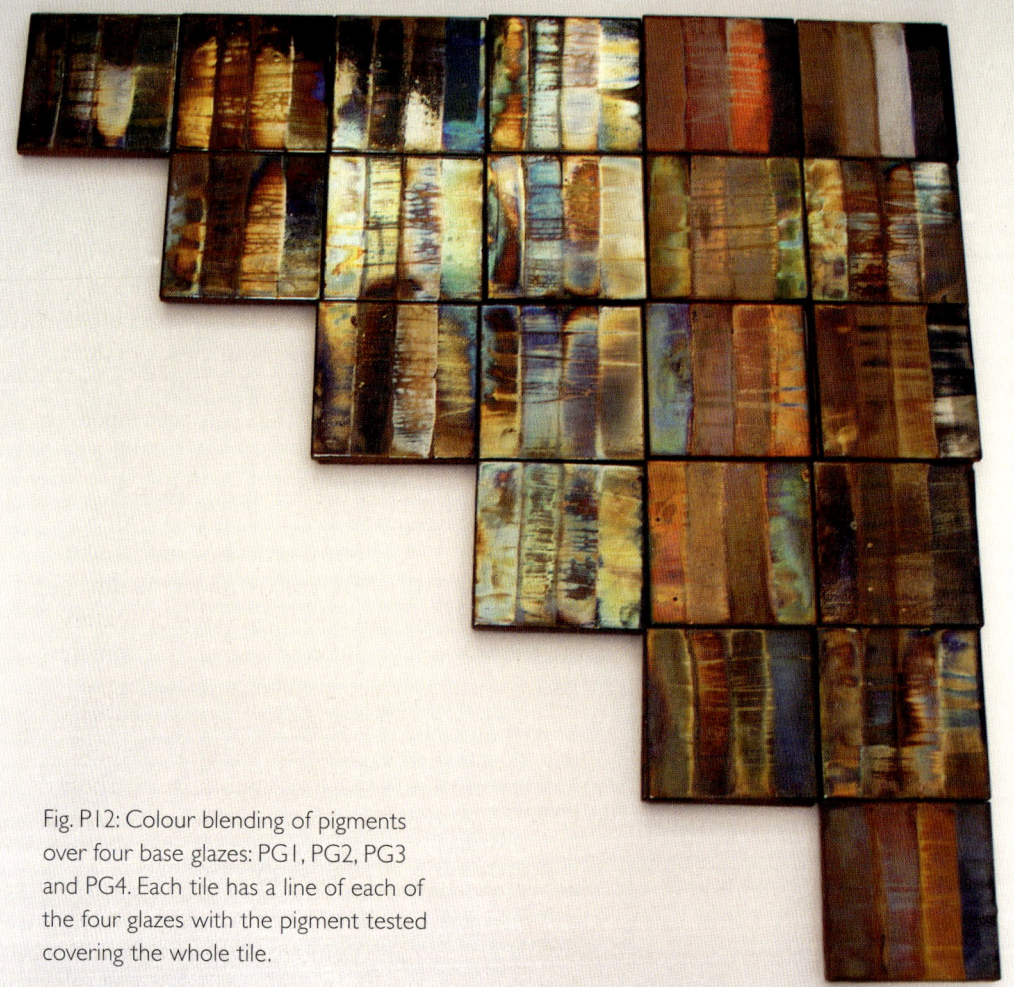

Fig. P12: Colour blending of pigments over four base glazes: PG1, PG2, PG3 and PG4. Each tile has a line of each of the four glazes with the pigment tested covering the whole tile.

Chart for Fig. P12

Test 1	Test 2	Test 3	Test 4	Test 5	Test 6
Burnt umber 50 Silver nitrate 10	Red ochre 50 Silver nitrate 5	Red ochre 50 Silver chloride 10	Red ochre 50 Silver nitrate 20	Burnt umber 50 Copper sulphate 10 Tin oxide 5	Burnt umber 50 Bismuth nitrate 5
	1+2	1+3	1+4	1+5	1+6
		2+3	2+4	2+5	2+6
			3+4	3+5	3+6
				4+5	4+6
					5+6

(eg: 2+4   red ochre 50, silver nitrate 5, tin oxide 5
+ red ochre 50, silver nitrate 20
equals red ochre 100, silver nitrate 25)

Colour blend for lustre pigments

When you start collecting pigment recipes, they will become like glaze recipes, as you won't know when to stop. I find that by using a colour-blend chart for pigments (the same one I use for blending glaze colours), I can develop a large range myself and see what reaction each additive has on the others. In Fig. P12, along the top line you can put various different pigment recipes – for example, red ochre with silver, or with different amounts of copper, or with kaolin and bismuth. Each of these combined mixes (each top row recipe) will be mixed 50:50 with every other recipe, to give six mixes resulting in 21 different pigments. This testing doesn't require 21 mixtures being weighed only 6! As it is only the top line that needs to be weighed and mixed, the other tests are then a 50/50 mix by volume only. The process doesn't take long but the information on how different mixes react with one another gives a picture that random mixes will not give. You can do more or fewer than six mixes along the top line.

In the example in Fig. P12 there are four base glazes – PG1, 2, 3, 4 – applied in lines on each tile which has been glaze-fired, then the tile is covered with the pigment mix from each test as per the chart. From weighing up six tests, 84 different outcomes arise: 21 pigment tests multiplied by the four glazes on each tile gives you 84 pieces of information. In tile six of the photo you can see that the lustre recipe had no real response and the four glaze lines can be seen. In the other test tiles the vertical lines of different tones/colours are the result of the pigment reacting differently to the four glaze bases.

If more sets of the blends are made and applied to tiles, you can then fire them using different temperatures between 630°C (1166°F) and 700°C (1292°F), the information will be more helpful, giving a better understanding of the pigment mix and firing temperature needed for different glazes. Note that the surface colours will alter according to the viewing angle and light source. The individual glazes are the first layer and run across each tile in four strips. These are then fired, and then the pigment tests are painted on over the four base glazes, each pigment covering all four base glazes to show the response. The range of colour and lustre developments varies greatly with each pigment mix applied to the four glazes.

Materials like silver are expensive, so you don't need to mix 100g amounts; a 25g mix will cover a large area for both testing and use. Arrange small containers (plastic cups) in the same configuration as the chart, numbering all the cups from 1 to 21 so that if the cups

Pigment mixes from the top line of Fig. P12
Each recipe is mixed 50:50 with each other one in turn.

1	2	3	4	5	6
Burnt umber 50 Silver nitrate 10	Red ochre 50 Silver nitrate 5 Tin 5	Red ochre 50 Silver Chloride 10	Red ochre 30 Silver Nitrate 20	Burnt umber 30 Copper sulphate 10 Tin 5	Burnt umber 50 Bismuth 5

are mixed up later you will know which mix is which. In the top cups add the pigment recipes you have decided upon (see Fig. 12 for the mixes used here); 25g of each is sufficient to test with (if need be as it makes the sums easier, you can measure out each one to 100g then divide by four). It is important to add the same amount of fluid (vinegar) to each cup. Add the vinegar first, then the material, then stir the mix until it is the consistency of thin cream. Do one and measure the vinegar added, then add the same amount to the other five cups. An oil-painting brush is excellent for mixing.

If you need/want to calcine any of the pigments, first weigh up the recipe of the pigment and then mix it with water or vinegar. Pour the mix into a small glazed fired bowl (or a thick mixture can be poured on to a fired glaze tile) and then fire the mix to 650°C/1202°F. Then hand-grind with a pestle and mortar.

Calcining is useful because the pigment is finer and you often get a better or stronger response (see p.49 for more details).

Set cups as in the layout of the tiles in Fig. P12 with the six test mixes on the top line. Remember to number the cups 1 to 21 this way they can be stored after testing and used for future retesting if needed. If the pigments dry out, just add more vinegar and mix.

- With a teaspoon take cup number 1, and place a spoonful in each of the cups in the next row down from the mixes (cups 7–11). Now the second row has one teaspoon in each cup.
- Next take cup 2, place one spoonful into cup 7 in the second row (immediately underneath cup 2), and then place one teaspoon in each empty cup along the third row, cups 12–15.
- Next take cup 3 and place one spoonful into cups 8 and 12, the two cups in the column running down from cup 3 (they will already have a spoonful each from cups 1 and 2). Proceed to the third row across (empty cups 16–18), placing one teaspoon in each.
- Follow the same pattern with the remaining cups, until with cup number 6 you place one spoon in all the cups below it (11, 15, 18, 20, 21). Cups below the one you're taking the mix from will already have a spoonful of mix, while those in new rows across will be empty.

This whole process, though it sounds long-winded, will take much less time than weighing up 21 tests. Each cup is then applied to a glaze test. Mark each with the cup number and the colour-blend number. If you do more than one pigment colour blend, for easy identification give it a letter or number to go with the tile number.

From 7 to 21 all the tests are a combination of two of the tests from the first row (cups 1–6). To mix any of the tests from 7 to 21 add together the two numbers to make that test, e.g. test number 13 is made up of equal parts from cups 2 and 4, while test 18 is equal parts from cups 4 and 6 (see pigment colour blend chart).

After the lustre firing use a marker pen to add the firing number from your logbook, which you should keep for future reference so that you can repeat promising mixes. It is very important to record the details of each test: glaze, pigment, firing.

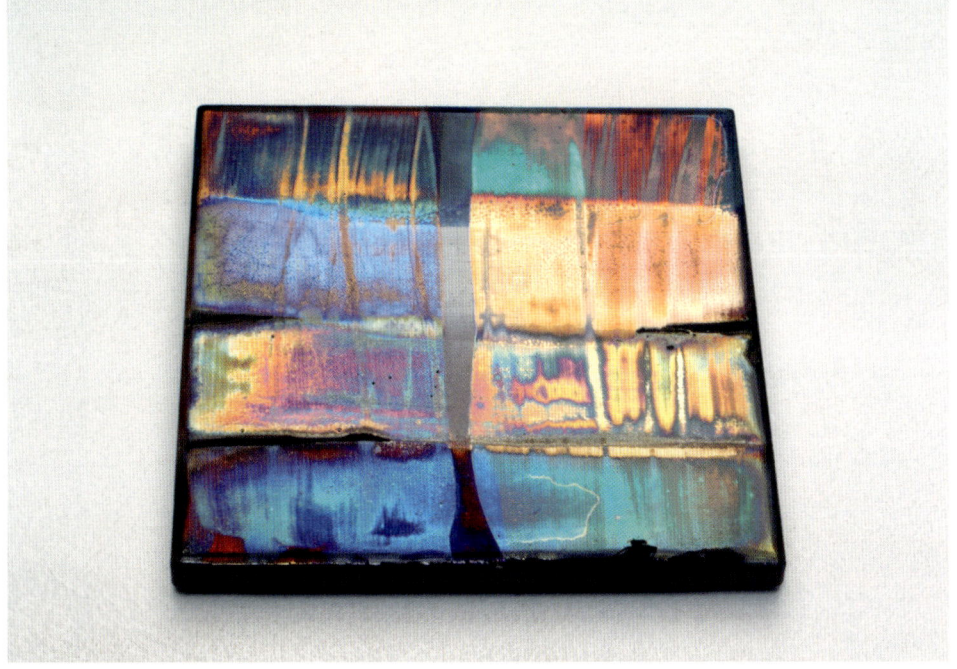

Fig. P13: (Left) pigment (burnt umber 10g, silver nitrate 1g) not calcined, (Right) calcined; both applied vertically over horizontally applied glazes PG1, 2, 3 and 4.

Calcining the pigments has various uses. Traditionally, it helped in breaking down the copper and silver after the metals had been put into acid (the silver and copper came from coins), by using either acetic acid (distilled vinegar) or sodium chloride (salt solution). Copper with acetic acid forms copper acetate. The pigment mix is mixed and ground with an iron-bearing clay then calcined (by firing at about 600°C/1112°F) to break down the metals (copper/silver) further, and then ground again, usually combined with vinegar in a pestle and mortar.

Vinegar on its own has only 4–18% acetic-acid content; the vinegar is believed to assist in two ways, firstly as a flocculant, then in the firing of the lustre, giving off carbon dioxide, which is believed to help in reducing the metals.

On the left in Fig. P13 is an uncalcined pigment, while on the right the same pigment has been calcined and ground.

The finer the mix can be ground, the finer the metal particles and the more readily these will create a more active pigment. You can see a degree of difference between the two. For me it isn't which is better but what you are after in surface colour and finish. You can use both mixes.

A number of potters like to calcine their pigments, feeling it gives them better quality and colour results. You will find a preference for copper, sulphate, sulphide, nitrate and acetate, all of which are soluble in water and vinegar mix. When calcined they turn into copper oxide, but the nature of the mix gives a finer particle of copper, which is important to the development of the lustre. This also applies to a pigment mixed with copper salt and not calcined; the copper is finer in the mix solution. Others use copper carbonate or copper oxide in their pigments, especially when the pigment has 30 to 70% of copper with the carrier. This is the same for silver, with the use of nitrate, oxalate (which will decompose at 140°C/284°F, giving off carbon dioxide), sulphide, chloride (which can help with haloing) and acetate.

When the copper, silver salts and carbonate are calcined, they will change to the oxide form. Heat a small amount of copper carbonate with a flame and it will turn black, to oxide. Traditionally, the washings (pigment residue washed off the pots after the lustre firing) of the pigment after the firing were kept and fed back into the mix.

Firing

The firing of the lustre plays a very important part in the development of pigment lustres. Here the slightest changes in temperature, reduction or time of cycle can alter the outcome. This can sometimes be for the good, and sometimes for the bad. But I never see the bad, as whatever the outcome it is your pointer, guide and reference as to what has happened in the firing. Keep good records of the firing schedule, keep graphs for quick comparison along with comments as to the density of the pack, and draw rings from past firings. These factors can have a big effect on the outcome of the firing result. If you have a light pack with your test firing and then you pack the kiln full of pots, the result will almost certainly be different. The number of pots and shelves contribute to the heating and cooling of the kiln and the flow of gases through the kiln, and all of this can change the results. To get to know the kiln, conduct tests with pigments in all parts of the kiln along with cones to give you feedback on temperature variation and different

degrees of reduction in different parts of the kiln.

Temperature is very important! You will find reds work better in the hotter areas and silver yellow-golds in the coolest.

The rewards when you hit the right firing cycle for your glaze make you feel so good. You become an alchemist, a sorcerer, a changer of metals. It is pretty exciting when it happens! The firing process can't help but be successful once you know both the window of reduction and reduction cycles needed.

It is most important to record what you do during the firing even if it is the smallest change like the damper being opened by 2cm (¾in.) instead of 3cm (1¼in.); or perhaps due to a phone call the time between reduction cycles was 15 minutes instead of the 7 minutes you had intended; or maybe the kiln was light- instead of dense-packed. These can all contribute to the outcome of the lustre. A big one is if you use a different pyrometer for a particular firing, it can be 20°C/36°F higher or lower than another pyrometer, which can dramatically change the outcome in colour development and surface quality.

This is not meant to panic you, but to stress the importance of keeping a record of events, in this case the firing. I fully believe in deliberately changing the variables. Change one element in your normal cycle for a different cycle and the results will be quite different, either better or worse, but you will learn and acquire innate feeling for what you do when you change settings, damper pressure, temperature, primary and secondary air, packing configuration, the temperature at which you reduce, the length of reduction time, etc.

It is very exciting how even small changes can alter the outcome of the lustre. You may find you only need one or two glazes and one or two pigments; different firing cycles will give you all the different results you seek.

By recording your firings, you will set a benchmark by which – and this is the important point – you can repeat your results. I can't stress this enough.

If you work in a vacuum, with no knowledge or guidance, it can be frustrating and unrewarding, but only from the failures and the information the firings give you, and by working with and narrowing the variables, will you come to understand them and learn to control your lustre results. There are no easy formulae; if there were, potters and industry would have long ago learned to produce lustre as easily as a cobalt-blue glaze. But they didn't!

With pigment lustres and lustre glazes you need to be able to control the temperature and the atmosphere in the kiln (and hence the reduction).

To fire your lustres, use two forms of information gathering: a pyrometer (use the same one each time as they do vary one from another), as at this temperature 10°C/18°F can make a difference to the outcome. Your pyrometer may not read exactly but that is OK. It becomes your main point of reference for temperature rise and fall. If it is 20–30°C/ 68–86°F out, you will learn to begin reduction at 580°C (1076°F) (if it is reading under that).

To benchmark your pyrometer, use cones in each firing; they measure heat work not temperature. The rate at which you fire a kiln will determine the temperature at which a cone will bend.

Using cones 022, 021, 020 and 019 for each firing, you can note when the first cone goes down. In the case of 021, firing at 60°C/108°F per hour this occurs at 602°C (1116°F), while firing at 150°C/270°F per hour the same cone will bend at 614°C (1137°F). Note the temperature reading on the pyrometer. You now have a point of reference.

You may be asking why have cones in every firing when you know the temperature from looking at the pyrometer. To give you an example, when I reduce in my electric kiln I can set the temperature at 635°C (1175°F) and cone 020 goes over during firing. I know then to begin the reduction cycles, and after one hour I am still reading 635°C (1175°F) but cone 019 has gone over. Heat in the kiln has been working on the cones and glazes, and this can easily lead to overfiring of the glaze or pigments, such that the pigments might start to fuse to the glaze (see Fig. P14), so you need to keep a close eye on the cones.

Cones are very important markers in the firing as they will indicate the actual amount of heatwork in the kiln (as opposed to simply the temperature). The degree of reduction you obtain in the kiln can be also seen and used as a benchmark. Very heavy early reduction and the cones will be black or grey and inflated-looking. Other firings with reduction later and not as heavy and the cones will not look like this. All observations should be noted down in your firing log.

Each glaze will have a window of temperature that works best with a particular pigment or set of pigments. Both the degree of reduction and the optimum temperature window can best be determined through a series of firings. Have a large number of draw rings, each with a different glaze, e.g. 4–5 rings of 3–4 glazes, and apply a number of

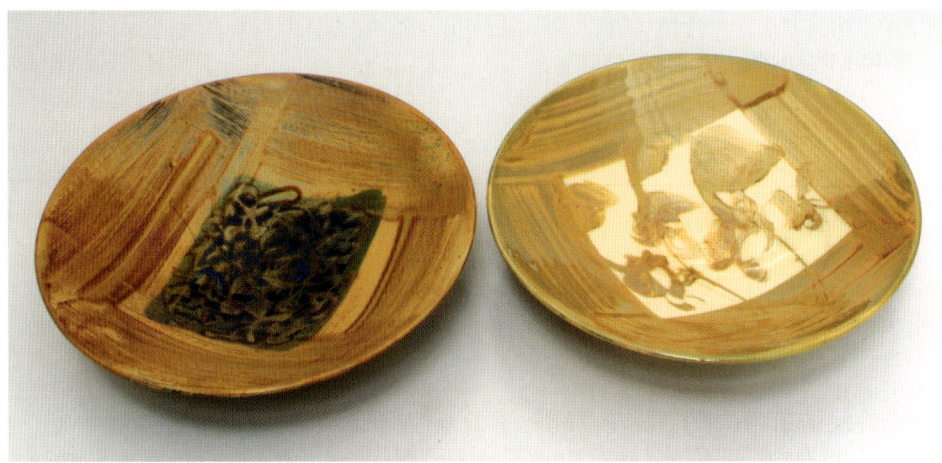

Fig. P14: The left-hand bowl has overfired pigment which has fused to the glaze. On the right is the same pigment and glaze but fired 25°C/45°F lower.

pigments to each ring. Then, in a single firing, beginning at a lower temperature starting at 600°C (1112°F) after three or four reduction cycles, you should start to pull rings out every 20°C/36°F. Go high enough in temperature that the pigments start to fuse to the glazes; this could be as high as 720°C (1328°F) so you can see the different results in different glazes.

You will notice that some glazes will be able to go higher than others, and you'll also see a change in lustre colour. Reds on the whole like a slightly hotter firing (up to 20–30°C/36–54°F hotter) than silver. But there is always a glaze that red works better in when cooler. I suggest you distribute cones throughout your kiln, especially in the first few firings. This will tell you where and by how much temperatures differ. You might find a 20–30°C/36–54°F variation. Put two sets of the same pigment tests in these areas for double feedback. The outcome will help you understand and build a picture of your kiln, glazes and pigments.

Take each glaze you want to test,

glaze a number of test pieces and source as many glazes as you like. The more you do, the more information will be gained. I find tiles or cylinders the easiest to use for this task. You can paint three or four different bands of glazes on a 15cm (6in) square tile, while on cylinders glaze can be applied down the length or around the circumference (see Fig. P3). You can group these in variations on a glaze base – e.g. the base glaze then additions of tin, zirconium and titanium – to see lustre response with the different opacifiers. Additions of metal oxides like cobalt or stains – e.g. black, yellow or green – will give further base colours. As seen earlier, the underlying colour is very important to the lustre tone or colour outcome.

Glaze at least six to ten tests at the same time. By having these tests already fired it will allow you to do a number of different test firings quickly and to vary your firing cycles and compare the results. It only takes a few minutes more to glaze six to ten tests than it does to mix up the glaze for just one, but at the end of the process you'll have a reserve of fired glazes for testing pigments and firing cycles.

Kiln types

Early lustre kilns were built specially for lustre firings. The best-known of these appears in drawings by Cipriano Piccolpasso and his description of a pierced muffle kiln, which enabled an even heat and smoking of the ware. A full description of Piccolpasso's muffle kiln can be found in his book *The Three Books of the Potter's Art*, but essentially it is a firebox directly under a chamber that has a muffle (a muffle is a chamber in a kiln that protects ware, normally sealed off from the flame and gas). In this kiln the muffle has holes cut into the wall. In this case the chamber is round in shape; the flame can't flow freely around the ware which helps to keep control of the heat and flame, and prevents it from directly touching the ware. The holes break up the flame creating a more even heating of the ware. Spanish lustre kilns were built along similar lines: a firebox underneath, a small opening in the top of the firebox into a larger chamber, with a number of vents spaced over the top of the kiln allowing control of the flame path and reduction by reducing the size of the vents, similar to the use of a damper in reducing the size of the flue opening.

The temperature we are aiming at is just at red heat (still quite low). Roaring flame isn't needed to obtain high temperatures. The emphasis is on the gentle, red, smoky flame. Spanish kilns were sometimes fired using rosemary bushes alone as fuel, giving a very smoky flame for the entire firing cycle.

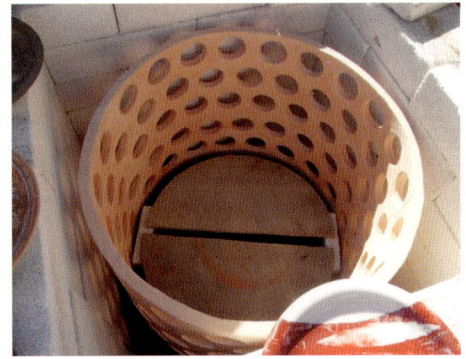

ABOVE AND BELOW Fig. P15a & b: A modern take on Piccolpasso's type of muffle kiln, showing a saggar with holes to break up the flame, allowing it to come through more evenly.

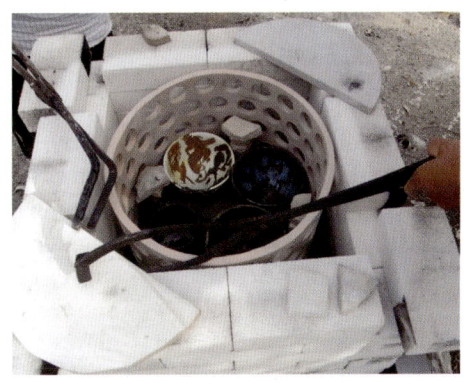

Wood-fired kilns

Traditionally, brick-built wood kilns have been used, like Alan Caiger-Smith's 100 cu. ft wood-fired kiln using willow wood. But today having a wood kiln in a studio can be difficult, as most potters live in an urban environment where wood is not allowed to be burnt – this is due to health concerns and smoke pollution (banned in a number of urban communities now). So gas is the next best way of firing pigment lustre. John Chiswell Jones and Bob Connery both use gas kilns.

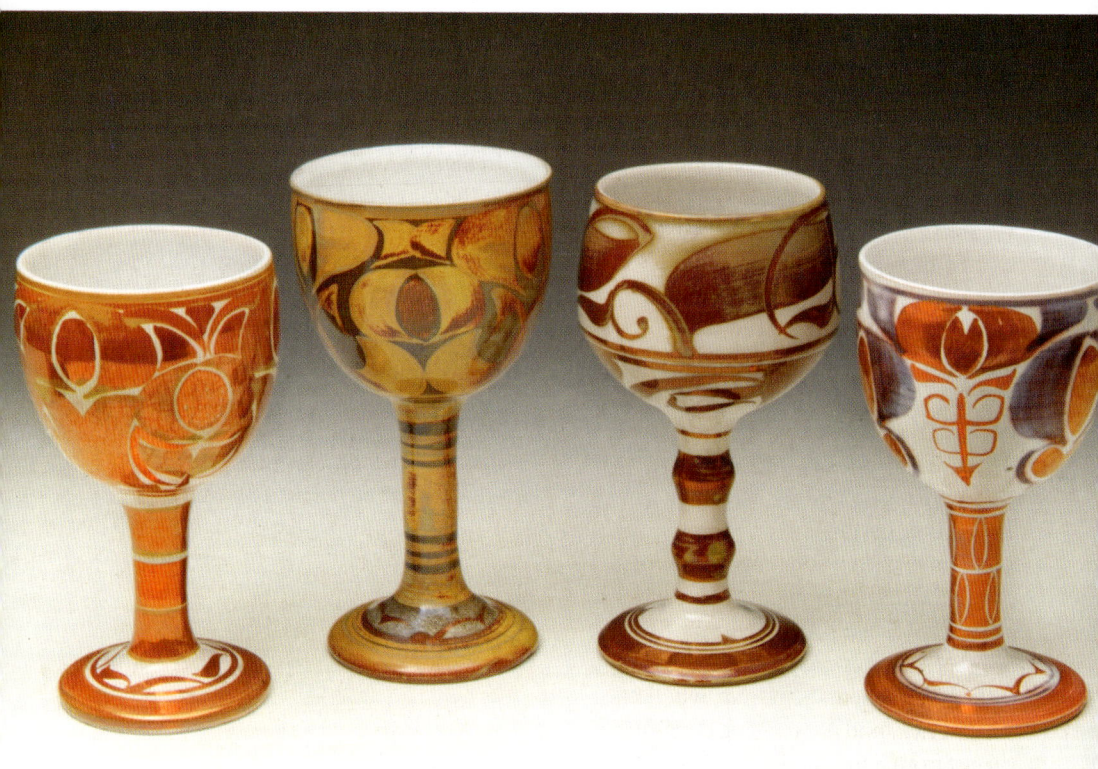

Fig. P16: Goblets by Alan Caiger-Smith, with a variety of pigments on different glazes fired in a wood-fired kiln. Ht: approx. 15–18cm (6–7in.). *Photo: Anne-Marie Caiger-Smith.*

Alan Caiger-Smith and Sutton Taylor both used wood-fired kilns for their lustre firings (though Sutton now uses a gas kiln). This isn't an easy process as at any time if too much wood is added the kiln temperature can climb too fast and too high, and you can easily lose the work from overfiring. So great care must be taken when adding fuel and in reduction control. It isn't like gas, where the gas can be turned down immediately and the heat source lowered. Once the wood is added it begins to burn, increasing the heat source and inevitably completing the combustion cycle, and the heat thus built up is far from easy to diminish.

Gas and electric kilns

A gas or electric kiln, on the other hand, will have a door that can be partly opened to help diminish heat quickly. If you have too much of an increase in temperature, you just open the door a little and dump the heat. **If your kiln has risen to as much as 600°C (1112°F), wearing protective gloves and face shield, open with care (Do not stand directly in line with the door!) and make sure that nothing flammable sits directly above the kiln or nearby. The door can safely be opened 5cm (2 in.).**

When firing pigment lustres in a gas kiln you may have to do a few simple modifications. The secondary air around the burner port (head and kiln) will need to be reduced. Ceramic fibre or pieces of cut kiln shelf can be used for this purpose, as when lit the flame fills the burner porthole. This reduces the secondary oxygen and allows for heavier reduction. When reducing a gas kiln, once the target temperature has been reached, close the primary air on the burners and close the damper by more than 95%; the gas pressure may also need to be increased, though by how much is a moot point. Close the damper and increase the gas until the flame starts to lick out of the ports as back-pressure increases, then light the unburnt gas coming out of the flue (this is an important safety procedure, so do not breathe in unburnt gas, and make sure the kiln space is well ventilated too). You will see the temperature drop. This is the first reduction cycle, which, depending on the kiln particulars (its size, whether fibre or brick, and the packing density), will last from 5 to 15 minutes. Then open the damper and burner (remembering to decrease gas pressure) and oxidize back up to temperature – this will take between 5 and 15 minutes depending on the size of kiln (and could be more). Once back up to temperature, repeat the process.

After two or three cycles it is time to draw a test ring from the kiln. Usually the test ring will comprise one or two glazes that you use in each firing as a point of reference, with two to four different pigments painted on each glaze. Another change you should make to your kiln is to enlarge the spy hole, or on a small kiln to open the door enough that you can easily draw out the ring. Repeat this process until the draw ring has developed lustre, then close down kiln.

NB: Make sure the gas has burnt out of the kiln: if you open the door while still in a reduction cycle, a ball of flame will come out! Turn the gas pressure down and open the flue, as this will quickly clear the kiln of unburnt gas and it can be opened safely.

In Fig. P17, a test ring is being removed from the kiln using a wire rod with a hook at one end. **Make sure you wear gloves and full face mask when doing this.** You can see in this image an electric kiln being reduced with wood. Note down the cones and test ring you have used for drawing out in further cycles.

In this electric kiln (Fig. P17) the shelf is made from thick wire-gauge mesh, which allows the reducing gases to pass

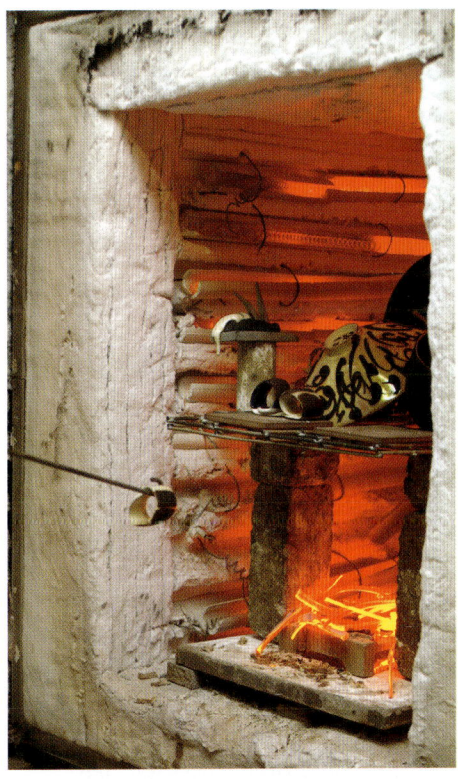

Fig. P17: Drawing a test ring from an electric kiln reduced with wood. Note that the shelf is made of thick wire mesh and the bowl is upside down to encourage haloes. *Photo by John Daly.*

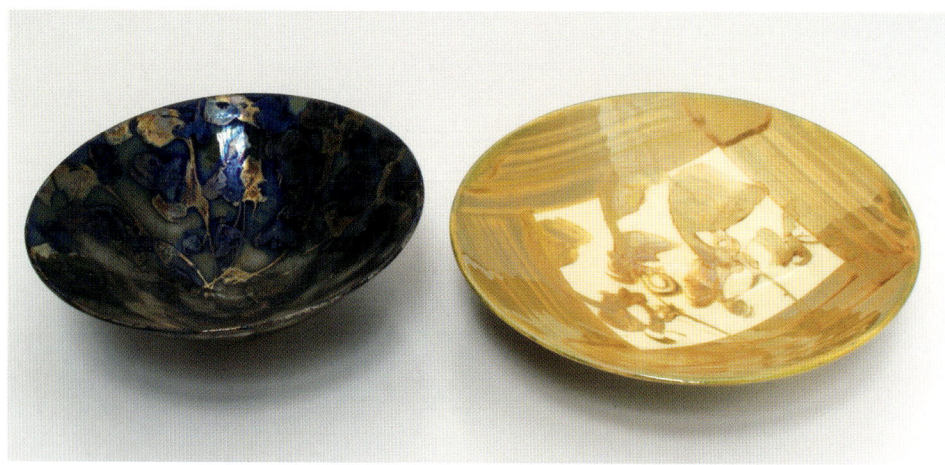

Fig. P18: Two bowls with P1 base glaze and pigment GD2. Both were fired in the electric kiln. *Photo courtesy of the author.*

easily through and around the pots. Many potters like the use of perforated shelves, but they are expensive. Remember that the temperature should be just red-hot. There are large kilns in Spain, used for firing large lustre pots, which use metal rods to create a stacking frame on which to place the work. Note also that the pots can be touching and stacked on end or upside down, as with bowls. This can help with developing haloes.

In Fig. P18 the bowls were glazed with P1 base glaze with GD2 pigment. Both were fired in the electric kiln. The left bowl received heavier reduction than the one on the right. The left-hand one can be seen in Fig. P17 at the front, turned face down, receiving the full reduction flame, which reduced not only the silver pigment but also the lead in the glaze. The right-hand bowl received lighter reduction cycles and was fired on a kiln shelf, protecting it from flame. The electric kiln allowed experimentation with forms of reduction, using wood introduced through a lower spyhole.

The top vent was covered leaving the smallest gap, while small pieces of finely chopped wood were introduced, usually three bundles per cycle (see Fig. P19 for an example of a bundle). A good smoky atmosphere was achieved.

After the firing the base of the kiln was vacuumed out. I have fired in this way in this kiln for over 20 years and have still not replaced the elements. There is no damage apart from soot around the kiln openings.

The wood needs to be small, as its function is to burn the oxygen, not to create heat. If too large it takes time to burn and will increase the temperature. Old bamboo blinds are excellent. Other ways to reduce in an electric kiln are with wood shavings and coarse sawdust (too fine and the sawdust will smoulder and burn very slowly), wrapped in paper bundles for easy handling. Alternatively, you can drip oil into the kiln. Mothballs have been favoured in the past but are not healthy to use; sugar is better. Gas can be used, but only very carefully. Use a small burner with the primary air closed (i.e. air

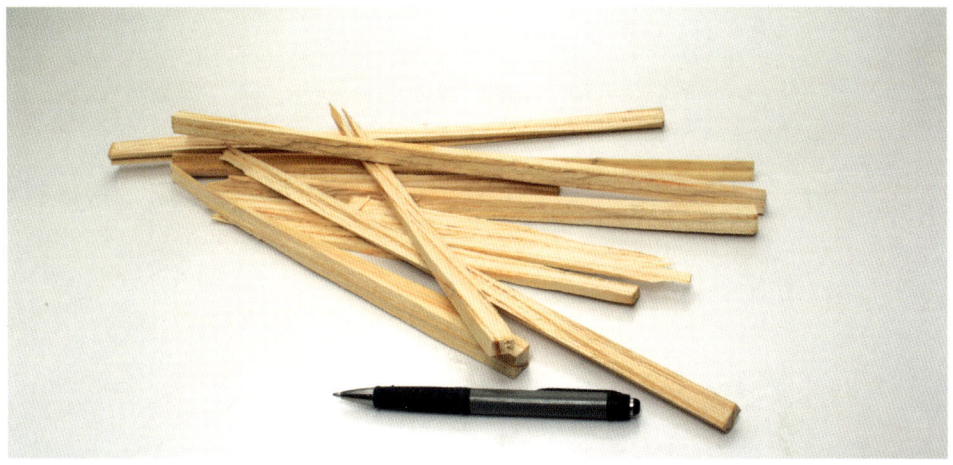

Fig. P19: The size of wood bundle sticks to be used as fuel for the kiln.

is introduced at the bottom of the door, for which purpose you may need to enlarge the bottom spy hole). When introducing the gas into the kiln, make sure the burner is alight, then after a minute light the excess gas coming out of the top vent and keep the vent open. This also produces good results. It is essential that you work in a well-ventilated space; I have a flue suspended over the electric kiln.

Some potters purge the kiln with nitrogen first before the reduction cycle. Margery Clinton used this method, with two pipes going into her electric kiln: one with nitrogen, the second natural gas.

Cycling of reduction for pigment lustres

For the (metal) lustre layer to develop on the surface of the glaze, a series of reduction and oxidisation cycles is needed. (It has been found that the thin layer of metal that produces the lustre develops under a nano layer of the glaze, see the end of Chapter 1 for more details.)

A lustre surface will develop with as little as three cycles of reduction, though this depends on the length and degree of reduction and temperature.

Bob Connery currently does the first two reduction cycles with gas alone. To activate full gas reduction, he closes the primary air on the burner and then closes the damper until there is a small wisp of back flame at the burner port. The first cycle starts when cone 021 is down (or is well on the way), and lasts for 20 minutes. The first part of the firing takes five hours, with the last hour spent above 450°C (842°F) and rising very slowly until cone 021 is down. This is followed by two further reduction cycles of 15 minutes each using wood alone (four reduction cycles are done with a fifth very rarely).

Final top temperatures for all these cycles will vary, but Bob generally stops if cone 018 falls. Cone 017 is the guard cone and may fall at the very end or even in the cooling phase after such heavy reduction. Remnant fuel is enough to prevent oxidation. Reduction should drop the temperature on the pyrometer

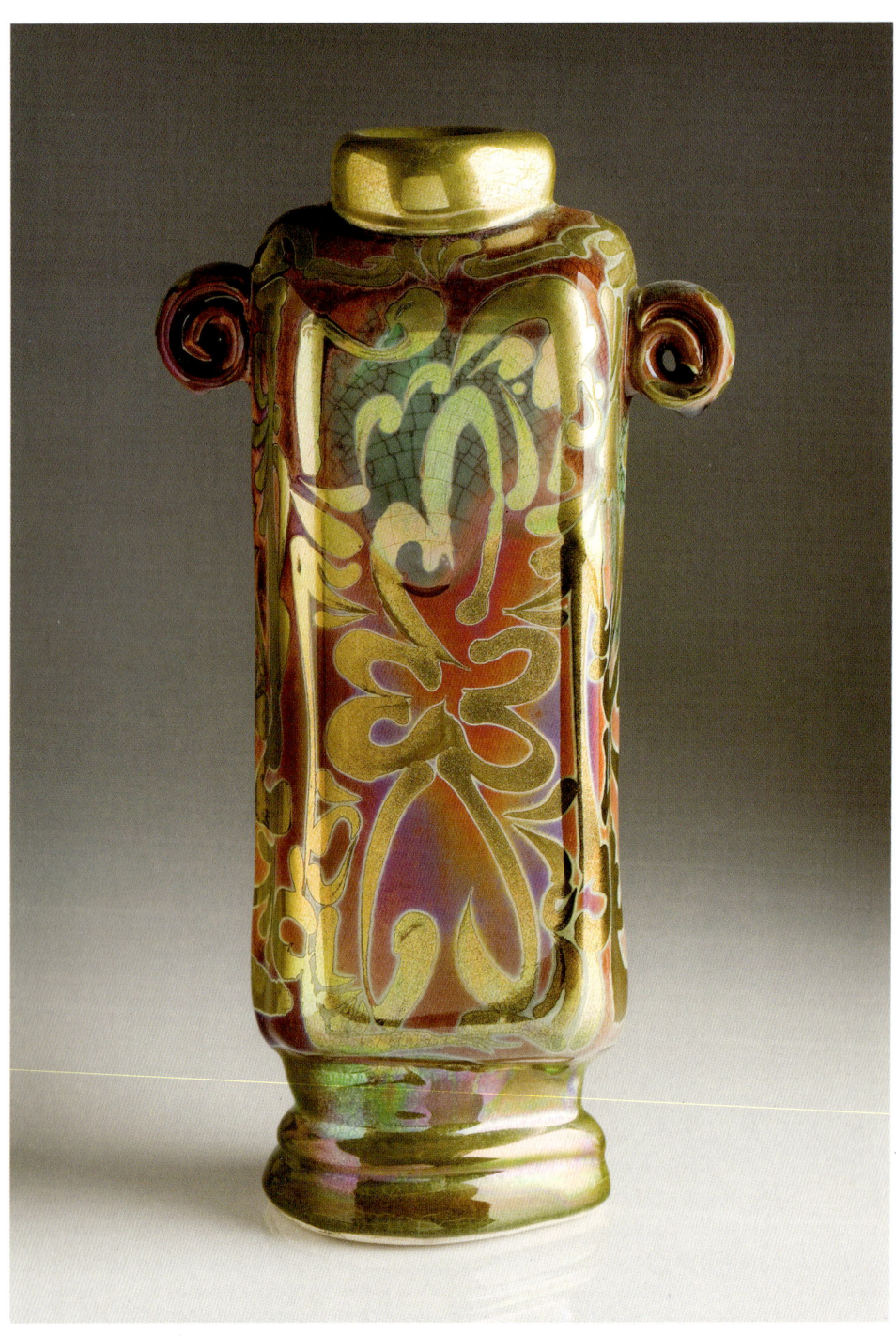

Fig. P20: by Bob Connery, 2010. High silver pigment decoration on a glaze altered by reduction (lustre glaze). Ht: 34cm (13½in.).

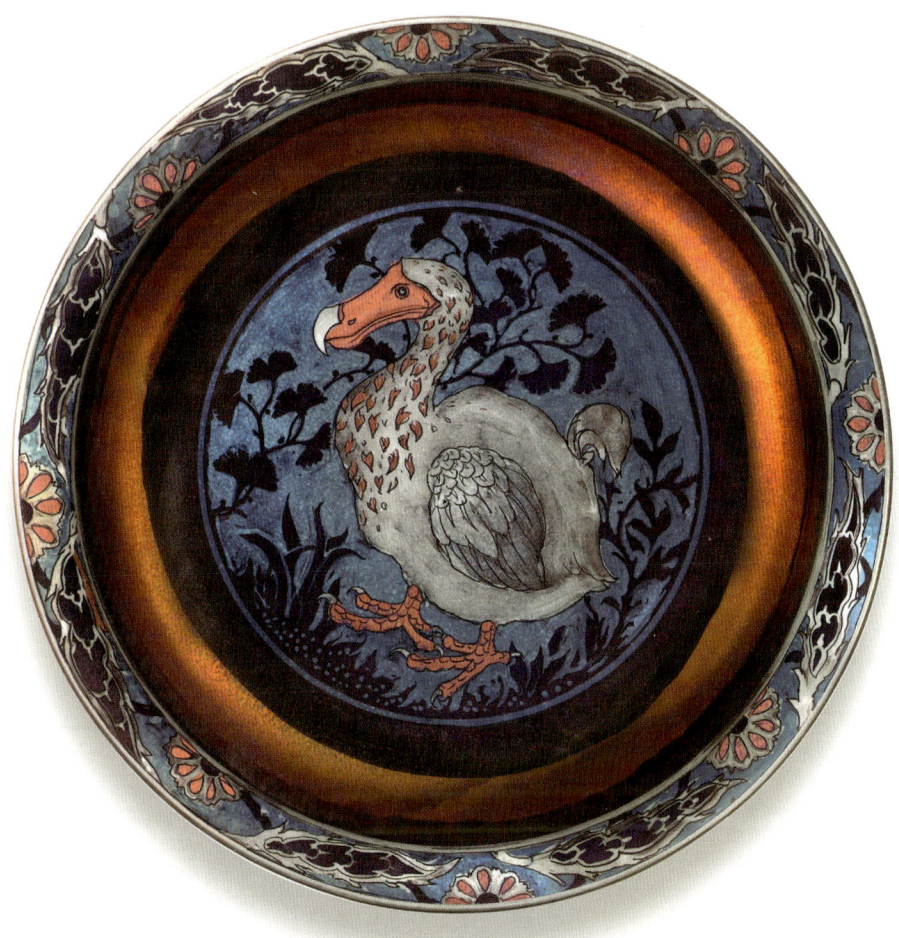

Fig. P21: *Dodo Charger* by Jonathan Chiswell Jones. Brush-decorated in silver, copper, and a mix of silver and copper clay paste; on a ground of copper and cobalt over porcelain. *Photo courtesy of the artist.*

by 60°C (108°F), and the oxidation cycle should take around 10 minutes to regain and increase temperature back to the temperature where reduction will begin again for the next cycle. The temperature of later cycles may not fall so drastically and care needs to be taken not to let the kiln rise too quickly when you begin the oxidation cycle: the kiln can easily go past the top temperature for the glaze and pigment.

Jonathan Chiswell-Jones uses a gas kiln with rather more than a cubic metre in packing space. The kiln is fired to a temperature of 674°C (1245°F), then four reduction cycles are carried out in total, achieved by switching off the air (burners use air and gas under pressure) and increasing the gas input. The first three cycles are 5 minutes each, while the last depends on the rings drawn from the kiln between each spasm. As Caiger-Smith points out, all this is best done in

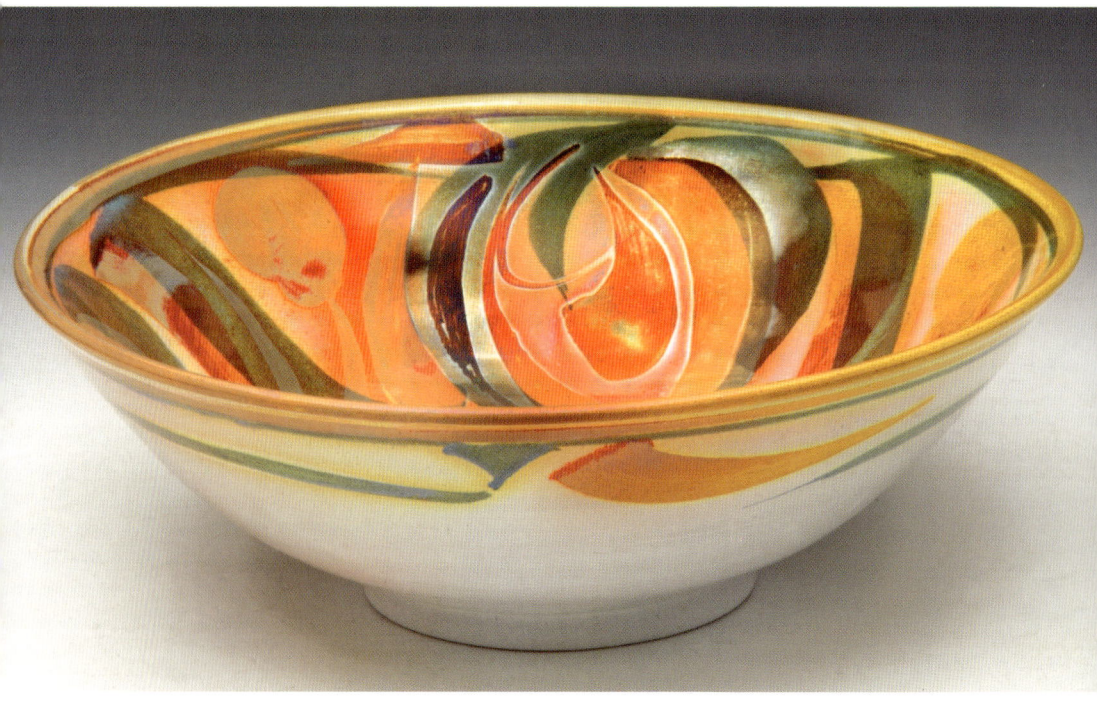

Fig. P22: Lustre bowl by Alan Caiger-Smith, 2005. 27 × 9cm (10½ × 3½in.). Note the halo around the decoration. *Photo courtesy of the artist.*

as short a time as possible. Of course, the temperature drops during reduction (about 30°C/86°F) and is then raised back to 674°C (1245°F) before the next cycle. The reduction is all complete in about an hour.

My best pigment is a mixture of all the brush washings used for past decoration. I am experimenting with pigments that contain no copper – just silver carbonate, clay, bismuth, and iron oxide. This can produce a beautiful pale blue given the right base colour and conditions, but I have not yet established the key variables.

In general when experimenting, I recommend settling on a glaze and a firing cycle. Then your tests of lustre pigments and underglaze colour, if any, will yield some consistent information.

I have 'wasted' many hours because I kept tinkering with the firing schedule, meaning that so many good early results became useless in the later, improved firing schedule. A logical mind would arrange the variables in order of generality. What I mean is: 1. The kiln. 2. The firing schedule. 3. The glaze. There are about seven in total. There is no point, for example, in doing extensive testing on the clay paste pigments if you then change the glaze. On the other hand, how can you assess a glaze for suitability unless you use the whole process? We can separate the variables, but they actually work in combination.

Alan Caiger-Smith fires in a large wood-fired kiln. Alan describes it as a cross-draft, updraft, downdraft kiln.

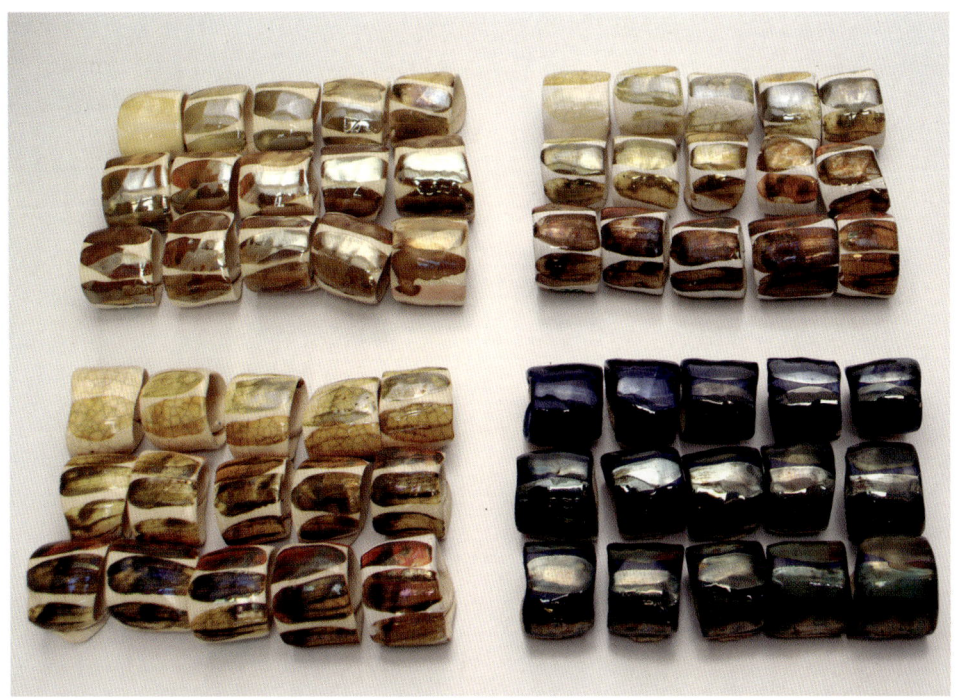

Fig. P23: Draw test rings combining glazes P1–4 and pigments GD1–4 over 15 reduction cycles. *Photo courtesy of the artist.*

The flame enters under the base of the kiln up into the chamber, then divides and goes out either side of the opposite end of the chamber. A lustre firing takes approximately 7½ hours in total; it takes around 6½ hours to fire up to 660°C (1220°F) at which point the reduction cycles begin. Depending on how the lustre is developing on the draw rings, there are around eight cycles of reduction.

The use of willow wood gives a long, gentle flame. A lustre firing can take two days to pack, with the care taken in where the different lustres are placed within the kiln, as well as consideration of the flame and gas flow, being all-important. Bowls on which Alan would like the development of a halo around the decoration are placed upside down on pieces of small shelf so as to lift them off the shelf itself.

To determine the optimum number of cycles for your glazes and pigments, do a firing with a large number of test rings. Have at least three different glazes with three to four different pigments on each ring. Line them up on the same shelf for ease of drawing. In Fig. P23, there are 15 rings each of four base glazes – P1, P2, P3, P4 – and each test ring has a varied thickness stroke of each of pigments GD1, GD2, GD3 and GD4, representing 240 separate pieces of information from a single firing. After every reduction cycle a test ring of each glaze was drawn from the kiln. What can be seen from this exercise is the increased development of the lustre after each cycle. As the process advances beyond the tenth cycle, the lustre starts to dull – on P2 and P4 in particular with silver pigment, where the reds become stronger. The silver can be seen to begin to develop a surface colour after one cycle, building into a properly reflective lustre after around six to eight cycles. The red starts to develop on P2 and P3 from eight cycles onwards. In other kilns I have found that the colour can take fewer cycles to develop.

These rings were fired in an electric kiln with the temperature controller set at 630°C (1166°F) and cone 020 three quarters bent over when the first cycle was begun. Each cycle was ten minutes with three bundles of sticks three minutes apart. Then the top and bottom vents of the kiln were opened and cleared for 5 minutes. The process was repeated for each cycle, with a ring being drawn after each one (normally, a few cycles are completed before the first test ring is drawn). The cycles went past what is considered a normal reduction temperature and time, but information was gathered on how glazes and pigments react to a longer firing and greater heat.

After the 15 cycles, with the kiln still reading 630°C (1166°F), cones 019, 018 and 017 had all gone over, by the work of the heat. This represents around 720°C (1328°F) in temperature. At this level of heat, the silver becomes dull and overfired, but the reds develop. The 240 separate results from this one firing are a lot to observe and digest, but they offer a thorough picture of the work of heat on the glaze and pigments and in reduction.

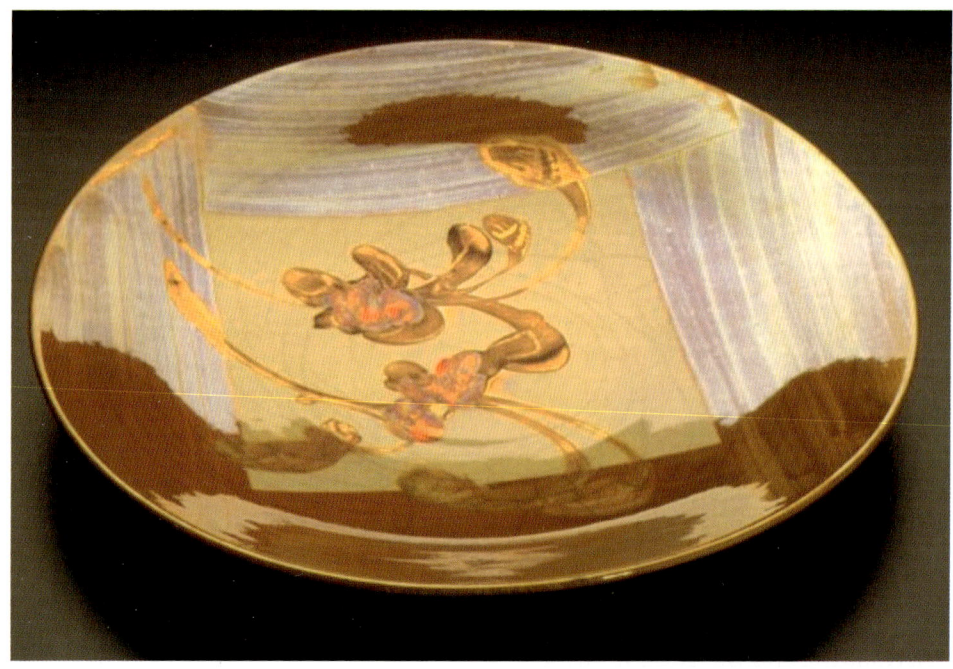

Fig. P24: Silver pigment-decorated bowl by Greg Daly. Glaze P1 and GD2 pigment. Dia: 30cm (11¾in.). *Photo by Russel Baarder.*

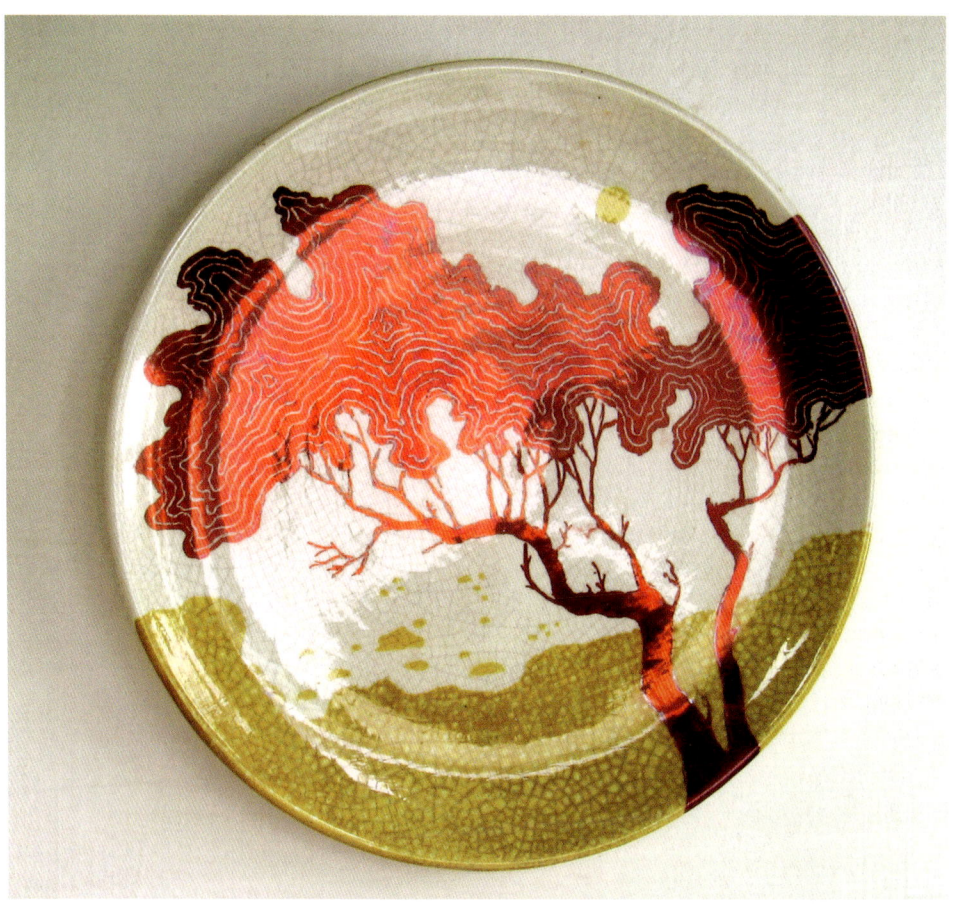

Fig. P25: Platter by Ferenc Halmos (Hungary), 2008. Dia: 32cm (12½in.). Silver and copper pigment lustres on a clear alkaline glaze, one reduction cycle at 690°C (1274°F). *Photo courtesy of the artist.*

Conclusion

Record, record, record! Observe, observe, observe! A given pigment will react differently on different glazes, so test each pigment initially on a number of glazes, vary the thickness of application, and distribute the same test throughout the kiln and in changes to firing cycles. Note down this information on the tests themselves, then line up the tests and compare. This will give you all the information you need to develop your pigment lustres.

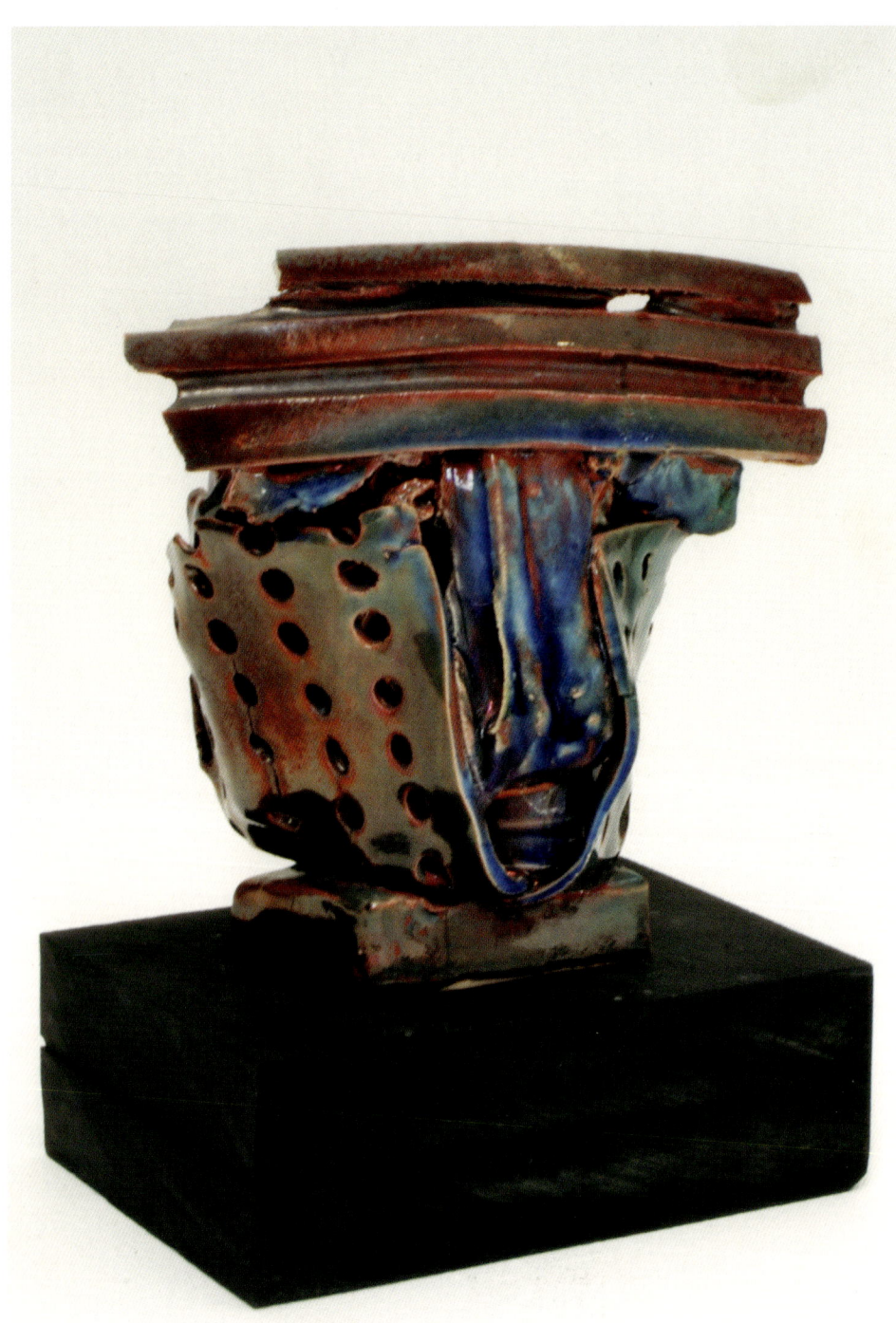

Fig. LG1: *Veiled Pretense by* Rod Bamford, 1988. Porcelain, high-soda copper porcelain glaze, reduced at 800°C (1472°F) on cooling. 12 x 9 x16cm (4¾ x 3½ x 6¼ in.). *Photo by Greg Daly.*

Chapter 3

Lustre glazes

Lustre glazes (also known as in-glaze lustre and flash lustre), as with pigment lustres, are about creating a thin layer of metal on top of the glaze. In pigment lustres we have seen that the pigment is the carrier, holding the metal compounds on the surface of the glaze which transfer into the glaze during the reduction cycles. However, with lustre glazes the glaze surface is reduced, with the metals already part of the glaze.

During reduction only the very top layer of glaze is reduced. This can be seen in Fig. LG2, where the centre tile has been acid-etched, which takes off the top layer of glaze to reveal the unreduced green copper glaze. The right tile is the copper glaze before reduction.

With pigment lustres there is a small window during which you can reduce the pigment, but with lustre glazes the window is larger and responds to different degrees of reduction for the final colour (see Fig. LG19). The plus side is if you don't like the result, the piece can be re-fired with more or less reduction and at a different temperature. If the work looks terrible after firing (reducing too low can cause the surface to look black, muddy), you can re-fire back to glaze temperature, reoxidising the surface to start all over again. The glaze itself isn't reduced, only a thin layer of the surface of the glaze; when firing back up to temperature the surface will reoxidize. This could not happen if you reduced a glaze as it melted to maturing temperature, because the colour would be locked into the glaze's glass matrix.

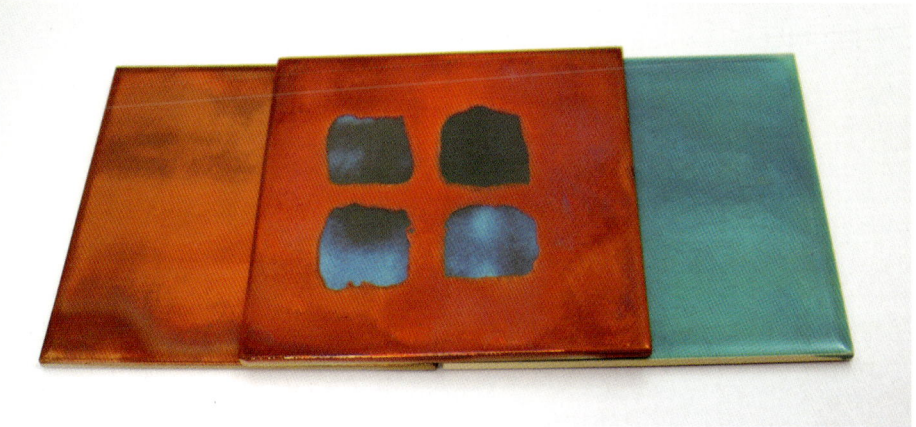

Fig. LG2: Etched lustre glaze showing the thinness of the lustre layer. *Photo by the author.*

What is needed to create a lustre glaze effect? Answer: a glaze, usually earthenware, containing (either singly or in combination) copper, silver and bismuth metals (in the form of carbonate, nitrate, sulphate and oxide) which when reduced will result in a lustre upon cooling. It sounds simple and it can be. Begin by using the base glazes already developed for the pigment glazes as a start (see PG2 and PG3 in the chart, p.38). High-lead glazes don't work that well, as the reduction makes the glazes very grey and muddy (see Fig. LG5 on p.71). Here you are reducing the metal lead in the glaze, which will take over from the other colourants.

The best base glaze to begin with is an alkaline one using alkaline frits or alkaline materials like gerstley borate, bicarbonate of soda, or borax (borax frit is better than soda ash as a sodium source). Raw borax and soda ash mixed in a glaze will crystallize in the glaze slop but these materials are also water soluble. There are two main reasons for making a frit, the first being to render soluble, non-soluble materials like borax and soda. Melted with silica and other materials like calcium or alumina into a liquid, this is then poured into a water bath. This quick cooling creates a shattered glass that is then ball-milled to a powder. Now the materials will not cause a problem when using them. The second is to render dangerous materials like lead safe to handle and use, in such forms as lead bisilicate. In Fig. LG1, Rod Bamford has based his lustre glaze on bicarbonate of soda with copper over a cobalt glaze, reduced at 760°C (1400°F). Line-blending silica and a clay like kaolin into a frit or combination of frits will give you a base to work with. Choose frits and materials to use that are easily obtainable for you.

This process is fast, and will give you information with little work. Use bisque tiles, making them at least 15cm (6in) square; or you can purchase them for this purpose. Small tests will not give you enough surface space to give you good enough feedback. It is important that, when you blend the silica and kaolin (usually in four or five tests in sequence all on one tile), the original information can easily be compared with the additions. These tiles I fire in an upright position, allowing me to see if there is any glaze movement (see Chapter 2, Fig. P3). Tile crank supports, used like a toast rack, are good for keeping them in position, with the added benefit that the tiles don't take up so much kiln shelf space during firing. The lustre firing also employs this method, where the tiles are in a vertical position and the response to the kiln's atmosphere is better than if they were lying down flat on the shelf.

Mixing the tests

While testing for a base glaze I find it important to add a metal colourant at this stage like copper or silver. You will observe the change to the lustre with the increase of the silica and kaolin. This also alters the softening temperature of the glaze and the temperature at which you need to begin reducing it. The reduction cycle happens on the cooling of the kiln not the upward part of the cycle. Either fire the glaze to maturing temperature, allow the kiln to cool and then reduce, or do another firing (a third firing, after the bisque and glaze firings) up to the temperature you want to reduce down from.

A number of outcomes can be seen and compared on a single tile. To obtain the most from a testing, I find it easy and best to glaze at least three tiles of the same test. Why? Because it will only take you an extra minute to paint a line of glaze on two more tiles (or more if you like), and it also allows you to fire the tests in different firing cycles and degrees of reduction to compare the different outcomes. Testing just a single tile locks you into one result. This lustre technique is as much about firing as about composition of the glaze. A normal oxidized glaze test is fired to the temperature you customarily fire to, and you have the result. A reduced glaze is a little different, and the outcome of your glaze can vary according to the degree and length of time of the reduction.

Now to look at fluxes. Frits or materials like gerstley borate (borate of sodium and calcium) blend in with silica and kaolin. Why use silica and kaolin? You need to add a refractory material to raise the melt of the glaze, in this case to cone 03 (1080°C/1976°F). As most frits are low-temperature fluxes they melt below 1000°C (1832°F). Silica will also act as a glass former (though not to the same extent as at higher temperatures) and it will also help with crazing, an inherent problem with alkaline glazes, while the kaolin or another clay (silica or alumina) will add a plastic material to aid in glaze application and suspension in water (vinegar as a flocculant can be added to help glaze suspension). You can choose other materials, but I have kept it simple and practical to begin with.

The temperature for lustre glazes isn't fixed. I have chosen an earthenware temperature, but you can decide at what temperature you would like to work. Keep in mind that this is a glaze that can

be used over an already fired stoneware and porcelain pot, re-glazed and fired to a lower temperature. My first foray into using this technique was to re-glaze already glazed stoneware pieces, because at the time I was preoccupied with high-temperature work. I found it can lead to interesting finishes – for example, a red lustre glaze decoration on a black Tenmoku vase.

If you are going to glaze more than one test tile, I would suggest you double the mix. As you are taking a small amount of glaze out of the mix each time you glaze a test tile (before adding the material for the next test), the percentage of the materials in the mix will gradually change. The amount of original glaze material will gradually decrease in relation to the amount of new materials being added. After you apply one test sample to a tile, you will add the next ingredient into the mix, then apply this and so on. It makes sense therefore to start with a larger quantity of glaze mix in order to decrease this variable.

The dominant metals for developing lustre in the glaze are, as with pigment lustres, copper and silver. Bismuth is also an important lustre former when added to copper and silver, but on its own is colourless and gives a mother-of-pearl effect. Applied over another glaze, such as a dark blue, it will bring that glaze alive. The forms these metals can take are as follows: copper oxide, copper carbonate, copper nitrate and copper sulphate, with the copper being present in the fused glaze as a colourant; I find copper carbonate is fine to use. Some people feel that the copper sulphate form is more desirable, but used in lustre glazes it will naturally turn to copper oxide upon firing. While in pigment lustre the use of copper sulphate can be very important, as it consists of fine particles when dissolved in vinegar and it releases sulphur in the firing (thus helping the pigment reaction with the glaze), here it is fired all the way up first and melted, and doesn't, I feel, have a significant impact on the final result. However, when applied with a brush it can be prone to bleeding, so less concentrated solutions are easier to use in this case. With silver and bismuth, carbonates and oxides are available, but the nitrate form is cheaper and easier to obtain.

The method for mixing the lustre glaze tests is quick and easy. We are going to line blend in silica and kaolin (in the same proportions as Chapter 2) using silica 40% and kaolin 60%. Weigh these separately and dry-mix them together, then place the ingredients (40g silica and 60g kaolin) in a lidded container with approximately 60% free space, and shake for a minute. When this is done, leave the lid on for a few minutes so you don't get a cloud of dust. Now we are going to add to our initial 100g frit, trial amounts of 5g of the silica/kaolin mix. So your first test should consist of only 5g of the mix, and then you should continue to add +5g silica/kaolin mix for each test, up to 20g (or higher if you wish). On your test tile remember to apply the first line of just 100% frit before adding the silica/kaolin. Additions can be made to a single mix as you go, or you can do it more slowly and weigh up each test (decreasing the flux as you first add 5g silica/kaolin to 95g flux; then 10g silica/kaolin to 90g flux; then 15g silica/kaolin to 85g flux; then 20g silica/kaolin, etc.). The straight additions are easier and quicker, with the proviso that when you have settled on the best result you must then reduce the recipe

back to make it add up to 100. Do this by multiplying each ingredient by 100 and divide by the total, as follows:

Frit: $100 \times 100 = 10000/120 = 83$
Silica: $8 \times 100 = 800/120 = 7$
Kaolin: $12 \times 100 = 120/120 = 10$
Total: 120   100

Process

First place the 100g of frit/flux into a container holding a little water. This helps to wet the materials as they go in (adding water to a dry mix makes it harder to mix the material from the bottom of the mix). Add more water if needed. Because you are aiming for three distinct thicknesses in application, and the first is very thin, make the mix a little on the thin side. There isn't a ratio I can give you of water to materials, so add it gradually. The two frits used here might weigh 100g, but you will notice that the mass is different. Lead bisilicate is a much smaller mass, as lead itself is a heavier material than the soft sodium borosilicate frit.

To mix the test, I use a nylon 2.5cm (1in.) brush. The nylon brush has a spring in it that allows you to push down and break up any lumps, and it bounces back and is easy to wash; or you can use an electric hand-blender. The brush is also used to apply the glaze test. Why use a brush and not pour? Well, the brush is quicker, and it may apply the glaze more unevenly, but this inconsistency will give you more information once the test tile has been fired.

Before I begin applying the glaze test I mark the back of the tile with information about the glaze composition and any additions. You have a large area on which to mark all this down rather than a number for the test that relates to an entry in a book. This way, everything you need to know is on hand (you can lose the book, but the tile still has all the information on it). After the reduction firing, mark information about the firing on the back of the tile in felt pen, such as when temperature reduction occurred and for how long. You may have three to five tiles of the same mix, which you can now easily identify and compare. This is so important. Another aid in preparing your tile, if you are going to apply three or more mixes, is to mark off the strips evenly with a felt pen or pencil. If not you may find the last one or two mixes don't have much space on the tile.

For the first test, take 100g of frit/flux and metal (copper carbonate; I suggest 1–3%). For the second test, add 5g quantities composed of the same silica/kaolin mix (40g silica, 60g kaolin) repeating this addition between four and six times for each test.

The frit and colourant is then mixed with water. For the first test apply three distinct thicknesses of frit (without additions) to the test tile. For the second test, add 5g of the silica and kaolin mix, blend it with the frit (or flux), apply to the same tile and repeat; this will not take long to do. Then fire to your glaze temperature.

All these glaze tests given here were fired to cone 03 (1080°C/1976°F). Note that you should brush the thicker application at the top of the tile when this is fired vertically. This allows space for the glaze to move, which may happen with the 100% frit mix and with those mixes containing a low amount of silica and kaolin. Firing vertically will give you an idea of the fluidity of the glaze in case you need to take care when applying it to a pot. Additions of copper, silver and bismuth in

these first tests are important in finding a working glaze that gives you the results you want. This system of testing will save you time and avoid duplication, resulting in working base glazes and lustre surfaces derived from the additions of copper, silver and whatever else you choose. This will save you time in mixing up individual glazes and help you to develop a base glaze you can use successfully yourself. You can choose any frit or flux to do these tests with. Even a combination of two frits can work – I suggest a 50/50 mix. Start with the frits and low-temperature fluxes you have on hand. Add copper, silver and bismuth to a base and see the response. Copper is cheap and easy to obtain, so try this first. You will find that different base glazes (using different frits) will respond differently and give red to copper colours. Once you have a base glaze that gives a result, start adding silver and bismuth for more results.

In Fig. LG3 there are six different line blends all based around copper response in the glazes. The first tile (top left) takes a mix of 100g soft sodium borosilicate frit, 1g copper carbonate and 4g bismuth. The first line is this mix on its own, and three other lines include additions of a mix of 40% silica and 60% kaolin in increasing amounts of 5, 10 and 15g. A cherry red right through the tests, the first line – without any additions of silica and kaolin – is fluid and has a blue tint coming through. Very little crazing occurs even after the addition of 15g silica/kaolin (the fourth line). This would be a good tile to take as a starting point.

The first tile at the bottom left takes the third base glaze from this tile and applies it to pigment lustre glaze PG1. You can see that the underlying glaze has gone grey from the reduction of the lead in the

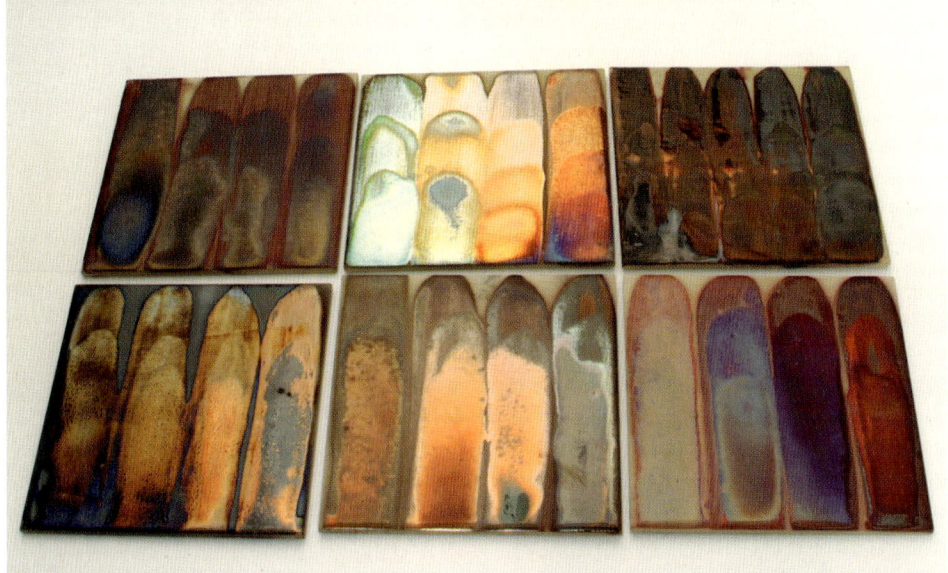

Fig. LG3: Six copper lustre test tiles and 24 glazes.

glaze back to the base metal. This is only a surface greying. Copper additions to the base glaze are 0.5, 1, 2 & 4. The copper glaze gets richer and more coppery as the copper percentage in the glaze increases.

The tile in the centre of the top row has the same copper additions but with a different base comprised of 50 parts soft sodium borosilicate and 50 parts gerstley borate, together with 6 parts silica, 9 parts kaolin, 2 parts silver nitrate and 4 parts bismuth nitrate. The silver and bismuth in this base glaze will produce a blue, but a small addition of copper gives a green iridescence (1g), or gold (4g), or purple-blue gold (6g). The tests from this tile, if fired through different cycles will give a very broad and colourful palette.

The bottom-centre tile has the same additions as the tile above it but the base in this case has no gerstley borate, just 100 parts soft sodium borosilicate, together with 4 parts silica, 6 parts kaolin, 2 parts silver and 4 parts bismuth nitrate, and (from right to left) copper carbonate additions of 1, 2, 4 and 6g. The smaller additions of copper give

pinks, but 4g gives a rich ruby red, and 6g a coppery red.

The tile on the top right blends a soft sodium borosilicate frit, in 10g additions, into a 100g copper-carbonate base mixed with 6g bismuth nitrate. This produces matt pewter metallic surfaces with matt gold and coppery colours and, where thin on the edges, a bright ruby red. One worth exploring, you can try using any soft sodium borosilicate for these tests.

The bottom-right tile is the same as the bottom left but with no glaze underneath, with additions of copper carbonate in 0.5, 1 , 2 and 4g. Note that these copper tests included bismuth, which helps with the blue–red colours.

By comparison, in Fig. LG4, the same glaze base of 100g soft sodium borosilicate frit, 4g silica and 6g kaolin, with additions of only copper carbonate (i.e. no bismuth) in increasing amounts of 0.5, 1, 2 and 4g, produces a rich red coppery colour. Higher percentages of copper can be tested. Depending on the degree of reduction and cycle the 4g copper carbonate will go from a turquoise green when oxidized to a red/copper colour when heavily reduced, all the way to a pewter colour at temperatures below 600°C (1112°F). This is a very simple, effective glaze, but try substituting different frits/fluxes and see the results.

Anyone who has used tin in a raku glaze will have found that it can give a pearl colour and when reduced heavily enough a silvery mirror surface. This is when the tin has been reduced back to its metal. But only the top layer, a micro layer of the glaze, is actually being reduced. The left tile in Fig. LG5 is an alkaline glaze: 100g soft sodium borosilicate frit, 4g silica, 6g kaolin, with additions of 5, 10 and 15g of tin oxide. The degree of iridescence increases along with the amount of tin oxide, with a gold pearl colour developing on some angles of the silver-grey surface.

The tile on the right is the pigment glaze base PG1. The first test line is comprised of 100g lead bisilicate, 4g silica and 6g kaolin, with the addition of 10g tin oxide, then 2g silver nitrate, then 4g bismuth nitrate. As can be seen, there

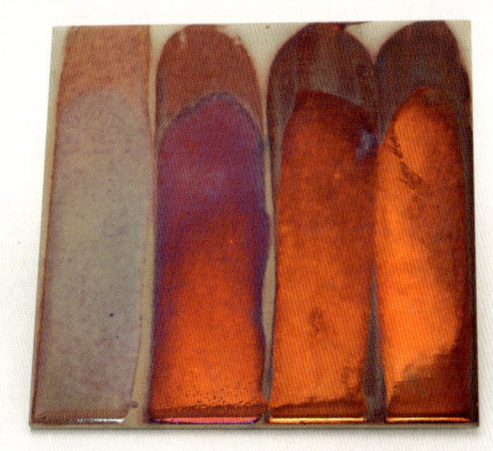

Fig. LG4: Copper additions to the base glaze.

is a predominance of greys, as the lead reduces to grey, especially with the base glaze on its own. The tin is also a grey, but with the addition of bismuth and silver a gold bronze develops where the tin is thin. The tile in the photo doesn't fully show this, as the light angle needs to be different for these colours to be visible, but from this test you can see that the use of a lead frit will lend a greying to the

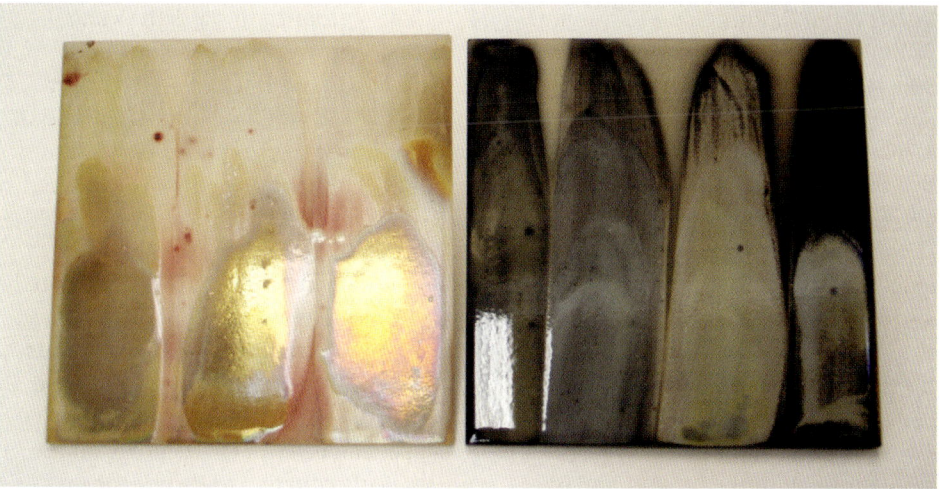

Fig. LG5: Tin responses in two different bases.

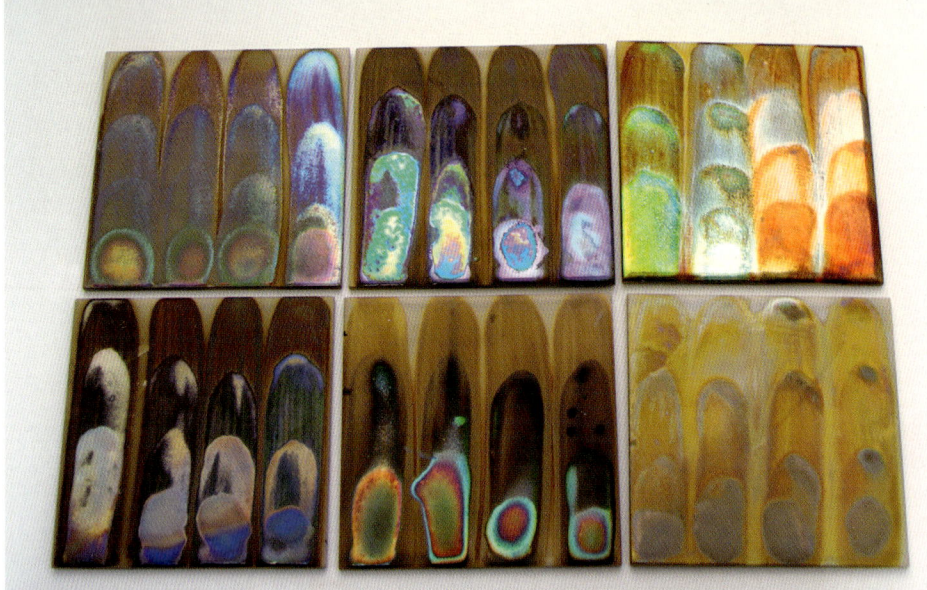

Fig. LG6: Silver-based lustre glaze tests.

glaze. Alkaline bases using frits or raw materials like gerstley borate, colemanite, lithium and bicarbonate of soda (my preference ahead of soda ash) are the base fluxes for lustre glazes.

The series of tests pictured in Fig. LG6 features a glaze containing silver nitrate and bismuth nitrate as the main lustre colourants. Beginning with the tile at the top left, the base is 50g soft sodium borosilicate frit, 50g gerstley borate, 2g silver nitrate, 4g bismuth nitrate and 1g copper carbonate with additions of the silica/kaolin mix 5, 10 and 15g. There is very little difference in this sequence of tests and no crazing. As the silica/kaolin increases, so does the iridescence. From a light coppery colour (where thick) it progresses through to silver-grey (where thick) assuming a blue copper colour where there is a thinner application.

The centre tile in the top row is similar but without the gerstley borate, and there is also a marked difference in the surface colours. The base is 100g soft sodium borosilicate frit, 2g silver nitrate, 4g bismuth nitrate and 1g copper

carbonate, with additions of silica/kaolin (beginning with the second test line) in amounts of 5, 10 and 15g. Beginning with a surface looking like a Christmas beetle, the iridescent green shifts to blue and then to mauve, with the increasing amounts of silica/kaolin giving a series full of changing colours. When viewed from different angles the surface comes alive with lustre.

The tile on the bottom left has the same mix on the tile, with the difference being that this tile was put through a heavier reduction, where the other tile received a lighter reduction (i.e. the reduction was later in the firing). This leads to two different results: the lighter reduction is brighter, glossier and more colourful, where the more heavily reduced tile has a predominance of silvery gunmetal with flashes, where thinner, of a coppery surface (due to the fact that both the silver and the copper in the mix have been reduced back to the metals on the surface).

The top-right tile, too, is full of colour, but this time the range is from iridescent green to copper. This tile is different in that a base glaze was applied to the tile and fired first before the glaze tests. This base is comprised of 75g soft sodium borosilicate frit, 25g lead bisilicate, 4g silica and 6g kaolin (PG3 glaze base with no tin). The glaze mix is the last test on the top left tile: 50g soft sodium borosilicate frit, 50g gerstley borate, 6g silica, 9g kaolin, 2g silver nitrate and 4g bismuth nitrate, with additions of copper in increasing amounts of 1, 2, 4 and 6g. The colours range from a green-gold through a silver-blue to a copper-bronze colour. It is worth noting here that the thin applications give just as much colour, from yellow to ruby red.

You can develop this variation of colour further from a glaze by the way you apply it to the work. Apply a base glaze first (different glaze colours and surfaces will give different results), then, using a brush that will give variation in thickness of application, you can build up an overall pattern. The use of a spray gun to apply graduated thicknesses will create a gradual tonal change across the piece; used in conjunction with stencils it will enable you to build up an elaborate pattern from just a few glazes. Combine a red glaze from this tile and a blue from the previous one and you could have a continual change of colour and tones across the work.

The tile on the bottom right is similar but has no copper, only silver. This tile has also been applied first with the same base glaze. The glaze test on top is 50g soft sodium borosilicate frit, 50g gerstley borate and 4g silver nitrate, with additions of silica/kaolin mix (beginning with the second test line) in increasing amounts of 5, 10 and 15g. The first impression is silver-greys where the application is thick and a yellow-gold where thin. This is very similar to the reaction of silver on a lead base glaze which we have in the top right tile, and it would be worth testing this glaze with an overglaze of copper-red pigment. As the red pigment needs a higher temperature than silver does, in this combination the two would suit each other for the purposes of obtaining the yellow-gold of silver and the red of copper pigment. This glaze when seen from a more oblique angle displays a full iridescent surface.

The bottom-middle tile uses a glaze comprised of 100g soft sodium borosilicate frit, 4g silver nitrate, with additions of silica/kaolin mix (beginning with the second test line) in increasing amounts of 5, 10 and 15g. Like the test to its right it is just silver (though the mix in the other test contains gerstley borate) and was applied over a base glaze. However, here the result is quite different, beginning with a gold coppery colour and moving to a blue. It has the look of heat-treated titanium jewellery. Where the application is thin, a brown with a green iridescence shows through. Even where the glaze is more thickly applied the colour range in a small area is like the eye on a peacock's tail. This glaze is worth careful thickness testing, to tease the full range of colours and effects out of it.

Tests in Fig. LG7 develop silver nitrate and bismuth nitrate further. The tile on the top left is just blue oxidised, while the tile to the right is the same mix but the silver and bismuth have been reduced, and thus changed, in the third firing of reduction. Cobalt, iron, chrome, nickel, manganese and vanadium are not affected at this low temperature post-reduction, in comparison with silver, bismuth, copper and to a lesser extent tin. These are the metals that give rise to lustres at this lower temperature, though you can use other oxides and glaze stains to colour a base with additions of silver and bismuth. Copper will have the tendency to take over, but other oxides can be used to moderate the result. Try a yellow glaze stain (or another colour stain) with silver. This will open up more possibilities in colour and effects.

The base for all these four tiles is 100g soft sodium borosilicate frit, 4g silica and 6g kaolin. The top two tiles also contained 2g silver nitrate, 4g bismuth nitrate and additions of cobalt oxide in increasing amounts of 1, 2, 3 and 4g. In comparing this tile (on the top right) with the other silver tests you can see the blue is stronger going from a teal blue through to a slate grey-blue. When this tile is moved around in the light it flashes like a blue mirror.

The bottom two tiles are the same glaze test: 100g soft sodium borosilicate frit, 4g silica, 6g kaolin, 4g bismuth nitrate and additions of silver nitrate in increasing amounts of 1, 2, 3 and 4g. However, these two tiles are quite different. The bottom-left tile has a glaze applied under the tests, comprising 75g soft sodium borosilicate frit, 25g lead bisilicate, 4g silica and 6g kaolin, with the result that the top glazes are taken into the melt. Where the glaze is thinly applied the yellow-gold develops across all the four tests, but where the application is thicker, it is iridescent from mauve to blue-green. On the tile without the base glaze (on the bottom right), the colours are stronger and more vivid, starting with a glossy mauve, moving through silvery blues to a deep electric blue. Where the application is thinner a brown dominates, though a green-gold shows through. As with other glazes,

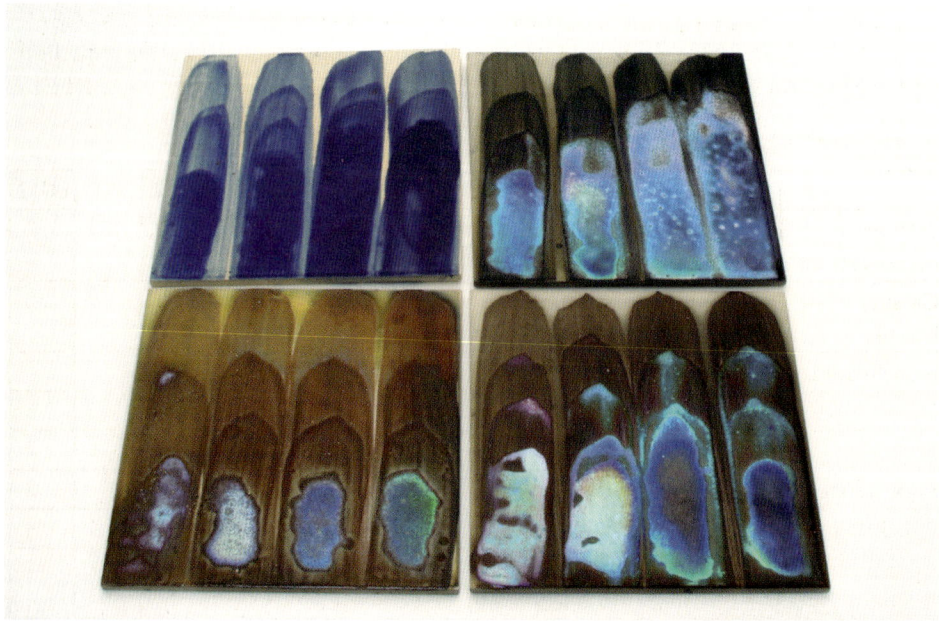

Fig. LG7: Cobalt and silver lustre glaze tests.

74

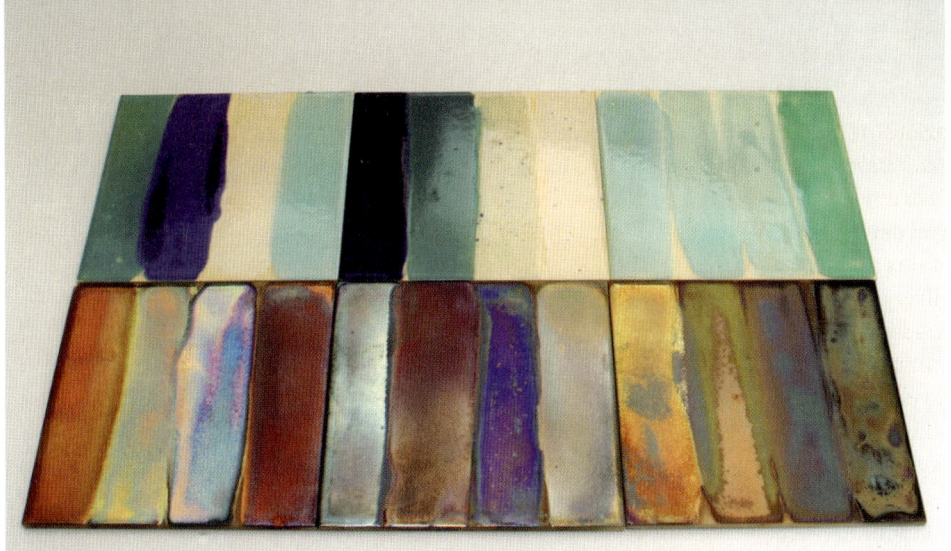

Fig. LG8: Twelve lustre glaze tests, before and after reduction.

thickness of application will certainly dictate the colour outcome.

When testing these glazes, it is so important to apply different thicknesses until you have decided what you are after. That way you will develop control over one of the elements.

At some point you need to select a few glazes from all this testing to take further. There are 12 glazes in Fig. LG8, which I have selected from the tests done so far.

The top line is what they look like after the glaze firing (oxidized) and the ones below are the same glazes reduced during a third firing, a huge change that can still be altered by the degree of reduction each glaze undergoes. The lustre glaze recipes are numbered left to right, 1–12.

In Fig. LG9 all the lustre glazes have been reduced to differing degrees, with the top line receiving a heavier reduction starting at cone 018 (720°C/1328°F)

Lustre glaze recipes derived from the tests

	LG1	LG2	LG3	LG4	LG5	LG6	LG7	LG8	LG9	LG10	LG11	LG12
Soft sodium borosilicate frit	50	50	100	50	100	50	100	50	50	100	100	50
Gerstley borate	50	50		50		50		50				50
Lead bisilicate									50			
Silica	6	4	4	6	4	4	4	6	4	6	4	6
Kaolin	9	6	6	9	6	6	6	9	6	9	6	9
Silver nitrate		3	2	2	2	2	4	4	3	2		2
Bismuth nitrate	4	4	4	4	4	3			2	4	4	4
Copper carbonate	1					6			3	1	1	1
Cobalt oxide			1		4							

75

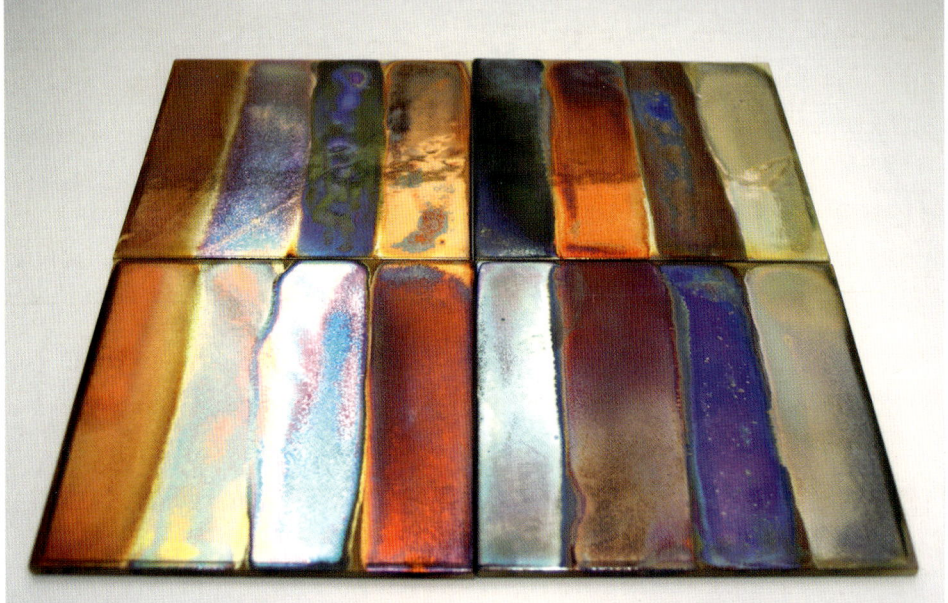

Fig. LG9: Eight lustre glazes with two different reduction cycles: top line heavier reduction, lower line lighter reduction.

at 150°C (270°F) per hour, reducing to 630°C (1166°F). The reduction process will be covered later. Note that the copper glazes in the front row are red in colour, and in the back row they are copper-red to copper, while the silver- and bismuth-based glazes are darker and more metallic. Those on the bottom line, with a lighter reduction, are on the whole brighter, shinier and more lustrous. Both reduction cycles were for 10 minutes.

What effects would result if the glazes were applied over other glazes? In Fig. LG11, three base glazes were used with pigment lustres.

These glazes were applied first, vertically, then lustre glazes were applied horizontally on top. From top to bottom the lustre glazes used were LG3, LG6 and LG8. Glaze application was with a brush and, as you can see, a second and thicker application was made, which accounts for the different colour in the centre of each glaze. Applying the glazes only takes a few minutes, so do more than one as you

Pigment lustre glaze recipes (Fig. LG11)

	PG -2	PG -2	PG -4
Soft sodium borosilicate frit	100		
Lead bisilicate	100	100	
Silica	8	4	8
Kaolin	12	612	
Cobalt oxide			4
Black stain		10	

can test them in different reduction cycles to give you more feedback. There are three glazes underneath and three across them on top, plus the second application of lustre glaze, giving you 27 pieces of information for only a few minutes' work. Repeat this process with other glazes; with one reduction firing you will have a large number of finishes to begin working with.

A helpful hint when looking at this type of test is to take a piece of paper and cut a hole –either round or square

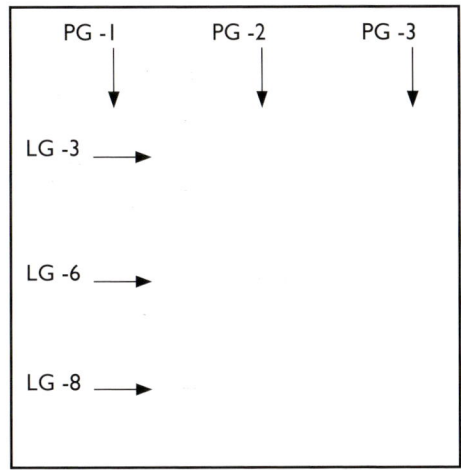

Fig. LG10: Tile application: first application of glazes down; second across.

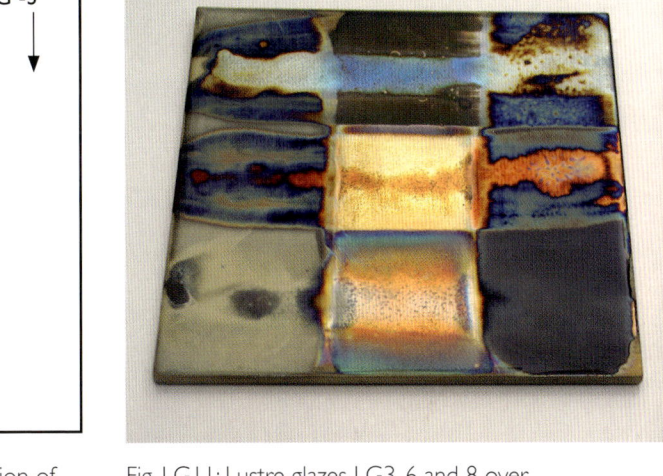

Fig. LG11: Lustre glazes LG3, 6 and 8 over three base glazes.

BELOW Fig. LG12: Lustre-glaze vases (left to right): PG4 glaze first then LG1 sprayed over in varying thicknesses; then the same pigment glaze with LG5; then with LG4; then with LG1 fired with one burner reducing and one burner on an oxidizing flame.

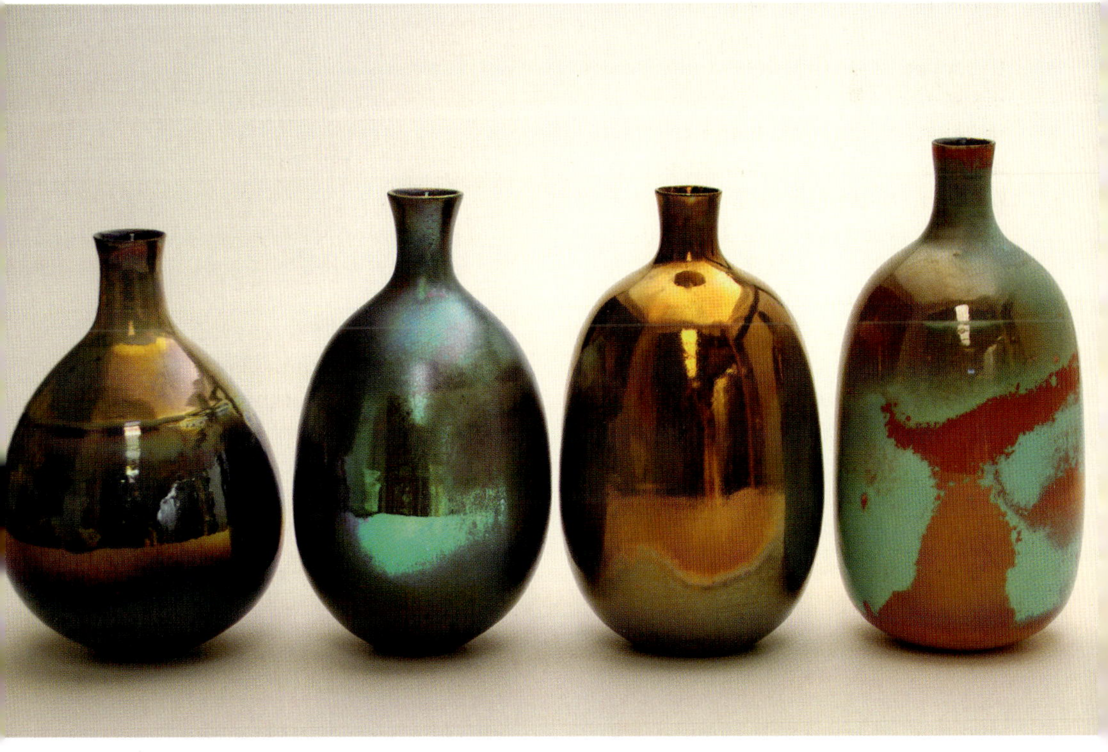

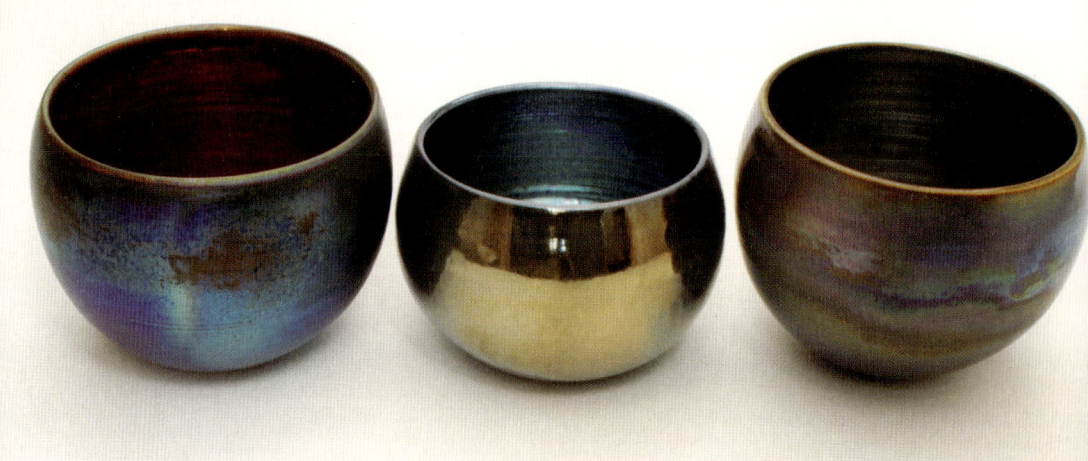

Fig. LG13: Lustre-glaze bowls (5 glazes) (left to right): Outside LG-7/inside LG-1; outside LG-9/ inside LG-7; outside LG-5/inside LG-4.

– 4cm (1½in) across; this will act as a window which you move across the tile surface. When you first look at the tile, it will be seen as pattern and colour, and much will be missed. The use of the smaller window will frame small areas so that you can see more clearly aspects that could easily elude a more general assessment. This little technique helps train the eye to see possibilities.

The lustre-glaze testing so far has used silver, bismuth and copper as part of the glaze mix. But another way, which suits decorating with lustre glaze, is to apply copper, silver and bismuth to the raw glazed surface via brushwork, stencilling, sponge pattern or airbrush. This can lead to a different surface finish. In Fig. LG14 the glaze-fired tiles have been decorated with a brush using the following mixes, and were diluted with 50ml (17 US fl.oz) of water for repeat concentration of the solution.

In Figs LG15 and 16 we see the finished reduced results. The two sets are the same, save the base glaze. Both are alkaline, with the lead glaze turning a dark black-grey from the lead being reduced. Cobalt was used as a modifier of colour as in the lustre-glaze test, in this case cobalt nitrate, which is water-soluble and can give very weak cobalt blues.

You can try any coloured or clear glaze. These (LG17) are but two examples using different glazes with the same decoration.

Chart for Figs LG14, LG15 & LG16

Copper carbonate 5g Silver nitrate 2g	Silver nitrate 2g Bismuth nitrate 2g	Cobalt oxide 2g Silver nitrate 2g
Copper nitrate 5g	Copper carbonate 5g	Copper carbonate 3g
		Cobalt nitrate 1g Bismuth nitrate 1g

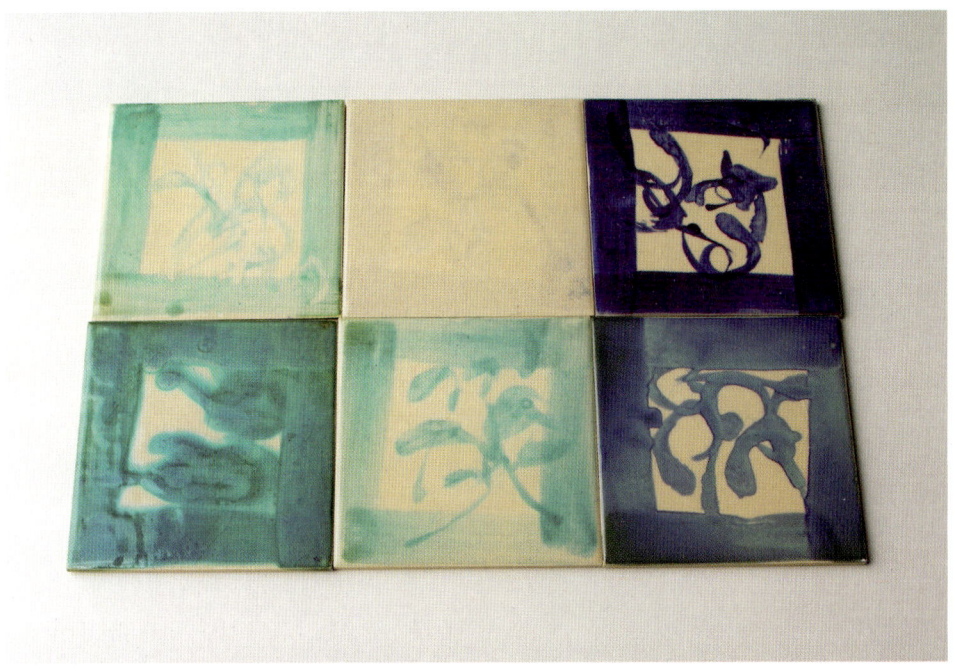

Fig. LG14: Base glaze PG2 with copper, silver, cobalt and bismuth mixes brushed on (see chart for the mixes, p.78), before an oxidized glaze firing.

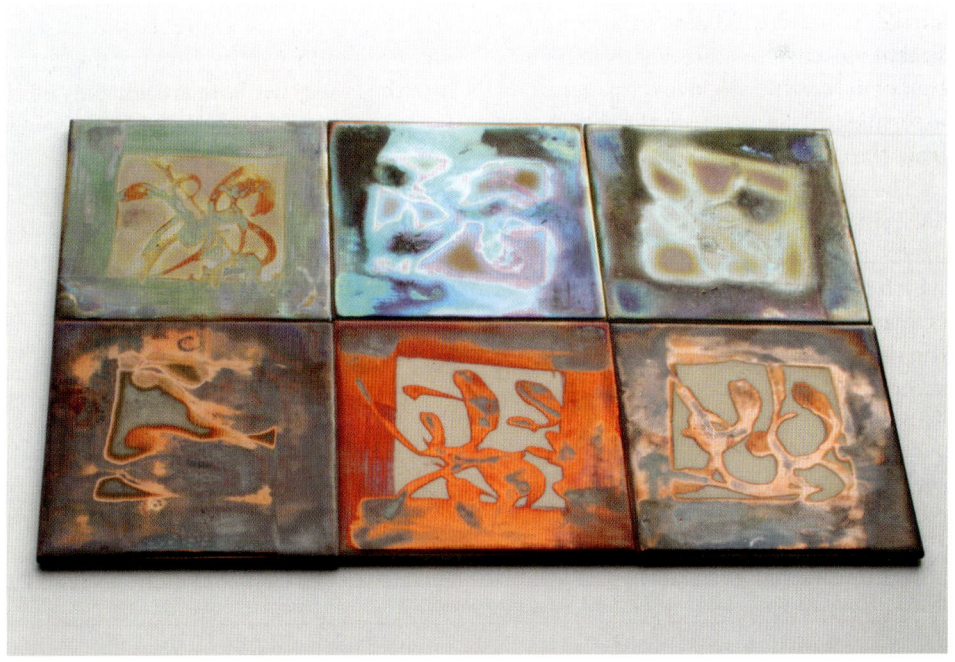

Fig. LG15: Glaze base PG2 reduced, applied to tiles from Fig. LG14.

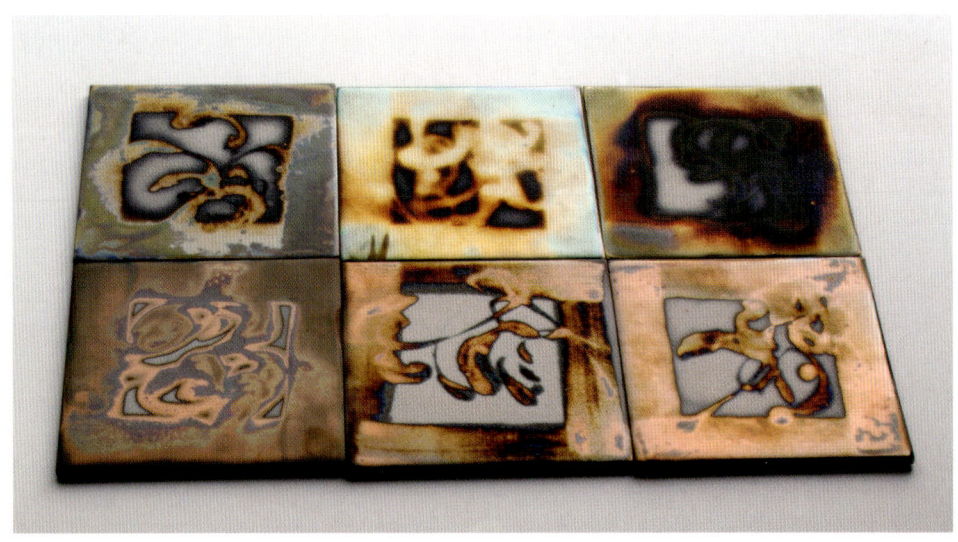

Fig. LG16: Glaze base PG3, reduced with the same mixes as LG15.

	Fig. LG15 (PG2)	Fig. LG16 (PG3)
Soft sodium borosilicate frit	100	50
Lead bisilicate		50
Silica	4	4
Kaolin	6	6
Tin		10

BELOW Fig. LG16A: Example of a platter with brushwork using silver and copper by Catherine Bennett, 2010. Dia: 36cm (14½in.). *Photo by Greg Daly.*

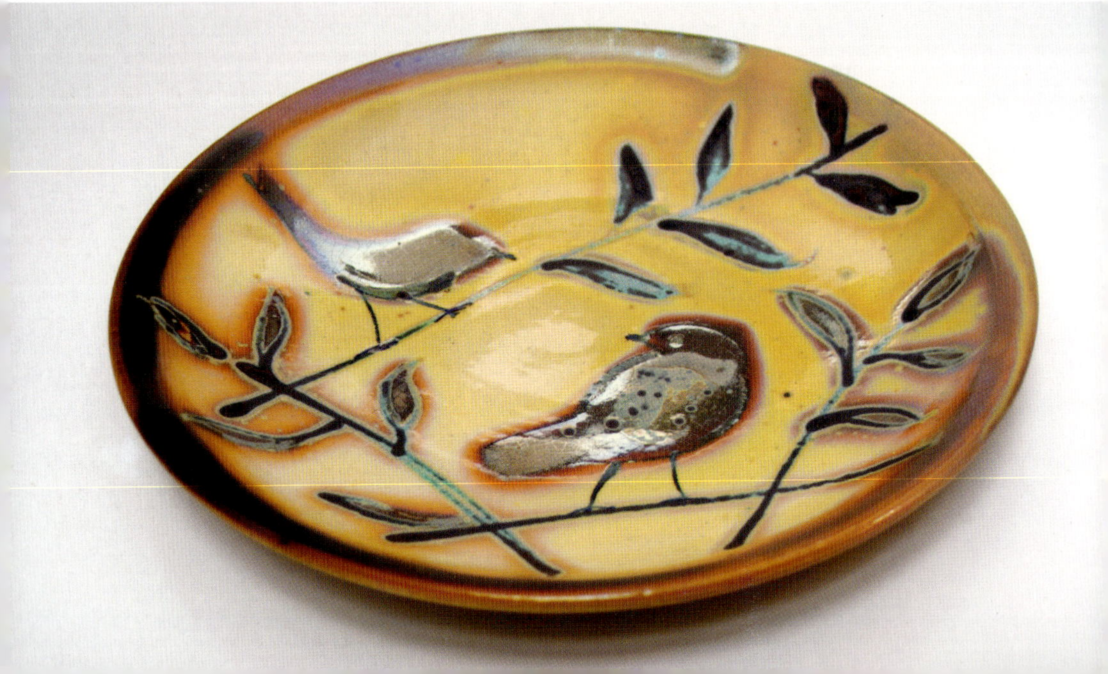

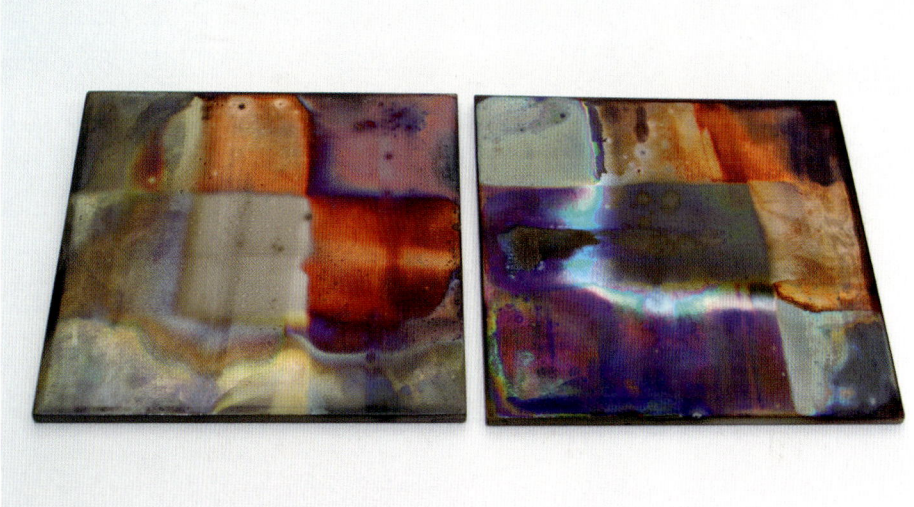

Fig. LG17: Washes of copper, bismuth and silver over two glazes in a grid. The left tile has a PG3 base glaze, the right tile a PG2 base.

In Fig. LG16A we see reduced silver and copper brush decoration. As the silver, bismuth and copper nitrate are soluble you will notice a haloing effect as the solution bleeds out from the brushwork. The plate by Catherine Bennett, along with silver and copper, has black stain in the decoration to define the composition. The copper and silver give the colours and tones, and the copper halo effect can be clearly seen.

You can continue to apply the solution of silver, bismuth and copper over the raw-glaze surface using a grid, in which they are applied over and under each other. Fig. LG17 is an example of this grid testing.

A wash of the ingredients listed below is applied across the tile in one direction, then a second wash in the same order is applied across it in the other; the first one horizontally, the second vertically. Divide the tile into as many divisions as you have ingredients you want to test (in this case there are three). Bear in mind that if you make the divisions too small they will bleed into one another.

Line 1: 6g copper nitrate or sulphate with 50ml water
Line 2: 4g bismuth nitrate with 50ml water
Line 3: 4g silver nitrate with 50ml water

A drop of food dye can be added so that you can see where you have painted the copper, silver and bismuth, as it can be hard to see where you have brushed it on. Remember to wear protective gloves, as the materials are water-soluble and can easily be taken in through the skin. With a broad brush, apply three solutions in order horizontally across the tile. Then rotate the tile through 90 degrees (these tiles were rotated anticlockwise; it doesn't matter which way you turn them, as long as you remember to mark the backs); you will see the lines of the application you have just done running vertically. Now repeat in the same order – in this case copper, bismuth and silver.

On the tile each of these materials will have crossed over each other and diagonally each will be on its own: on the top right is copper over copper; in the middle is bismuth over bismuth; at bottom left is silver over silver. You can see how the two different bases respond differently to these three materials. With copper and bismuth overlapping in the middle row on the right, the one on the left-hand tile is a rich red while the one on the right-hand tile is a copper colour. Likewise with the silver brushed over the base glaze that includes lead, we see silver and yellow-gold developing, while over the pure alkaline glaze the silver overlapped by silver bismuth gives a blue–mauve iridescence. All this information should be on the underside of the tile: the base glaze, the order in which solutions have been applied (with arrows showing which went under and which over) and a firing number for later reference. A number of the same glaze-solution combinations should be tried; if you have three or four of each you can try different reduction cycles and compare the results. This way you get a large return for little work. Fig. LG18 represents the test translated onto a pot.

As with pigment lustres, it is important to know at what temperature the lustre glaze softens (in this case to allow reduction to the surface of the glaze). In the test you have just done the base glaze will soften at different temperatures and through a series of reduction firings will give slightly different (in some cases quite different) results. If you begin reducing at under 700°C (1292°F) some of the mixes with higher percentages of silica and kaolin will not fully respond, with only a partial reduction of the glaze taking place; whereas the softer glazes with less silica and kaolin will respond. Reduction test firings with reduction started at 50°C (122°F) will give more of a result on the higher silica and kaolin additions. There is no correct result, just different outcomes. This will build into a broad palette of colours and finishes derived from just a few glazes.

You can use all forms of glaze application or decoration in applying these glazes. But the cost of materials like silver and to a lesser extent bismuth will probably stop you mixing up a large bucket of the glazes to dip the work in. Pouring the glaze is one option, but skill is required to achieve an even application with a glaze that offers different colours. Spraying the glaze is one of the best options, though the overspray waste can be costly. I find a small touch-up spray gun has a smaller spray pattern and is the best for this purpose: you can control the spray application with very little overspray.

As these materials are corrosive, thorough cleaning of the gun and any other apparatus used is essential. A face mask and gloves need to be worn, and even eye protection, in case of any glaze overspray containing silver or bismuth. The gloves protect the skin: if you get the slightest bit of glaze on your hands and don't wash immediately, dark black areas will appear where the glaze is in sunlight; these indicate where silver nitrate has come into contact with your skin. Like photographic film, your skin is light-sensitive.

Another application method is to paint the glaze on, but with earthenware and low-firing glazes the clay content is very low, so the

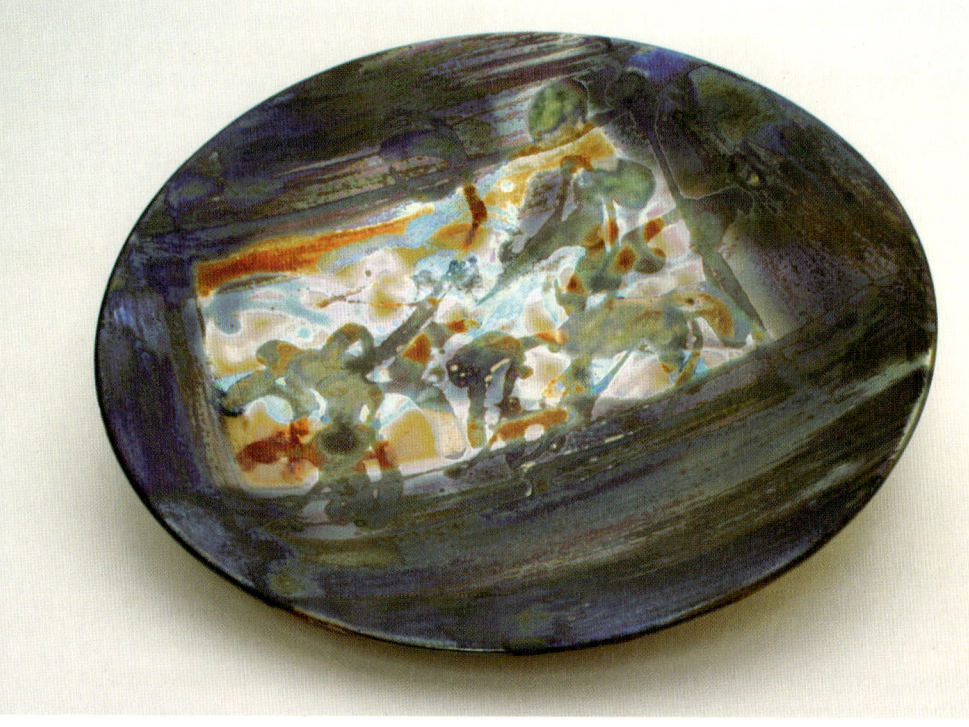

Fig. LG18: Washes and brush decoration of silver and copper over PG2 base glaze.

glaze application is very patchy. As soon as the brush touches the bisque surface the water is drawn in and the brush dries, which militates against an even application of the glaze. But the addition of a painting medium like CMC (Carboxy Methyl Cellulose) to the glaze has the effect of slowing the absorption of the water into the pot, giving time for the glaze to be applied evenly across the surface; two to three coats may be necessary to build up the desired thickness. Allow the glaze to dry between coats until the surface moisture disappears. Other mediums like gum arabic can also be used in place of CMC. Most ceramic suppliers have a number of mediums.

I prefer making up a thick mix of medium with the consistency of honey, as it can easily be thinned down. To your glaze mix (whose ideal consistency should be that of cream) add the medium in small amounts, mix in and test on a bisque surface. If the glaze dries quickly add more, repeating the test until the glaze doesn't dry instantly but stays paintable for around 30–40 seconds at least. You might need to add a little more water to thin down the mix. I find each mix is a little different. You will find glazes with silver nitrate in them may make the medium go lumpy. Use an electric blender or, if there is a problem with application, try another medium. If you're spraying or pouring, adding vinegar to the glaze as a flocculant will prevent the glaze from settling.

Firing of lustre glazes

As with the pigment lustres this is a very critical part of the finished result, controlling the final lustre colour and effect. But the nature of this type of lustre is that if you don't like it you can refire the work until you achieve a result you do like. This usually means taking it back to the reduction temperature range, but if it gets too dark and muddy you can always refire the piece back to full glaze temperature again.

You can do the whole process in one firing. Fire the kiln up to a normal glaze-firing temperature, turn off the gas and allow to cool. Then relight the burners, primary air closed, damper 95–98% closed (this will vary from kiln to kiln: if the flame starts to back-burn out of the burner port, open the flue up further) for the lustre reduction cycle. The temperature at which you relight for reduction will vary according to the result from your test glazes. The reduction cycle will also vary depending on that result. I have found a short 5–10 minutes gives results, while 10–15 minutes gives the lustre more depth. With a large spyhole, using a torch will allow you to watch the lustre develop. Then allow to cool. If your firing is not successful you can refire and repeat, either at a higher temperature or with heavier reduction. If the surface goes muddy, or metallic with too much reduction, you can refire back to glaze-firing temperature and begin over again.

All these glazes have been fired to cone 03 (1080°C/1976°F). If you are firing in a brick kiln, the latent heat can cause a problem when you try to reduce the glaze upon cooling. When you relight the burner for the reduction cycle the kiln will either sit on the temperature or climb a little. If you have a fibre kiln this is usually not as much of a problem, as the fibre doesn't act as a heat sink.

The second, and I find the better, way to reduce a lustre glaze is a separate third firing, which I feel gives you better control of the reduction cycle. You need to fire up to a temperature where the glaze softens. Starting the reduction too early, you will find only sections or rims are reduced. Most glazes need temperatures in the range between 650°C (1202°F) and 850°C (1562°F). Unless you are trying to reduce a cone 6 (or higher) glaze, going higher doesn't achieve anything. Try it yourself and see. You might have a glaze that likes a higher temperature at which to begin reduction. In Fig. LG19, seven test rings represent seven firing cycles. The top line is LG6 glaze, the bottom line LG7. The first ring is not reduced, but from there the sequence is 600°C (1112°F), 650°C (1202°F), 700°C (1292°F), 750°C (1382°F), 800°C (1472°F) and 850°C (1562°C).

With the copper glaze the reduction doesn't have much effect on the glaze under 700°C (1292°F), but above that mark a coppery red develops into a ruby red as the temperature rises. With the LG6 glaze recipe the copper turns into a metallic grey at 850°C (1562°F) when the reduction cycle is commenced at this temperature. The colour is green when reduced at a higher temperature (850°C/1562°F) for a cycle, the reason being that the temperature is high enough for the surface that has been reduced to become re-oxidized on cooling. To stop this from happening, reduce down to 730°C (1346°F) at the temperature where you find the best results.

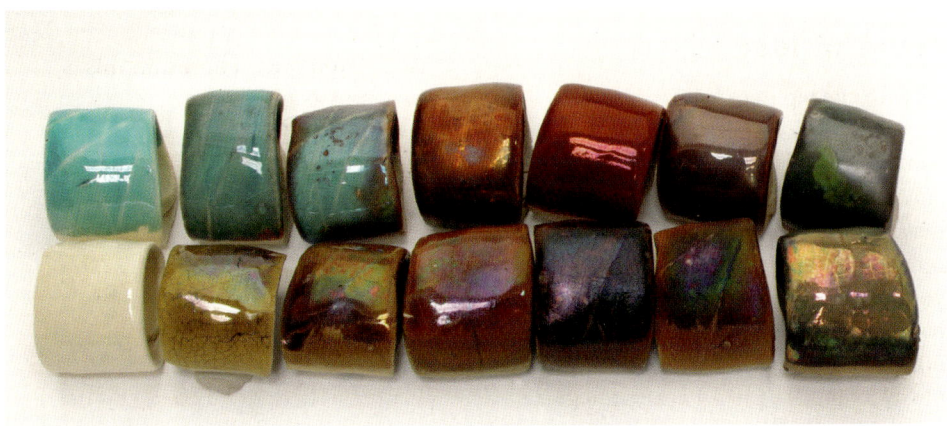

Fig. LG19: Lustre glazes LG6 (top row) and LG7 (bottom row) reduced at 600°C (1112°F), 650°C (1202°F), 700°C (1292°C), 750°C (1382°F), 800°C (1472°F), 850°C (1562°F).

These results, once the right temperature had been reached, were reduced down to 630°C (1166°F). You should be looking at 15–20 minutes for the reduction and for the kiln to make the drop in temperature. In a fibre kiln, where there is no mass in the structure, it can take less time. If it looks like the temperature is dropping down in 5 minutes, slow it down and take at least 15 minutes, because the glaze surface needs time to reduce. But, of course, the amount of reduction time does have an effect on final colour and surface quality, so experiment by varying the duration of the reduction cycle. I don't reduce under red heat because I find the glazes tend to develop too much of a metallic muddy colour, sometimes trapping the carbon and leaving a lizard-like glaze if taken well under 600°C (1112°F).

The bottom row is lustre glaze LG7, with the addition of silver. As with pigment lustres, to begin with the silver reacts at a lower temperature. At 600°C (1112°F) the resulting colour is a yellow-gold, then we move to a green-gold, a mauve gold-blue, then to an electric blue, then to gold and blue, and finally

to a gold-green. Remember, for this test reduction stopped at 730°C (1346°F). The change in colour and lustre surface will depend on the temperature at which you reduce. Fig. LG19 only shows the results of two lustre glazes over 120°C (248°F). But the degree of reduction will also affect the final outcome. You can play with one glaze and by changing the temperature at which you choose to reduce, the duration of the reduction cycle and the degree of reduction, you will have a broad variety of colours and lustre surface effects.

Fig. LG20 is a lustre crystalline-glazed platter with copper and silver by Ferenc Halmos which was first fired to 1250°C (2282°F) and was then put through a cooling cycle to promote crystal growth within the glaze. Finally, it was put through a lustre reduction firing in a gas kiln, showing that a high-temperature crystalline glaze can be transformed into a lustre glaze. Sometimes Ferenc reduces his lustre glazes with oil instead of gas.

These tests were all done in individual firings, but you could try reducing at a low temperature and pulling out a test ring, then firing higher, reducing, pulling

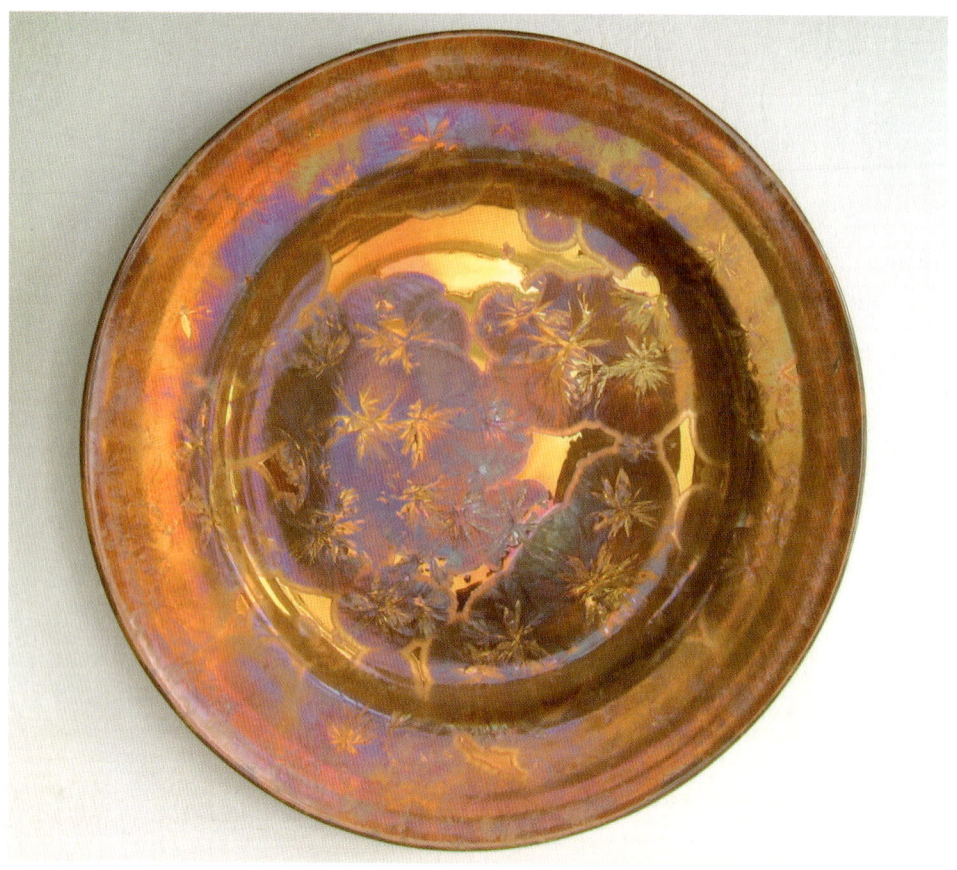

Fig. LG20: Ferenc Halmos (Hungary), 2009. Reduced lustre crystalline glaze, dia: 46cm (18in.). *Photo courtesy of the artist.*

another test ring, etc. I suggest when doing such tests that you use a number of glazes, as they all react slightly differently. There is no correct reducing cycle, only different cycles for different results.

What methods are there to reduce the kiln for lustre glaze? A wood kiln would be good, but we don't all have a small one of those. Electric kilns are one option, but how do you reduce in an electric kiln? Well, first I would like to alleviate the fear that it will damage your elements. One of my electric kilns, which I have regularly reduced in for over 25 years, still has the

same elements, though it has been used for firing only at low temperatures not stoneware temperatures. Give the kiln and the elements a vacuum after each reduction firing.

As for fuels to reduce with, some makers use mothballs. Beatrice Wood was said to have reduced with a combination of mothballs and wood in an electric kiln. My experience is that they gave little real reduction, and thus are less well suited to the copper glazes than to the silver ones, which don't need as much reduction and then you have the added problem of vapours from the

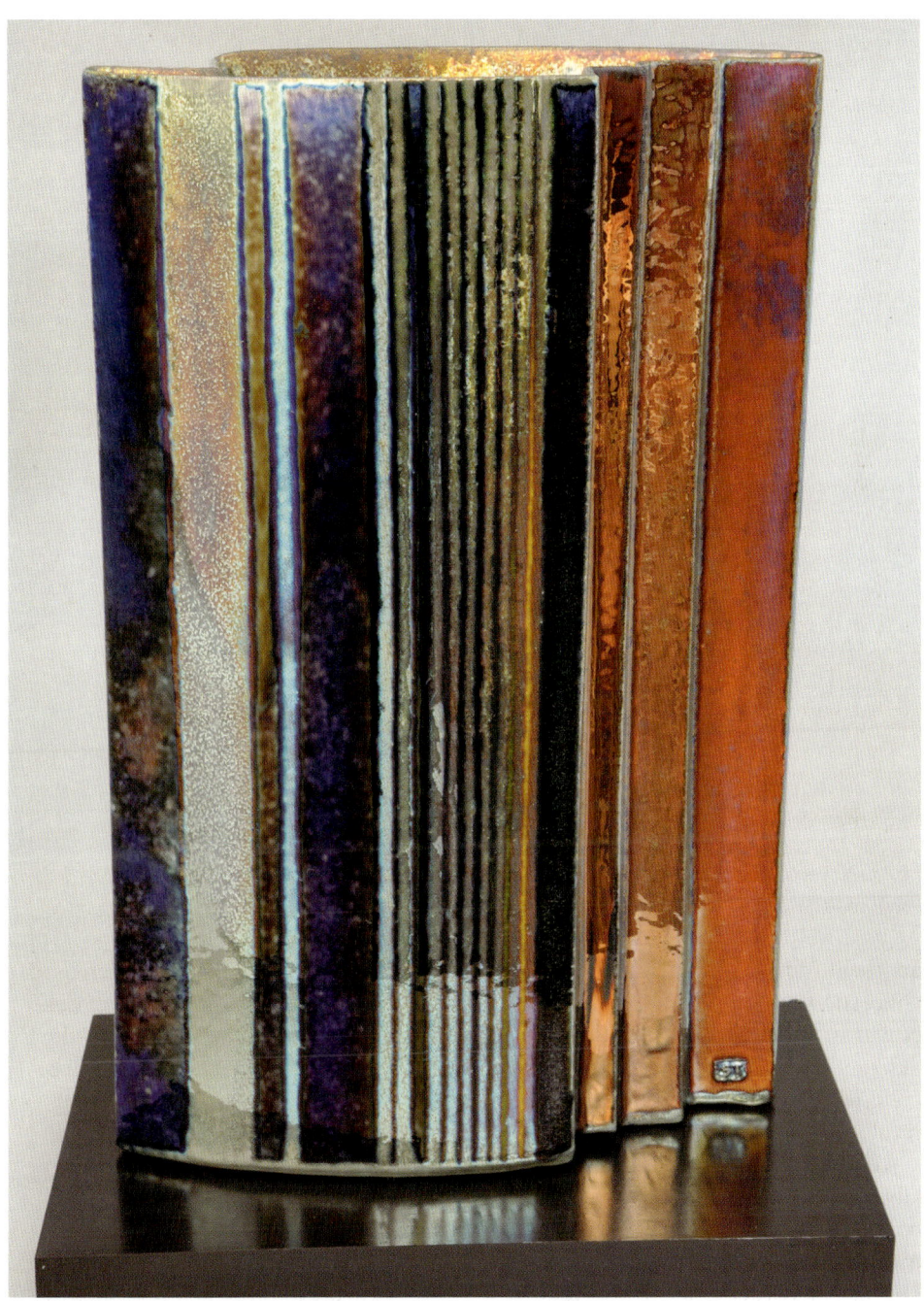

Fig. LG21: *The Light of Dawn by* Sutton Taylor. Underglaze slip containing cobalt, copper and silver. Base glaze fired to 1150°C (2102°F); inglaze lustre fired in separate firings at 1075°C (1967°F), 975°C (1787°F) and 940°C (1724°F), with reduction at 750°C (1382°F), 730°C (1346°F) and 720°C (1328°F) respectively. 51 × 33cm (20 × 13in.).

mothballs, which give off dangerous gases. Wrapped up in parcels, sugar is another possibility, it is a very successful reducing agent but creates lots of carbon smoke. Sawdust will only smoulder, though large wood shavings can be put into a paper bag to make it easier to introduce them into the kiln. However, thin pieces of wood are ideal, as they will burn quickly, reducing the kiln and creating fewer residual coals (see Chapter 2, Pigment Lustres). Where thicker pieces take longer to burn, a few small pieces thrown into the spy hole (preferably through a hole at the bottom of the kiln) every few minutes instead will burn rapidly, and there is little charcoal left to generate heat. This is my preferred fuel source for reduction in electric kilns.

In truth, there are also no real dangers with using wood that can't be easily avoided with a little care. **However, if you need to open the door to put in more wood (have a space below the bottom shelf in which to place it, as you only want the wood to be reducing the glazes, ash and coals can mark the glaze surface), if the previous batch of wood hasn't fully burnt, opening the kiln will introduce oxygen into the kiln, where there are unburnt gases, creating a fireball. So wearing leather gloves, a face protector and protective clothing, open the kiln door slowly and just enough to allow air into the kiln. You may see a flame come out of the top of the door, but this will only last a moment or two. Now you can open the door a little wider to put in the new wood.**

If you are using a gas poker or small burner to reduce the electric kiln with, have the primary air closed (a Bunsen burner with the air inlet on, then closed, is ideal to start with). This should be placed in the bottom spyhole (you might have either to make one or enlarge the one you already have). **With gas you need a vent at the top of your kiln or the top spy hole open. The opening needs to be around 2.5cm (1in.); experiment until you have got it right. And as you are introducing gas into the kiln you need an exit. The exiting gas also needs to be lit with a gas lighter, or you will have a dangerous situation (a build-up of unburnt gas).**

All these techniques for reducing in electric kilns need good ventilation and even a direct flue like a gas kiln. Please take this seriously, as not to do so could be dangerous.

In a gas kiln you need to reduce the opening where the burners enter the kiln, either with ceramic fibre or, as I do, using pieces of kiln shelf. You need to be able to reduce the secondary air, leaving only enough space for the flame to fill the reduced opening for the burner port. Too much secondary air will result in a light reduction and an increase in temperature (see Fig. LG23). When at reduction temperature, close off your primary air completely. In my kiln I fully close the flue and open the spyhole, allowing some of the gas to escape, which is then lit after reduction has started.

My kiln has four burners and in truth has too much power for low-temperature firing, so I block off two burners on each side, which I find gives me better control over the degree of reduction. You should also take note of your gas pressure, as different burners require different pressures. Above all keep a full record of all you do. A small thing may not seem significant but it can be. There is no prescribed pressure for a burner for any kiln; each has a different jet size and

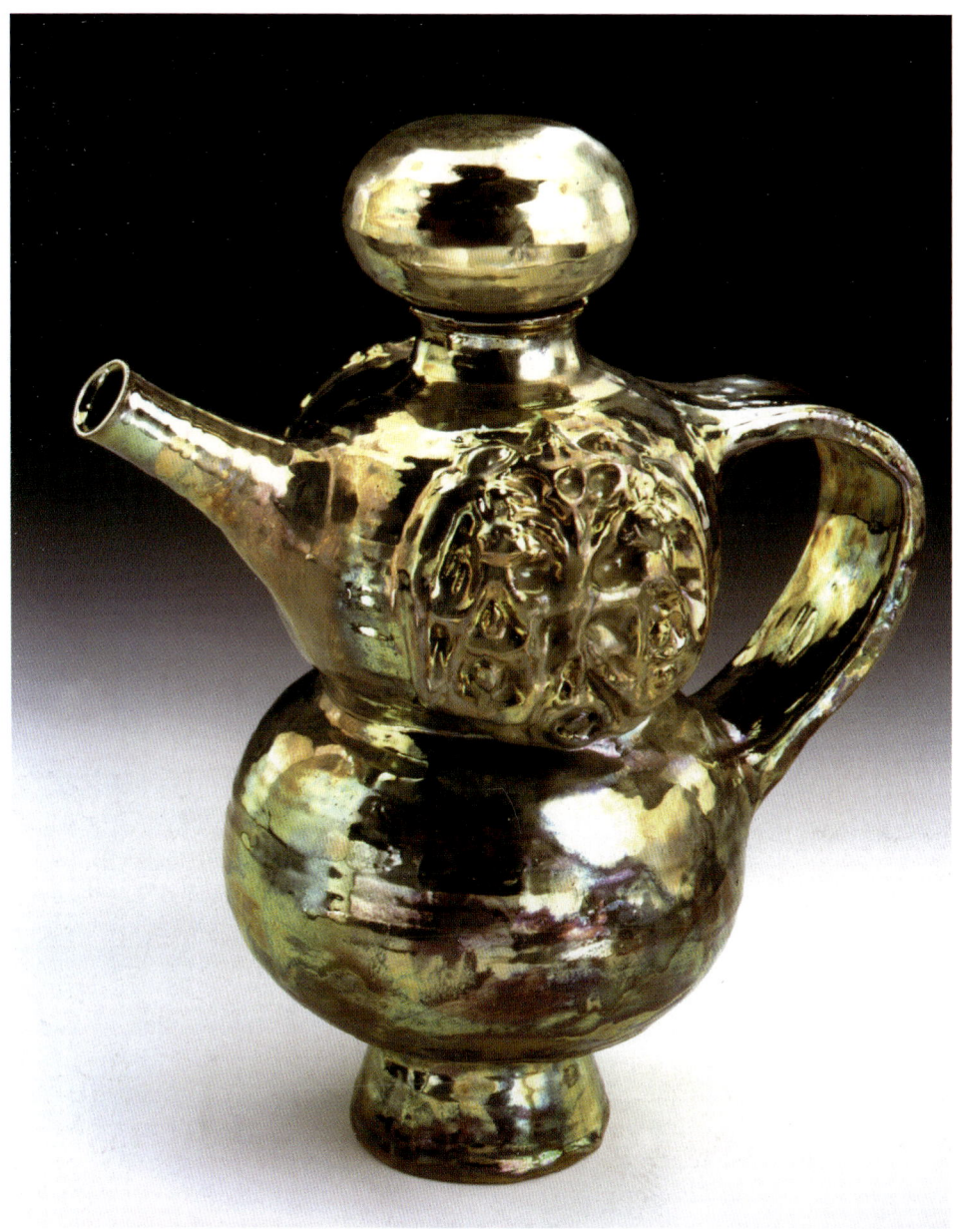

Fig. LG22: Beatrice Wood (1893–1998), gold lustre teapot, 1988. Earthenware with lustre, 35.5 × 29.2cm (14 × 11½in.). Collection of the Smithsonian American Art Museum. *Photo courtesy of the Smithsonian American Art Museum, Washington, DC/Art Resource, NY.*

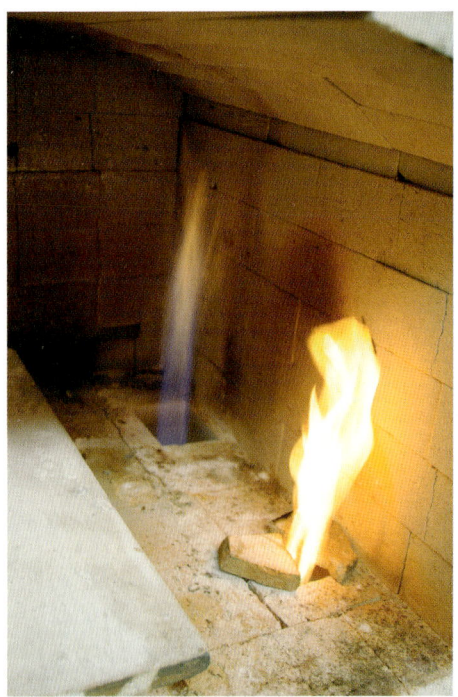

Fig. LG23: The yellow flame shows the burner port closed and a heavy reducing flame, in comparison with how it is normally seen on the left.

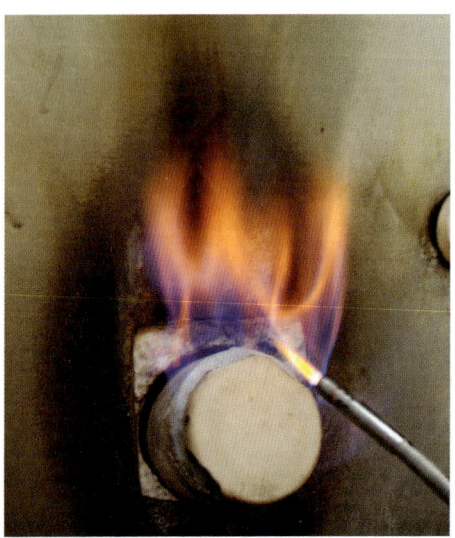

Fig. LG24: Lighting gas escaping from a spyhole.

nozzle. To help create a heavier reduction I also reduce the burner port size, just allowing the flame to fill it. Using kiln-shelf offcuts you can easily adjust the size of the hole, light the burner and close the primary air to observe the flame size and the space that you need to close down by. There is no danger to this. (See Fig. LG23).

The colour and size of the flame out of my spyhole is what I go on. The flame out of the spyhole is an orange for heavy reduction and a yellow-orange for medium reduction and a yellow for light reduction (see Fig. LG24).

Slight changes are what will alter your lustre glaze outcomes: differences in glaze thickness, slight differences in the temperature at which you reduce, slight differences in the degree of reduction (due in part to how densely you pack the kiln), slight differences in the temperature you reduce to. Think of these not as problems but like the strings of a musical instrument: play with them to get colour variations as you would play with an instrument to elicit different sounds. Some combinations you will find give a beautiful melody, while others simply make a noise.

It is important that you change one variable at a time. Staying with what you know works best. Then, once you have seen the results, change one aspect of the firing to see which changes can influence the glaze. It is important that you record everything you do in relation to the firing: for instance, the density of the kiln pack as well as the time it takes to get to temperature before you begin reduction. You would be surprised how these factors can change an outcome. If you go fast – say, taking 1½ hours to get to reduction temperature – and your kiln is

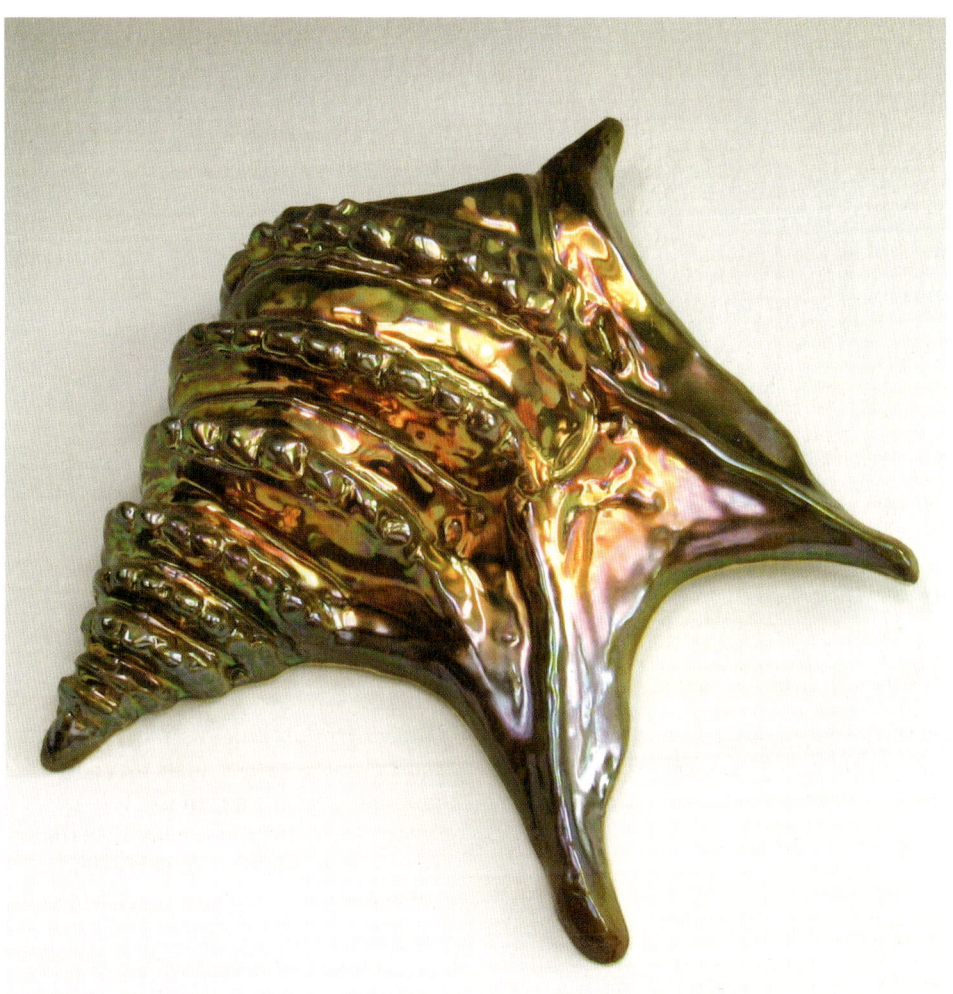

Fig. LG25: Lustred shell form by Ferenc Halmos, 2008. Inglaze silver lustre reduced with oil, 31 × 33cm (12 × 13in.). *Photo courtesy of the artist.*

made of brick, the heat penetration into the structure will be less than if you had taken four hours to get there. Once you begin reduction the faster firing will also cool down quicker to the temperature at which you cease reduction and finish the firing; whereas the latter, slower firing will take longer, and this can be a very important factor in determining the build-up of the lustre surface.

In Fig. LG2 the two (acid-etch test)

reduced tiles are slightly different in reds, the one on the left is more copper and the one in the middle a deeper red. Same glaze but different firing. The centre tile, which was etched to show the colour of the glaze underneath, had a shorter reducing cycle of only 10 minutes, while the one on the right had 20 minutes, though both were reduced to the same temperature.

If on your first attempt or later the

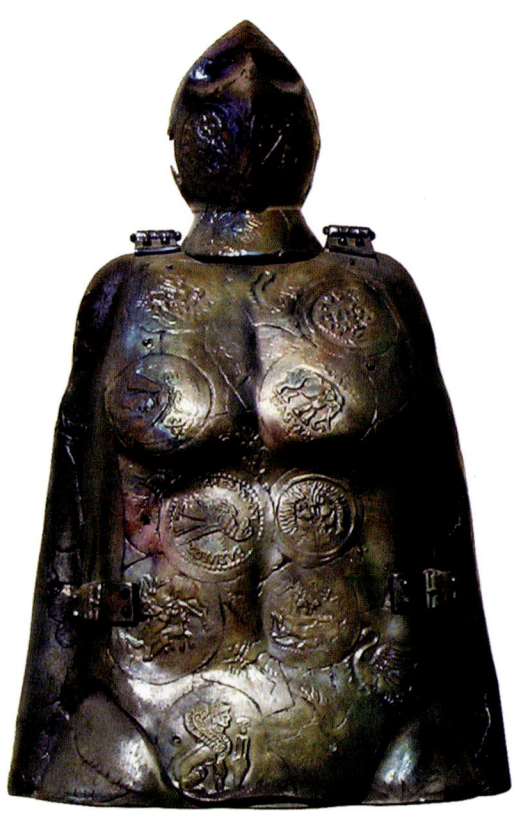

Fig. LG26: *Defenceless Human* by Kamuran-Sevim Çizer, 1996. Grogged clay with inglaze lustre using silver-bismuth lustre. Ht: 60cm (23½in.). *Photo courtesy of the artist.*

results aren't there, don't despair: the firing cycle changed even slightly will give you an entirely different result. Don't dismiss a lustre glaze that doesn't work first time. Thinking of your kiln and the way you reduce will transform your glaze in so many different ways. The difference you make can be very subtle, even going from a dense pack to a lighter pack.

As with all forms of lustre, there are other variables that affect how colour and surface turn out, such as the application method and the thickness of the glaze (for instance, if it is applied over another glaze very thinly so that the glaze underneath is also visible). The length and degree of reduction, whether a light yellow flame or a dark smoking flame comes out of the flue or spy hole (which may create an unpleasant

metallic finish), will make a difference to the colour and surface result, as will the kind of glaze you put over another.

With lustre glazes the beauty is that you can refire as many times as you like, until you achieve the result you are after. Numerous firing cycles can be tried. If it all gets too dark and over-reduced, the surface turning black-grey (usually from reducing down too low, e.g. under 620°C/1148°F), you can refire back to full glaze temperature, re-oxidizing the surface of the glaze again. Remember, when you reduce lustre glazes it is only the surface of the glaze that is reduced. The reduced layer of the metal lustre surface is only microns deep. Take a look at the work of Clément Massier and Zsolnay – all the colours are there.

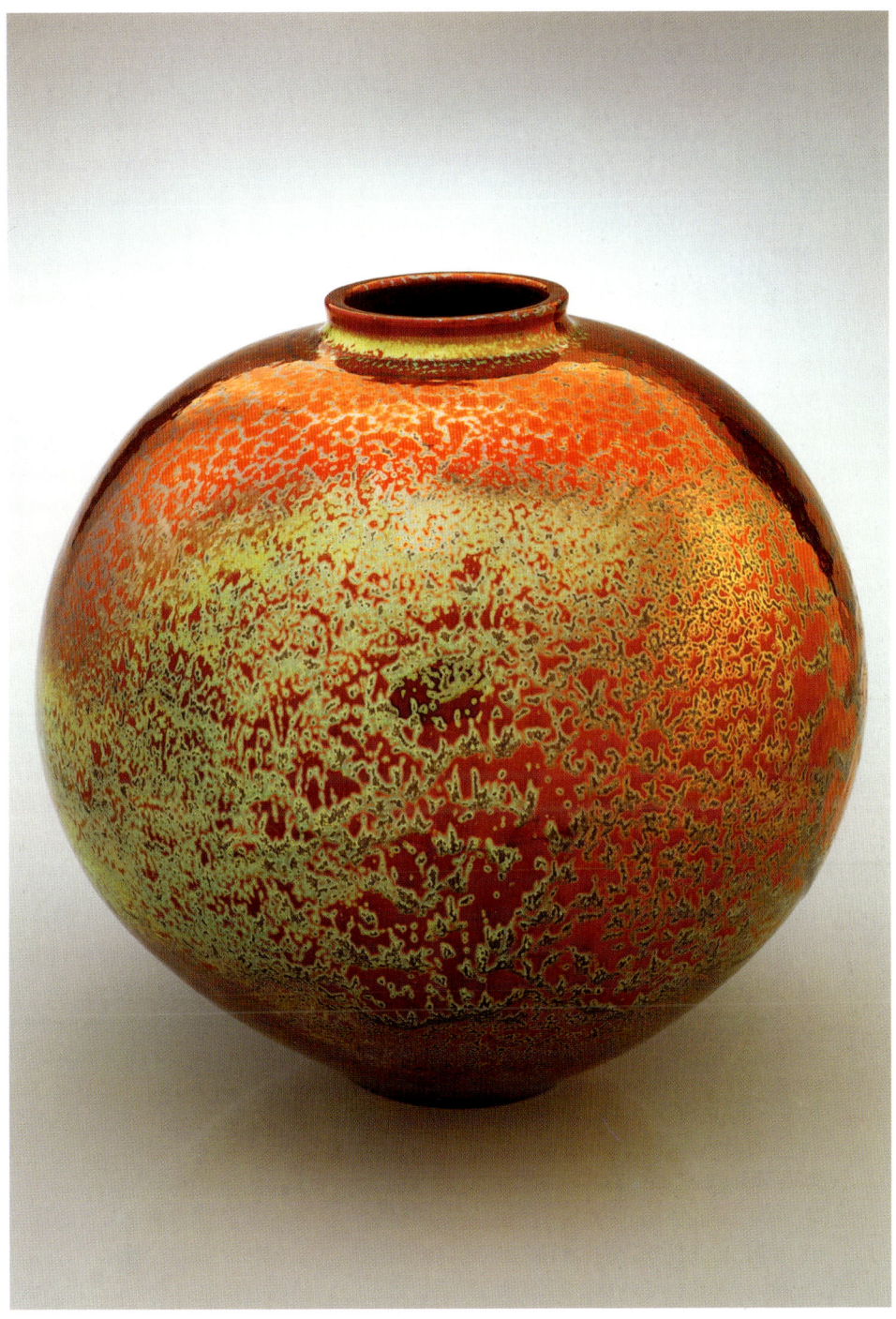

Fig. LG27: Lustre-glazed vase by Greg Daly, 1986. Copper, silver and bismuth lustre glaze.
H: 25cm (9½in.), dia: 27cm (10½in.). *Photo by Russel Baarder.*

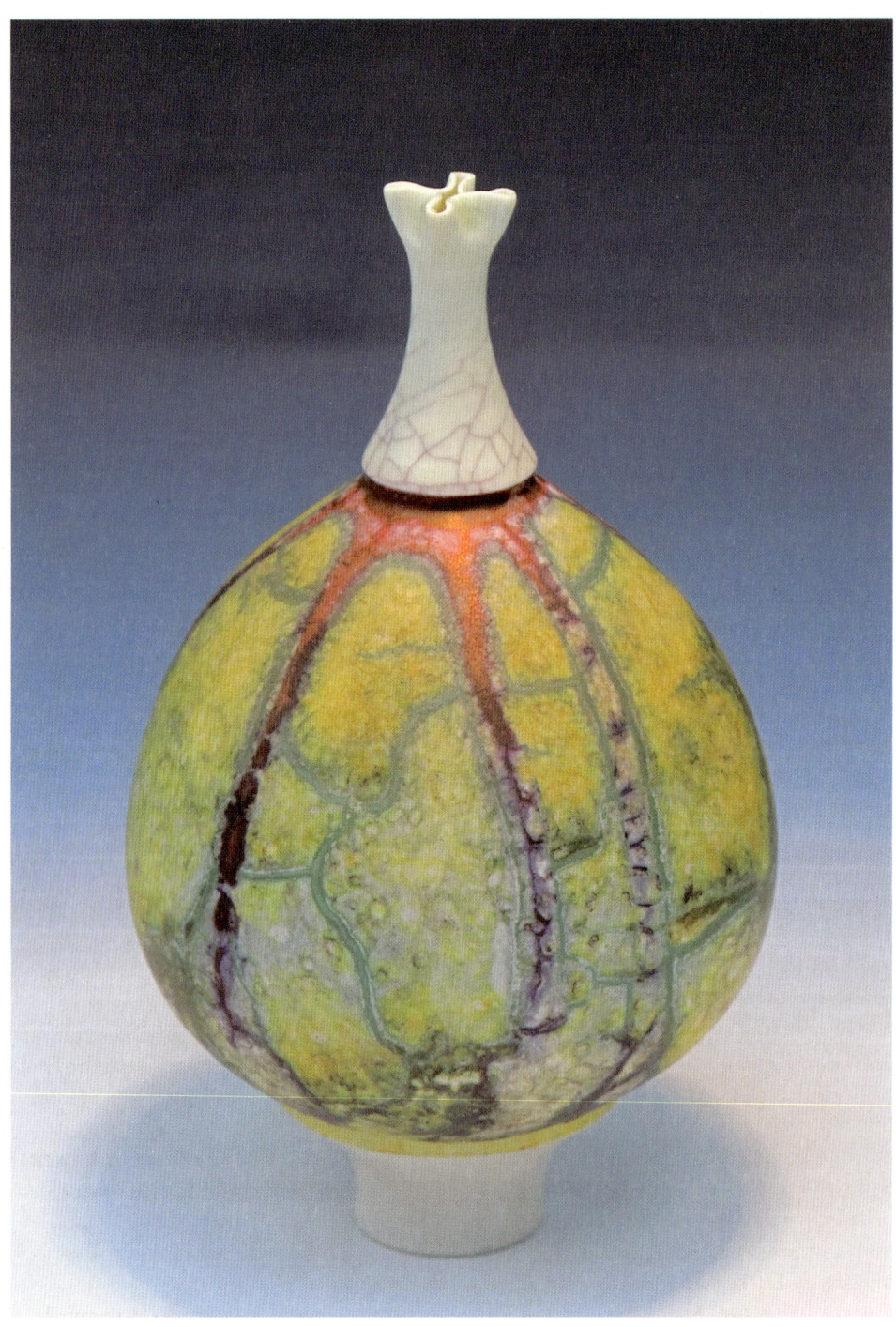

Fig. R1: Geoffery Swindell, porcelain vessel, 2004. Resin lustre first fired to 1280°C (2336°F), then lustre applied and fired to 760°C (1400°F). Ht: 10cm (4in). *Photo by the author.*

Chapter 4

Resin lustre

Like all other forms of lustre, resin lustre (sometimes called resinate lustres), a thin film-like coating of metal, is developed and fused onto the surface of the glaze. This form of lustre can be used either on earthenware or stoneware glazes. The technique is based on using a carbonaceous material, in this case melted pine resin, to which is added metal salts thinned with oil upon cooling. When applied to the fired glaze surface and fired to 700–800°C (1292–1472°F), the resin burns out, reducing the metal salts and depositing a thin metal layer on the glaze, creating either a coloured or colourless lustre. This form of lustre can be commercially purchased, and thus has become known as commercial lustre. It is important to remember that each of the different types of lustre creates its own surface finish and character. Resin lustre can be fired in an oxidizing atmosphere in an electric kiln.

These lustres can be classified according to two types: coloured and colourless. The coloured lustres are based on gold, cobalt, platinum, iron, uranium, chrome, nickel, manganese and copper, while the colourless lustres are based on bismuth, silver, lead, zinc, alumina and stannous (tin), for example. All the metals used in resin lustres are nitrate, acetate, sulphate or chloride forms of the metals. They need to be soluble in water. Nitrates, acetates, chlorides and

sulphates need to be handled with care, as you would other types of lustres. They are water-soluble, making them easily absorbed into the skin, so it is imperative that you use protective gloves. Oxides and carbonates are not soluble and cannot therefore be used in these lustres.

The colours obtainable with resin lustres range from mother-of-pearl, a colourless lustre that comes from bismuth, to a golden tone that comes from iron, to a greenish-yellow that comes from uranium. A small amount of bismuth with gold lustre gives a copper sheen. Adding more bismuth can create a blue shade.

The mixing and application of resin lustres can lead to some amazing surfaces that cannot be created with any other form of lustre. With pigment and lustre glazes, silver and copper dominate to give colour and effect; with resin, gold gives reds, pinks and purples, while copper gives blue and gold. The principle behind this type of lustre, and why it can be fired in an oxidizing atmosphere in an electric kiln, is that as the resin burns away it reduces the metal in the lustre mix back to its metal form. Cobalt, for example, when used as a metal in a resin lustre doesn't yield a blue colour but a silvery-grey lustre.

Resin lustres prepared from bismuth, lead, zinc, alumina, stannous (tin) and silver salts (nitrate, acetate, sulphate and chloride) appear colourless until light strikes the surface at an angle, whereupon an iridescent, mother-of-pearl, rainbow effect can be seen as light is refracted off the surface of the work.

Bismuth alone with resin forms a faint mother-of-pearl lustre (3g bismuth and 10g resin). When combined with zinc and lead it creates a strong mother-of-pearl: pine resin 10g, lead acetate 2g, zinc actate 2g, bismuth nitrate 2g.

Bismuth has two roles in a lustre: in a small amount it can act as a flux (it helps to stop the gold from simply rubbing off after firing), and in larger amounts it can give a mother-of-pearl effect to the colour.

Coloured resin lustres are developed using the following metal salts: gold for gold, pink, red and purple; palladium for silver; uranium for yellow or green-yellow; chrome for yellow; cobalt for brown to gunmetal; nickel for light brown; manganese for brown; iron for light brown to orange; copper for brown to red.

In most cases a resin lustre mix made from the metal salts will rub straight off after the firing. A low-temperature flux needs to be included in the mix, which in most cases is bismuth, though lead can also be used. An example is a silvery gunmetal lustre.

Recipe:

Pine resin	10g
Cobalt nitrate	3g
Bismuth nitrate	2g

If the bismuth isn't included, the lustre when fired will rub off. The inclusion of the bismuth doesn't alter the colour, but acts as a flux to fuse the cobalt onto the glaze.

There are both wet and dry methods of making resin lustres – two methods that Rudolf Hainbach describes in his 1907 book *Pottery Decorating*, which is in part reprinted in *Ceramic Glazes* by C.W. Parmelee. In both cases the resinate of a metal is prepared first, dissolved in oil of lavender or turpentine. The wet method is a drawn-out process and will be mentioned later in the making of gold lustre. The easiest process is the dry method, as follows.

Making resin lustre

The making of resin lustre is not a complicated procedure. You need a hotplate on which to melt your resin, and preferably a small ceramic bowl in which to prepare the mix. The lustre mix covered here is a cobalt lustre, which as we have seen is a gunmetal colour.

Place 10g pine resin into the bowl on a low to mid-heat. You need to melt the resin like you would toffee: not hot enough and it will form one sticky lump; too hot and it will burn.

Pine resin, sometimes called rosin or colophony, can be easily obtained from an art shop (it is used by printers), or from a music shop (it is used by violinists to help their bows grip the strings). I have also tried sugars for mixing with the metal salts in place of the resin, as you need a carbonaceous material that when it burns will reduce the metal in the resin solution. However, when I added the bismuth and cobalt the whole mix erupted like a volcano spewing out black ash, so this is obviously not suitable (bismuth is an oxidizing agent, or flux, as it acts as an oxidizing agent, helping things to burn) – you should not have the mix too hot). I have also tried acacia resin, which didn't melt, but using pine

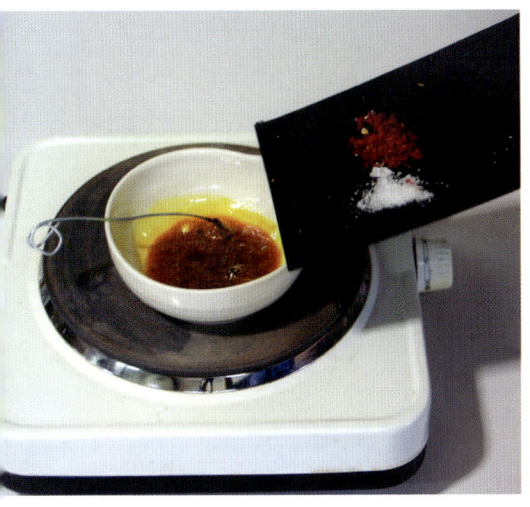

Fig. R2: Cobalt nitrate and bismuth nitrate are added to the melted pine resin.

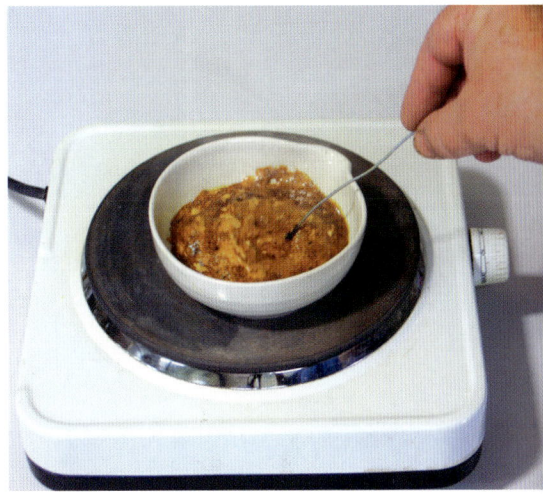

Fig. R3: The mix is stirred and will turn brown and froth.

resin was successful, so that's what I'd recommend.

The metal salts are cobalt nitrate, bismuth subnitrate, iron chloride, zinc acetate, lead acetate, gold chloride, palladium chloride, copper nitrate, stannous chloride, silver nitrate, uranium nitrate and potassium dichromate. Oxides and carbonates don't work with resin lustres, as the ingredient has to be soluble, absorbed into the resin solution.

When the mix has melted add 3g cobalt nitrate and 2g bismuth nitrate. As mentioned earlier the bismuth acts as a flux in the mix (see Fig. R2). If you just use cobalt nitrate it will work in terms of colour and surface, but will wipe off after the firing. At this point you will see why it is so important to be in a well-ventilated space, as fumes will be given off as you stir the mix. As you add the salts (Fig. R2), stir the mix and it will start to froth and give off nitrogen vapour (from the cobalt nitrate); it will also start to turn brown (see Fig. R3). Parmelee notes that 'when the mix turns brown, the lavender oil is

added slowly'. The first few times I tried this, the mix did turn brown and I added the oil to the mix, but the mix when fired was not lustre. What is not written is that you have to cook the mix until it goes from an opaque brown to a glossy brown-black, and depending on the ingredients this will take between 20 and 40 minutes.

When the mix has a glossy, dense colour, turn off the heat. Now you can add the oil, stirring slowly and continuously. For 10g resin you will need to add around 30–50ml of oil. The test is to put a drop from the mixing implement onto a tile. This cools it down so that you can check the viscosity of the mix: with too little oil it will be tacky, in which case add more oil to the mix. Note the black glossy look of the mix in Fig. R4 compared with that in Fig. R3.

If you are printing with the lustre or using stamps, a slightly thicker mix is better (if you are using a brush then make it a little thinner, and an airbrush thinner still); the mix can always be thinned later depending on your

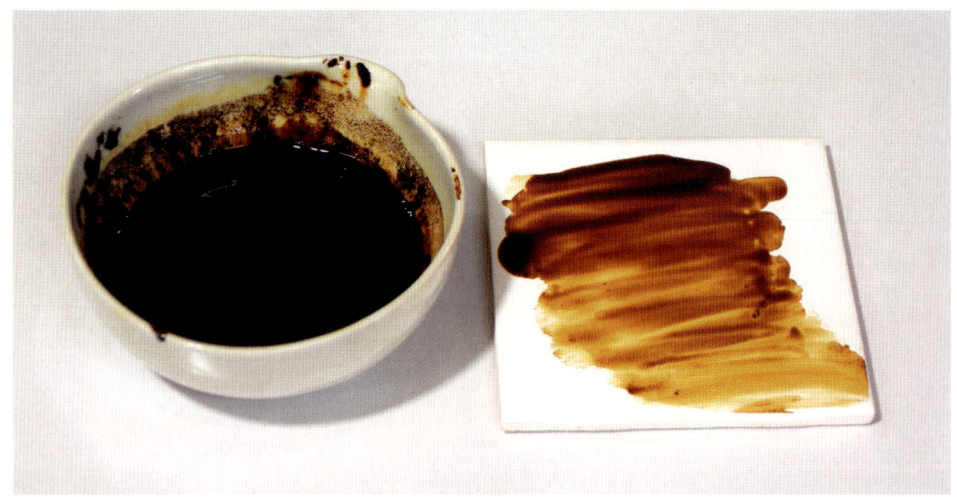

Fig. R4: The finished lustre. Note the glossy colour and the use of a tile to test the viscosity of the mix.

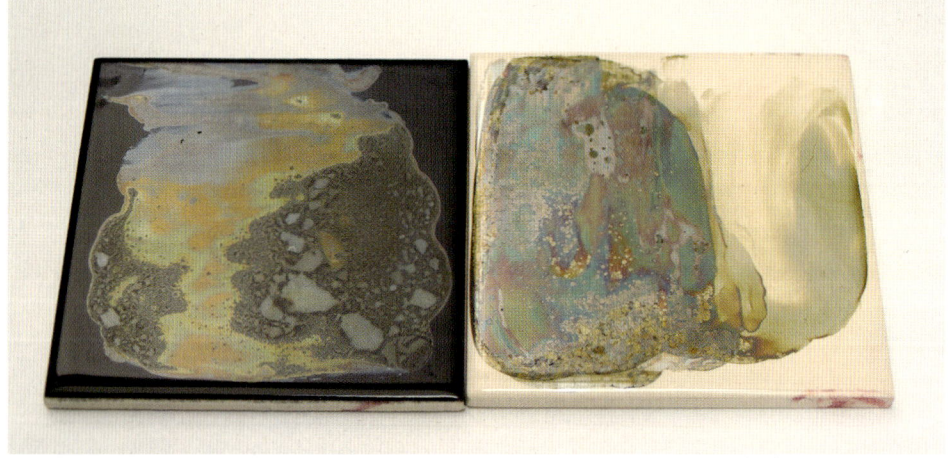

Fig. R5: The finished cobalt lustre on black and clear glazes, with varying thicknesses of application.

requirements. Lustres of this type can vary greatly according to how thickly they are applied. In Fig. R5, for example, the cobalt lustre colour on the tiles changes as the application of the lustre glaze thickness varies.

If the mix is left to cool without the oil being added, it will revert back to a hard lump of resin. The thinning agent traditionally used was lavender oil, but you can use most light oils such as eucalyptus, pure turpentine (not mineral turpentine) and French or Venetian turpentine, as well as clove, spike, rosemary, fennel and camphor oils. The main oil I use is eucalyptus oil, which is very similar in nature to lavender oil.

In commercial lustre toluene, nitrobenzene and chloroform are some of the solvents used, but I strongly suggest

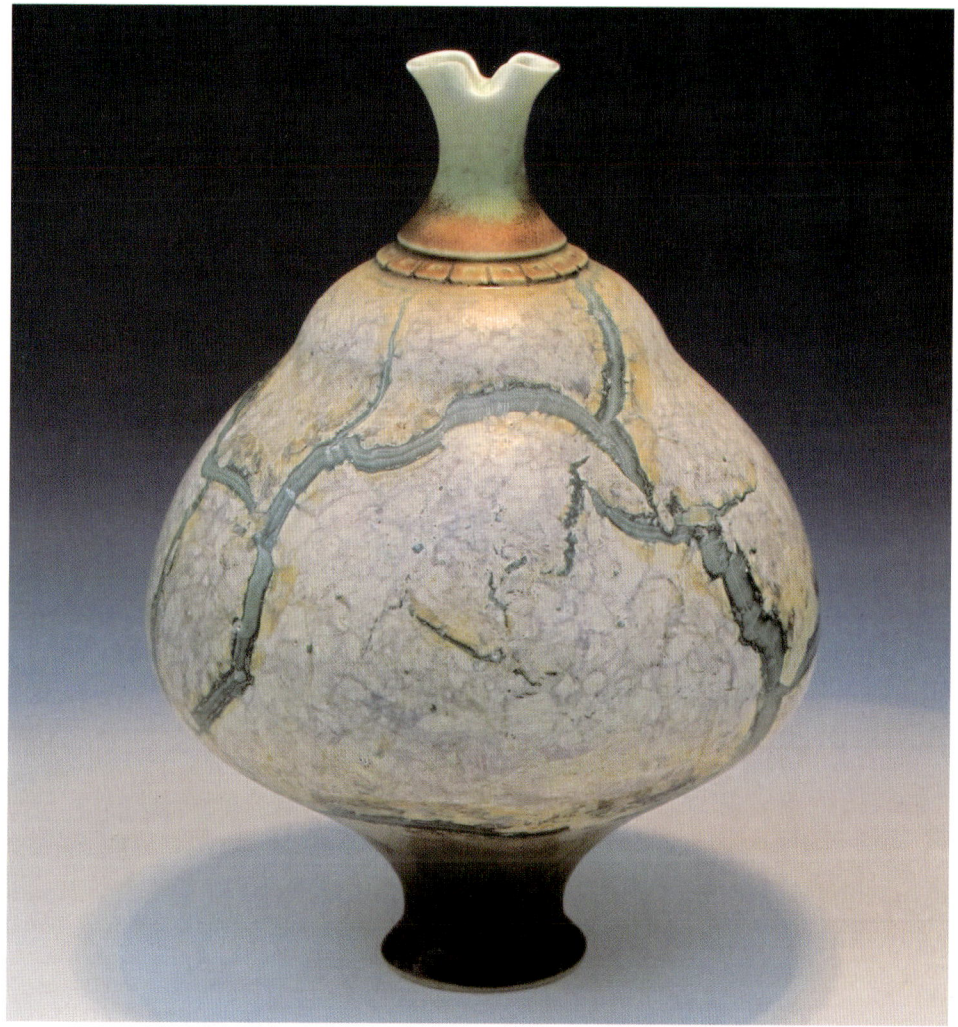

Fig. R6: Geoffery Swindell, porcelain vessel, 2009. Resin lustre first fired to 1280°C (2336°F), then lustre applied and fired to 760°C, 1400°F. Ht: 10cm (4in). *Photo by the author.*

not using these highly volatile solvents as they also have a carcinogenic association. They are used so that the lustre can be handled soon after it has been applied. Lavender and eucalyptus oils take longer before they can be handled, but they are safe to use and pleasant, too. Even so, it is important to wear a mask if you're spraying, as the mixture contains heavy metals. Place the pot on a tile or a broken piece of kiln shelf so that it can be moved easily into the kiln.

Once you have finished stirring the oil into the mix, cover it for 12 hours. This allows the undissolved particles to settle. At first it may appear perfect, but as it cools, particles will form and drop to the bottom of the mix, like they do in many saturated solutions. Pour off the top layer into an airtight container. Please note that if you use plastic, make sure that the oil or solvent doesn't dissolve the container! The mix can be kept for years. If it thickens, add more solvent. Hainbach suggests the residue left behind can be used again for the next mix.

When mixing your lustres you can use different solvents in each of the lustre mixes. When a lustre is applied using lavender oil and allowed to dry, a second lustre using, say, pure turpentine, (a thinner oil) instead of eucalyptus oil is applied over the first lustre application. This will break up the lustre, as different surface tensions between the oils will lead to one lustre floating and breaking up the other in a kind of vinegar-and -oil effect. This can be exploited for interesting decorative effects, similar to the work of Geoffrey Swindell (see p.94 and p.99). (There are also other oils you can use, such as light machine oil. It is worth experimenting.)

Spraying, painting and dabbing thinning agents like turpentine or paraffin oil over a lustre will create haloes and other patterns. The work of Geoffrey Swindell has explored this effect, as he notes:

I buy my lustre colours in small bottles ready-prepared by the manufacturer. It [the colour] is intended to be painted onto a shiny, glazed surface. After firing this would normally produce a lustrous iridescent colour surface. I paint it onto a matt glaze so that this pearlescent quality is lost but the flat colour remains. Whilst the fluid is still wet I airbrush paraffin and water onto the surface to break the tension and then add thickly brushed spots of other colours, causing them to marble together and form a random streaky pattern which is then fired to 800°C (1472°F) in an electric kiln.

In Figs R6 and R7 you can see 12 resin mixes; one set is applied on a white glaze and the other test on a dark blue. The colourless lustres can more easily be seen on the darker colour, but can also be made out on the white tile with the correct angle to the light.

Industry has adopted this form of resin lustre as it gave (good) consistent results each time. Commercially it is available pre-mixed in a bottle with ease of use in many colours and metals in hues including mother-of-pearl, greens, browns, blues, pink, reds, copper, platinum and gold, to mention a few.

Gold, as previously mentioned, will yield pink, red, purple, amethyst, blue, copper and gold, when mixed with bismuth in particular. The colour it gives depends on the thickness of application to the surface of the glaze: thick will give gold, while a thin application will give purples to pinks. Making gold lustre is achievable, but it is a long process necessitating the use of aqua regia, or 'royal water', a highly corrosive mix of hydrochloric and nitric acids in the ratio of 3:1. (It was so named because it can dissolve the 'royal' or 'noble' metals, gold and platinum.) One very good description of this long and complicated method for making gold lustre can be found in *Industrial Ceramics* by Singer & Singer (published by Chapman & Hall, 1963), but a much simpler method is explained here.

Today it is far easier and safer to purchase the gold % solution. Gold lustre solution is made in different percentages of gold, between 8 and 12% in the lustre mix. Commercially produced liquid gold may include turpentine, nitrobenzene,

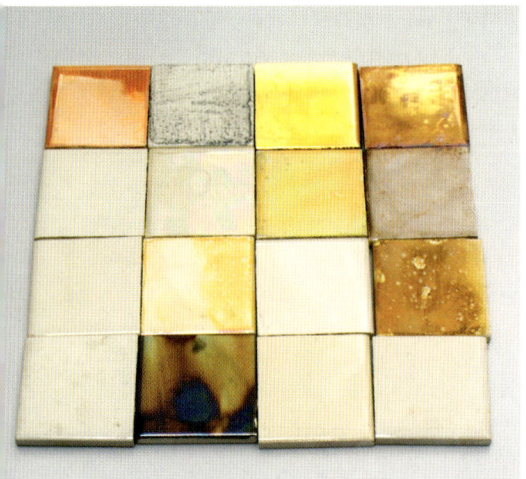 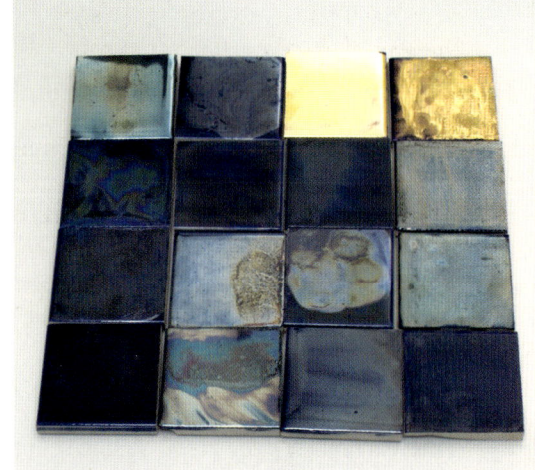

Fig. R7 & Fig. R8: 16 resin lustre mixes, all applied to two tiles: on a white glaze (left) and on a dark glaze (right).

Resin lustre test recipes

Iron nitrate 3g Bismuth nitrate 2g Resin 10g	Copper nitrate 3g Bismuth nitrate 2g Resin 10g	Gold lustre 8.5% Commercial	Gold lustre made with gold chloride
Zinc acetate 4g Resin 10g	Lead acetate 3g Bismuth nitrate 2g Resin 10g	Potassium dichromate 3g Bismuth nitrate 2g Resin 10g	Manganese 3g Bismuth nitrate 2g Resin 10g
Alumina acetate 3g Bismuth nitrate 2g Resin 10g	Uranium 3g Bismuth nitrate 2g Resin 10g	Bismuth nitrate 3g Resin 10g	Silver nitrate 3g Resin 10g
Stannous chloride 3g Bismuth nitrate 2g Resin 10g	Cobalt nitrate 3g Bismuth nitrate 2g Resin 10g	Strontium 3g Bismuth nitrate 2g Resin 10g	Cadmium 3g Bismuth nitrate 2g Resin 10g

chloroform and other solvents. In the gold lustre mix are rhodium (0.02–0.03%), chromium (0.035–0.08%) and bismuth (0.4–0.5%) along with the organic resin and the gold. The bismuth is to help flux the gold and the rhodium and chromium to make the lustre more durable.

Here is a second, much simpler way to make gold lustre as described in Hainbach's *Pottery Decorating*. First of all, purchase some gold chloride (though it can be expensive so look around; try photographic suppliers). You need a hotplate and bowl, and into the bowl you should place three parts linseed oil and one part (by volume) finely powdered sulphur (Fig. R8). Heat in a

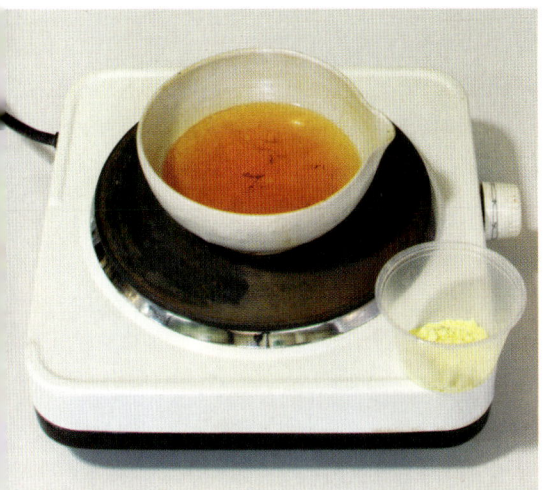
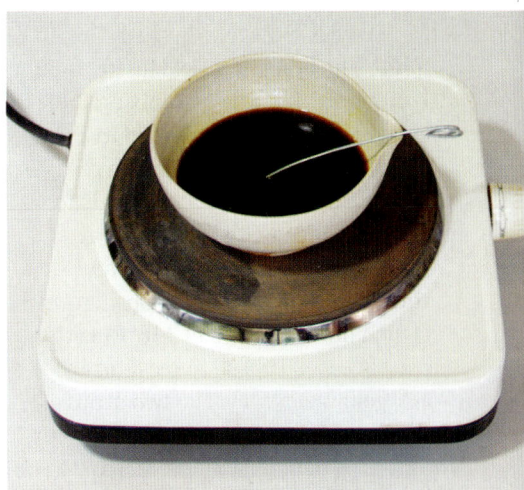

Figs. R9 – R10: The preparation of linseed oil and sulphur for the gold lustre.

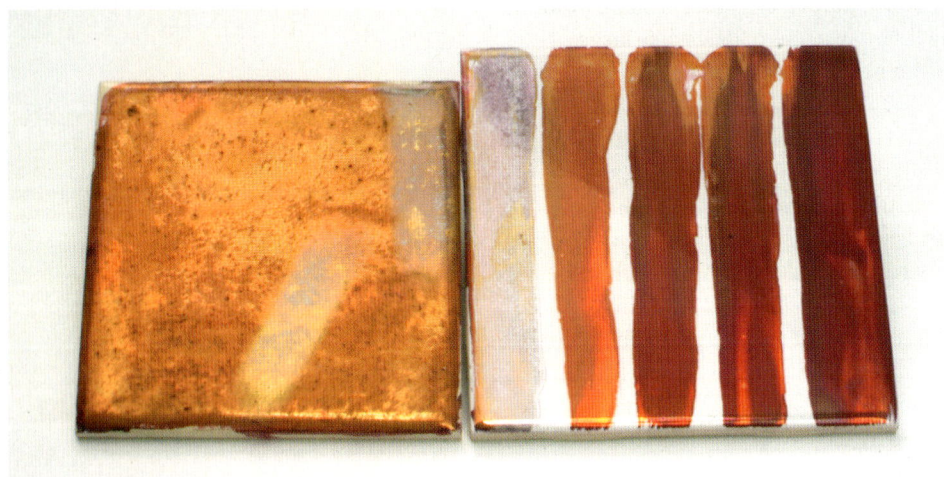

Fig. R11: Linseed oil, sulphur, gold chloride mix and additions of bismuth lustre.

similar way to the resin lustre mix. Stir to mix. Initially it will froth. Cook for approximately 30–40 minutes until the mix turns black (Figs R9 & R10). Then dilute with oil of turpentine until the mix can be strained through cheesecloth or a similar material. Mix 5ml of this mix with 2g of gold chloride. Palladium can be made the same way. In this mix it is the oil and sulphur that reduce the

gold during firing. If you use flowers of sulphur, wash the sulphur with water to get rid of any sulphur dioxide, then dry.

In Fig. R11 we see the gold lustre made using this method. Note the mark across the tile – this is where it has rubbed off. This tile was fired to 730°C (1346°F), but by firing at a higher temperature, 780°C (1436°F), the problem is overcome. The tile to the right has bismuth blended into the mixture of 5ml gold, linseed oil and sulphur. The first line is gold lustre, then two drops of bismuth resin mix are added. Then two more drops are added to bring the total to four drops of bismuth resin for 5ml gold. Another two equals six drops of bismuth added, then another two, bringing the total bismuth resin added to the 5 ml of gold to eight drops. The tile was then fired at 730°C (1346°F) with the surface well rubbed to see if any of the 100% gold wore away. The two drops of bismuth were enough to fuse the gold to the glaze by acting as a flux. Increasing the bismuth then changed the colour of the gold into a red-gold. This is because bismuth plays a dual role (a small amount will simply act as a flux, while large amounts will also affect the colour).

In Fig. R13(see mixing chart on p.104) the tile has gold mixed with a resin medium and three lustres. The first line mixes a medium made from resin and eucalyptus oil to dilute the gold lustre. The first mix is a duller bronze colour but by the end of the line the colour is a soft mauve-pink. The second line blend down blends in the bismuth lustre with gold lustre. The line blend of bismuth with gold starts from copper and goes to pink/purple. Note that the application varies in thickness, giving further tones and colours. The third line down mixes a commercial mother-of-pearl lustre with gold; the first mix ranges in colour from amethyst to a blue. The final line mixes gold with a tin lustre (stannous chloride); the first colour resulting from the two being combined is a deep purple through to a pink.

Don't go seeking a perfect mix – you'll obtain more information if you don't – but do try to have the application vary in thickness. You'll find a rubber glove

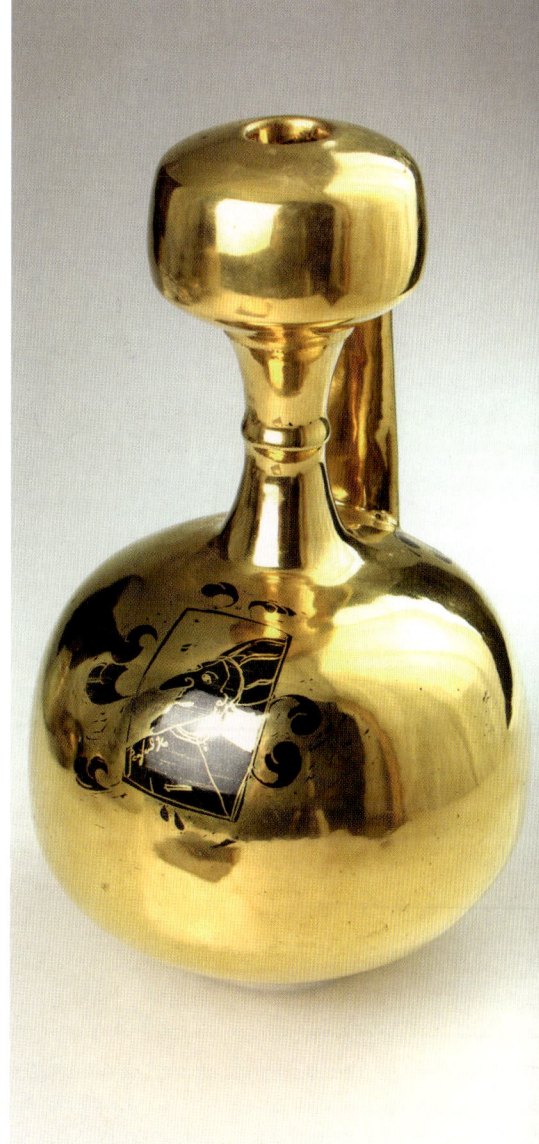

Fig. R12: Gold resin lustre vessel by Alan Peascod, with acid-etched decoration. Alan Peascod's work shows the use of a high-percentage gold resin lustre applied over a black stoneware glaze with acid-etched decoration. **(Hydrofluoric acid used for etching is highly dangerous and strong, I would suggest avoiding it.)** *Photo courtesy of the artist.*

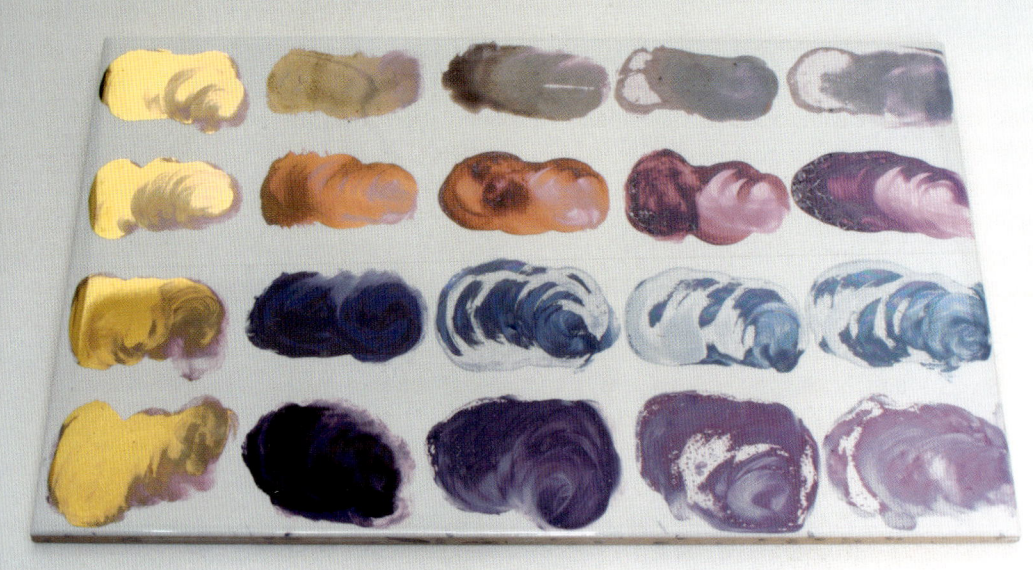

Fig. R13: A gold-lustre line-blend mix shows resin alone, then with three other lustre mixes (see the table for details).

Mixing chart for tile in Fig. R13

Gold lustre 8%	1 drop	1 drop	1 drop	1 drop
Resin and oil mix	2 drops	4 drops	8 drops	12 drops
Gold lustre 8%	1 drop	1 drop	1 drop	1 drop
Bismuth lustre	2 drops	4 drops	8 drops	12 drops
Gold lustre 8%	1 drop	1 drop	1 drop	1 drop
Mother-of-pearl lustre	2 drops	4 drops	8 drops	12 drops
Gold lustre 8%	1 drop	1 drop	1 drop	1 drop
Stannous lustre	2 drops	4 drops	8 drops	12 drops

on your hand is best, as you can mix in a circular motion and apply pressure to achieve a thin area of application. Using an eye dropper for measuring a small amount is accurate and reliable. Mark out the tile with a marker pen. This will help placement and mixing of the tests.

If you take each lustre in turn, smearing it down a glazed tile, you will see how important the application thickness is for colour change. Repeating this test on a number of different coloured glazes will lead to different fired results too. The thin application allows the underlying glaze colour to change the lustre colour. Remember that some lustres are colourless, so what is being altered by the coloured glaze and the lustre is the wavelength of light. A good example is the mother-of-pearl lustre. On a white glaze the result is a mother-of-pearl shell lustre, which when moved around in the light evinces a rainbow of colour. Applied on a black glaze the resulting colour is more like an oil slick, or the kaleidoscope of colour you see in petrol spilt on a wet road.

What I would suggest you do with all

resin lustre that you make or purchase is to take a glazed tile with a white or clear glaze and a dark-coloured (blue or black) glaze (preferably glossy, as the glossier the surface the more lustrous the surface will be) and test out your lustres on these glazed tiles. This especially goes for the colourless lustres like mother-of-pearl on a matt glaze, which will not be as effective as the light needs to reflect through the gloss surface, whereas a coloured lustre like gold will give a satin surface on a satin glaze and matt on a matt glaze. Try the lustres on the glazes you regularly use first.

In Fig. R15 we have a simple but effective way to see how resin lustres will respond under and over each other. This uses the same method as lustre glazes. In one direction the lustres are applied in a line across the tile, then in the same order they are applied down the tile. On the tile you will see that each lustre crosses over each of the other lustres and also itself. In this case seven lustres were used giving 49 results. If you do two tiles using the same combination of lustres, first apply the first lustre in the first direction to one tile, then fire, then apply the second lustre in the second direction and fire again. To the second test tile you apply both lustres in opposite directions and then fire once. The results will be different. The lustres on the first tile are fired separately and will not intermix but remain separate colours, whereas on the second tile, where they were applied at the same time, the lustres will interact more and be more likely to change colour. The outcome is 98 tests that take

Fig. R14: Lidded pot by Greg Daly, 1990. Gold lustre made with gold chloride mixed with an overspray of stannous and bismuth resin to create reds and gold. Acrylic paint used as resist decoration. Ht: 12cm (4¾in.). *Photo by Russell Baader.*

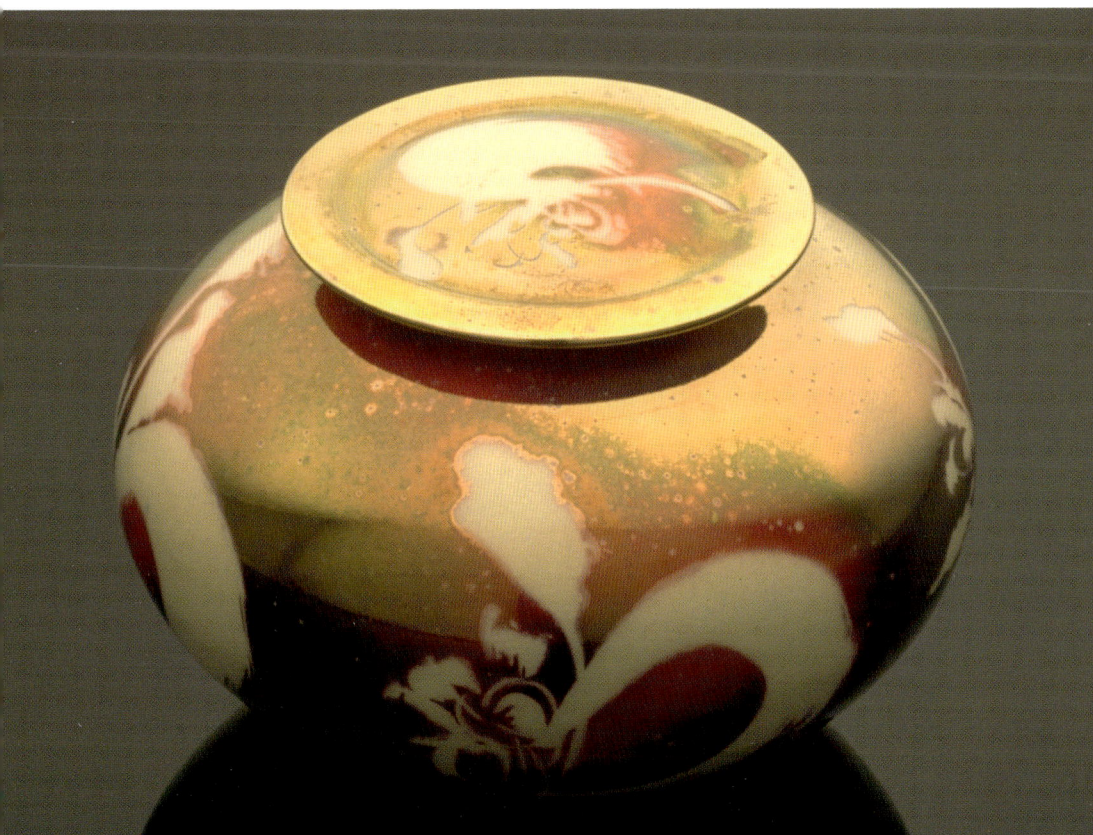

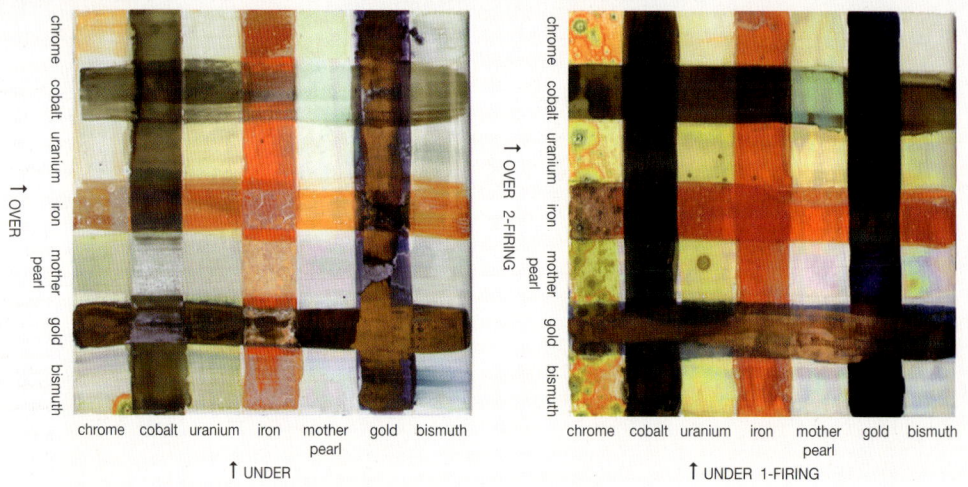

Fig. R15: Grid to test lustres under (horizontal application) and over (vertical application) each other.

Resin lustres used on the grid test

Potassium dichromate 3g Lead acetate 2g Resin 10g	Cobalt nitrate 3g Bismuth nitrate 2g Resin 10g	Uranium oxide 3g Bismuth nitrate 2g Resin 10g	Iron chloride 3g Bismuth nitrate 2g Resin 10g	Mother of-pearl (commercial)	Gold lustre (commercial)	Bismuth nitrate 3g Resin 10g

only a few minutes to do. The tile on the left had the lustres applied together and then fired, while on the right-hand tile, first one lustre was applied and then fired, then the second lustre was applied and fired.

As you can see, the latter has strong results in both surface application and colour, whereas the left-hand tile has had lustre applied too thickly in some areas, so that you have lustre lifting off as the resin burns and pulls it away from the glaze. As suggested in Chapter 3, take a piece of paper the size of the tile and cut a round or square hole 4cm (1.5in.) and move this over the test to help you see the results in isolation. Initially, you will only see a colour pattern and not what it contains.

I call this a colour blend, another easy way to have quick, effective feedback. I use it also for glaze-colour development and in pigment-lustre development. You decide on how many lustres you would like to test. The process mixes equal amounts of all ingredients, with eight resin lustres here giving 36 colour outcomes. It took approximately 20 minutes to do the 36 tests. Using a pen (which burns away) I mark off the tile in a grid pattern. The tile I used was a commercial white bisque tile approximately 30 x 60cm (12 x 24in.), a good size on which you can see a decent mix of each colour (this is important as little dots of colour will not tell you very much).

The top line represents the lustres on their own. The suggestion here and throughout the tests is that for the

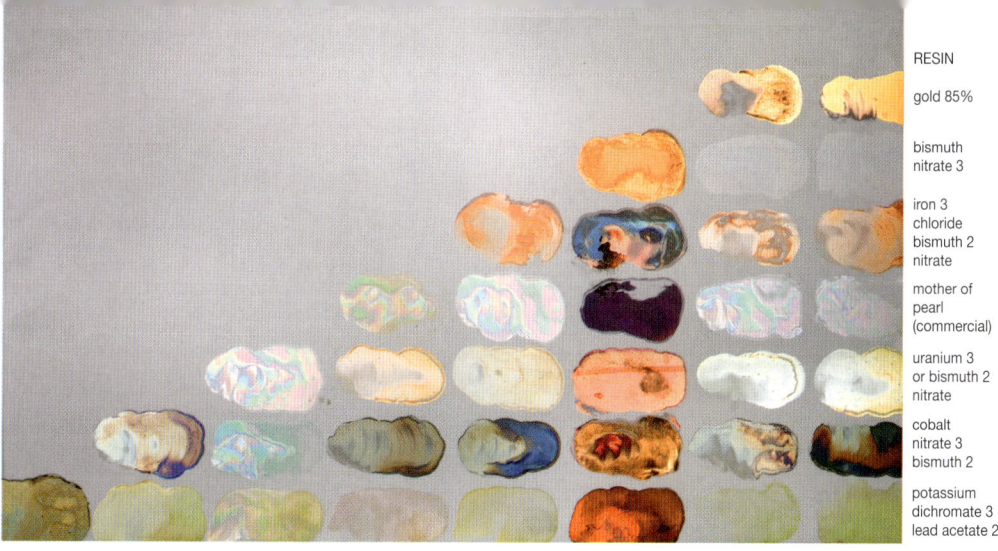

RESIN

gold 85%

bismuth
nitrate 3

iron 3
chloride
bismuth 2
nitrate

mother of
pearl
(commercial)

uranium 3
or bismuth 2
nitrate

cobalt
nitrate 3
bismuth 2

potassium
dichromate 3
lead acetate 2

Fig. R16: Lustre colour blend. A way to blend each lustre with each of the others.
Note: Uranium oxide is soluble, which is why it can be used to make a lustre.

Mixing chart for lustre colour blend for Fig. R16

Test 1	Test 2	Test 3	Test 4	Test 5	Test 6	Test 7	Test 8
Resin mix	Gold 8.5%	Bismuth nitrate 3	Iron Chloride 3 Bismuth nitrate 2	Mother of Pearl (commercial)	Uranium oxide 3 Bismuth nitrate 2	Cobalt nitrate 3 Bismuth 2	Potassium dichromate 3 Lead acetate 2

purposes of giving you more information you smear the lustre around or down to give a varying thickness to the application. Don't worry if you can only see a mere smudge, as even this much will yield colour. In box one I chose to use a mix of pine resin and oil, to dilute each of the lustres.

On the second line you should add equal parts of number 1 box with each box in turn 1+2, 1+3, 1+4, 1+5, 1+6, 1+7, 1+8 (see the chart above for details). One drop of each lustre is mixed with each of the others in a 50:50 ratio. The result in the second line will be half the strength of the mix. The third line across is gold mixed with the other lustres, 2+3, 2+4, 2+5, 2+6, 2+7, 2+8. Continue by following the chart. My suggestion is that with a marking pen, you divide up the spaces as per the chart and write in the numbers in each box as per the chart. You will find it easier to follow the pattern of mixing the first time. Somewhere on the test, each of the lustres is mixed with each others in equal amounts. If an interesting response happens between two lustre mixes, you can do a line blend to tease out the range of colours.

The outcome of this colour blend is a broader palette of colours than you can purchase.

Application of resin lustre

Before you begin applying lustre to a glaze surface, make sure the surface is clean of dust and grease. Your fingers may leave an oil residue that can affect the fired surface. Some people like to clean their surfaces down with methylated spirits first (turpentine is oil and can leave a resist on the surface). I am happy simply to clean the surface with a soft cloth. If it is dirty, however, a spirit glass cleaner can also be used.

After cleaning, watch where you handle the pots. Then you should also be careful after you have applied the lustre. Commercial lustres are made using highly volatile solvents that allow you to handle the work soon after application, but lustres made with oils take longer to dry, and handling them too soon could leave a fingerprint in the lustre after firing. I place the pot onto a bisque tile or kiln shelf before applying the lustre, especially all over, so handling the piece doesn't become a problem. The tile, with the pot sitting on it, is placed into the kiln and fired. Sometimes you need to deconstruct your actions in advance to work out the best plan to adopt in handling and decorating a piece.

Resin lustres can be applied via a number of techniques, the easiest of which is the brush. If you are applying a mother-of-pearl lustre, varying the way you apply it is advisable in order to achieve the best results. A coarse brush with a broad crosshatching stroke will give one effect, while a soft, even stroke will give another. It is worth testing out different methods on old pots or tiles. Use cheap and readily available commercial tiles to experiment on. Select a few basic colours and surfaces, including satin and matt tiles, to give you an idea of how the lustre will respond in different conditions. This initial testing doesn't take long, but will give you important feedback. Record on the back of each tile what you did and the sequence in which things occurred.

If you are using a gold lustre, it is very important to get the application correct or you can easily end up with pink patches or uneven colour. If you are adding a band of gold to a rim, begin by practising your movement with a dry brush to see if the surface is variable or not. If you are applying lustre to a dark glaze which makes it difficult to see, have a light positioned over your shoulder or on the workbench. The light will glisten off the line as you apply the lustre. It's important to load up the brush first. If you run out of lustre in banding the line, it is very hard to pick it up again. There are special brushes for lines, called liner brushes and cut-edge liner brushes. The latter were used in industry for the gold lines on plates and cups before a machine was developed. If you need to wipe off the line, use cloth or tissue doused with turpentine and clean it two to three times, as even a slight amount of gold left on the surface (especially a white or very light surface) will leave a blemish.

Mary Rich uses gold and other lustres to decorate her pieces, applied not to a high-gloss glaze but a soft satin glaze that gives a different finish. (Note: if the glaze is too matt and/or crazed, the decoration can bleed, so test first.) Mary Rich describes her process as follows:

My pots are thrown using Royale porcelain body. This is followed by a considerable amount of turning of the leatherhard pot to achieve the finished character of the piece. Then when dry I apply the desired colour by brushing on various oxides or combinations of prepared colours, body stains or slips using copper carbonate, manganese dioxide, cobalt carbonate and cobalt oxide. These are dried onto the clay before the biscuit firing. They will produce a wide range of pinks, as well as lavender blue-green, apple green, purple, turquoise, strong cobalt blue and dark viridian green. I use the same barium carbonate glaze for all my work. The glaze firing in my propane kiln goes to Orton cone 10, with a reducing atmosphere.

The pots are carefully examined after firing and, if satisfactory, are carefully washed to make sure there is no grease or dust. Their bases are ground with a carborundum stone. They are then decorated with liquid bright gold (10%) and lustres.

Lustres reflect the surface on which they are applied, so I aim to produce a sugar-almond semi-matt surface which I think best suits my work. All the decoration is hand-painted using ultrafine Japanese brushes. I use Chinese brushes and the more traditional ones from the Stoke-on-Trent potteries for banding and for the larger areas of gold.

Brushes and paper stencils or tape can be used to create a pattern. Laying down a number of lustres over each other in a single or in multiple firings can create amazing surfaces. Stamping is an interesting way of applying resin lustre.

Fig. R17: Four ways to apply resin lustre.

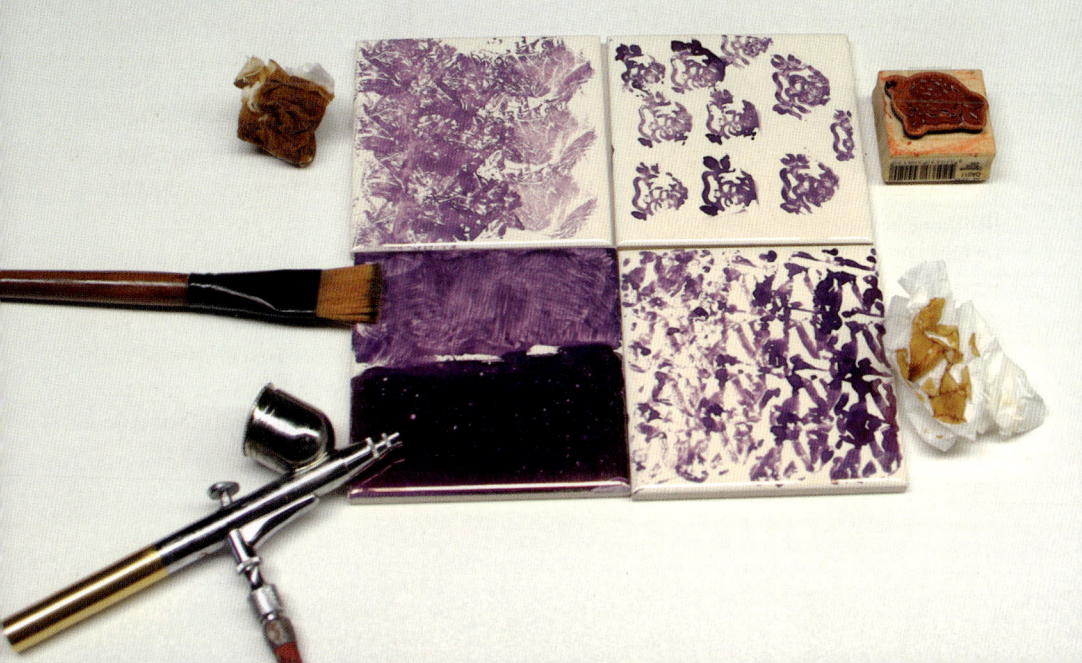

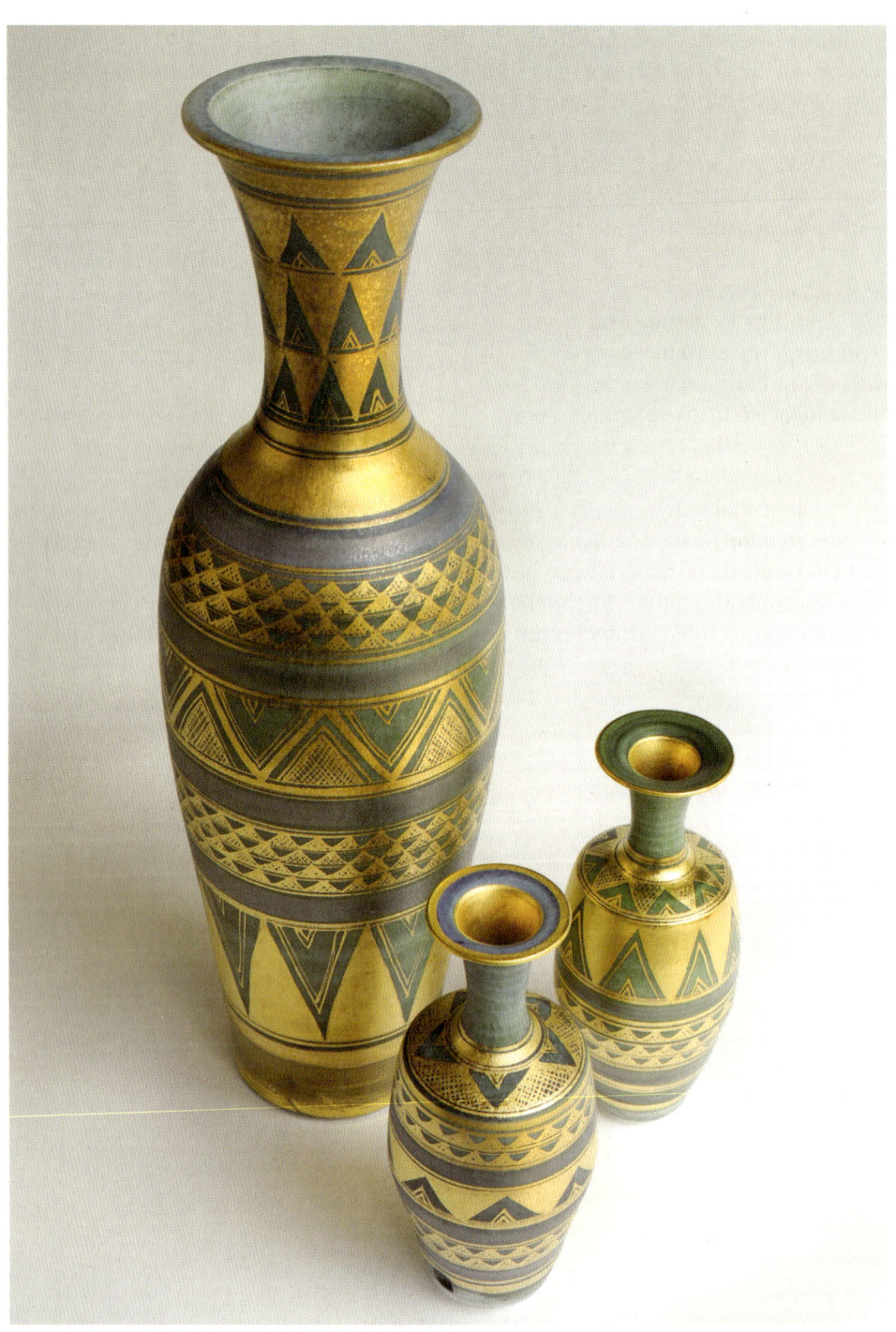

Fig. R18: Mary Rich, gold-lustre, brush-decorated porcelain, 2009. Ht: (large) approx. 30.5 cm (12 in.), (smaller) 13.5 cm (5¼ in.) and 12.5 cm (5 in.).

Rubber stamps or scrunched-up paper stamped on the surface of the pot can give a variety of interesting surfaces (see Fig. R18). Cut-up sponge stamps can also be used, but these can take up a lot of lustre so make them thin and back them onto board.

With an airbrush you can achieve a high level of control over application. A good fine airbrush can last for years if kept clean after each use. **When using an airbrush you need to wear a mask with a fume filter,** *not* **a dust mask. This operation needs to take place in a spray booth. Do not airbrush in your studio without full ventilation, especially when using commercial lustres, which contain solvents, making them very dangerous to your own and others' health. Resin lustres made from pure turpentine, lavender and eucalyptus oil are safer to handle and use, but a mask should still be worn as the mix you are spraying contains heavy metals and in soluble form can easily be absorbed into the body.** However, with a good mask and ventilation, applying lustre with the airbrush gives you control of subtle variations of thickness and tone.

John Wheeldon's lustre work uses stamping, brush and resist:

I feel that above all I am a potter who responds primarily to materials and processes, the exploration of which pushes my work forward. My involvement with raku developed during the late 80s because of a need to escape from the limitations placed upon me by the lustre techniques I was using. These were based on clean firings in electric kilns, and the relative sterility of this method coupled with a desire to use real fire pushed me towards raku.

My work is now mainly an exploration of the possibilities of using lustres applied to raku-fired terra sigillata surfaces. I have used lustres for many years but have only recently discovered their value as a decoration for raku where the metallic lustre and the smoked black terra sigillata combine to form a rich sensual surface. I am fascinated by the possibilities of this technique and the fact that it is achieved with just clay, gold and smoke.

My work is mainly thrown or press-moulded, coated with terra sigillata and bisque-fired to 920°C (1688°F). I apply precious-metal resinate lustres to the surface using a variety of methods – rubber stamps, brushes and resists amongst others. I also use smoke-resist slip in combination with the lustre on certain pieces. These are then fired in a raku kiln and smoked in order to achieve a rich black background and also to enhance and modify the colour of the lustre.

An interest in history also informs my work, although it may not be immediately apparent as the influence is often subliminal. The forms of much of my work refer to pieces from prehistory, especially the Bronze Age.

Over the years I have also collected pottery shards from gardens and fields, which span a period from Roman times to the 19th century. I find the marks left by the potters on these fragments – a fingerprint, a drag mark left by a dry sponge, a piece of wood used to score a pattern, the evidence of the tools that were used – so eloquent. We leave the same marks on our own work today. They are like a language left by potters to be read by potters.

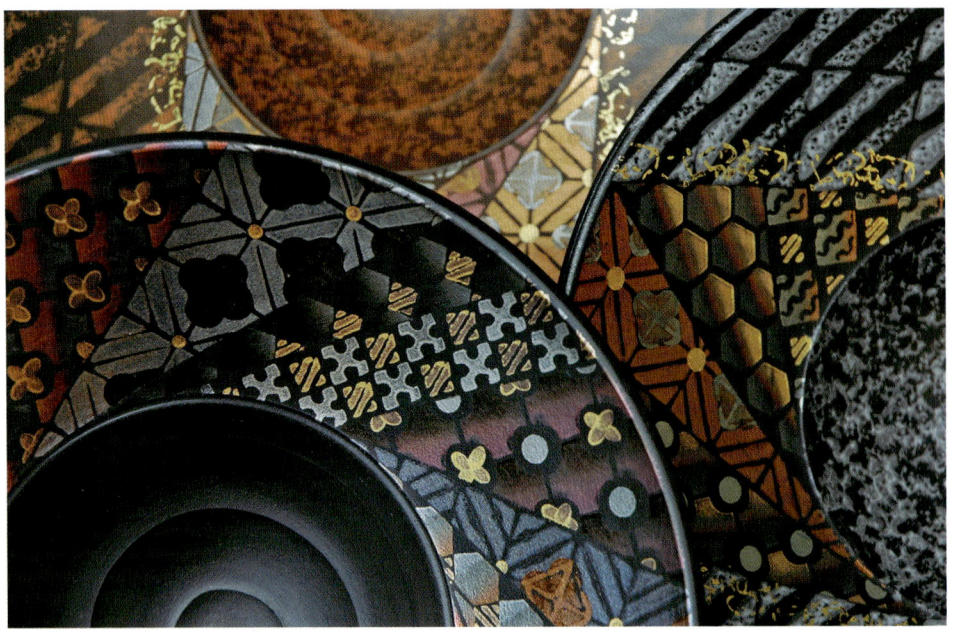

Fig. R19: Lustred bowl group by John Wheeldon, 2008. Created using precious metal lustres on terra sigillata surface using rubber stamps, brushes and resists. *Photo courtesy of the artist.*

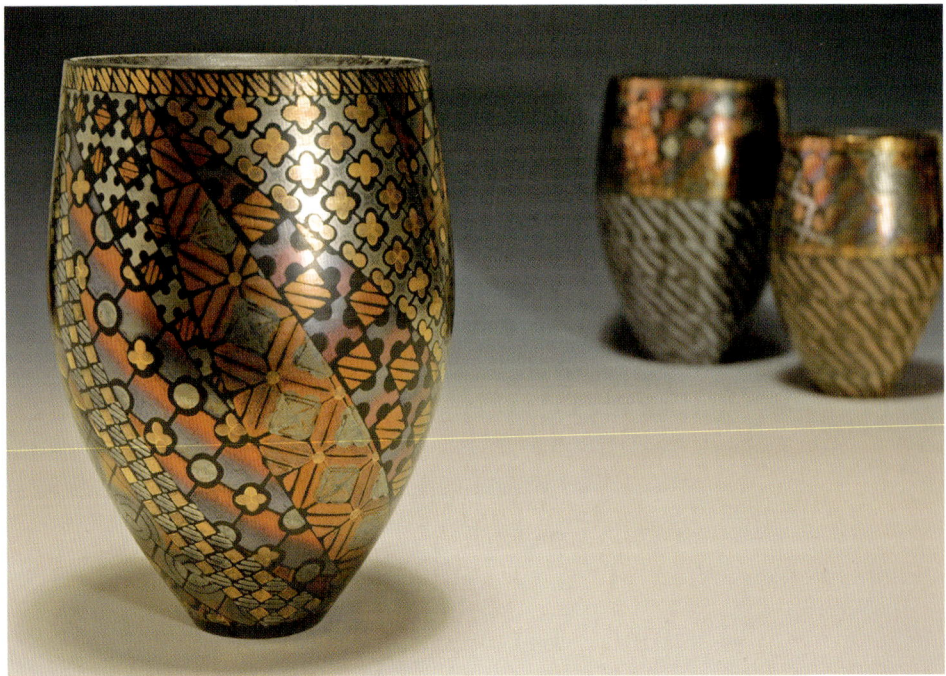

Fig. R20: Lustred vessels by John Wheeldon, 2009. Created using precious metal lustres on terra sigillata surface using rubber stamps, brushes and resists. *Photo courtesy of the artist.*

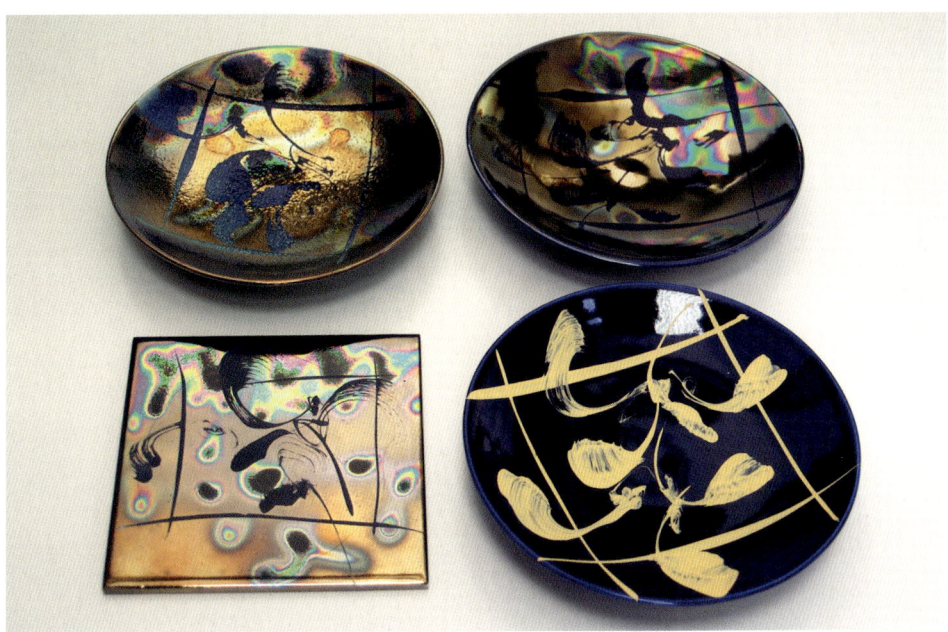

Fig. R21: The use of acrylic house paint for resist & airbrush lustre application.

Resist decoration methods

A number of materials can be used for resin-lustre resist, such as gesso, white-out, and latex; wax, however, can't be used, as when it melts it becomes a solvent and will dissolve the lustre. Two materials I prefer are matt house paint (it contains titanium dioxide with a binder) (see Fig. R19 for an example of a plate decorated using this technique) and clay slip made from any fine clay. The beauty with slip is that it allows you to sgraffito back through to the glaze, giving you fine lustre lines when it is washed off after the firing. Tapes and label stickers are also resist materials you can buy to use with commercial lustres.

Apply the resist material using brush, stencil or stamp to mask out where the lustre is not to go. The undecorated negative space thus becomes the decorated lustre space. In applying lustre with a brush over slip resist you might find that you pick up some of the resist decoration if you aren't sufficiently gentle, so make sure to use a soft brush or an airbrush for lustre application. There is no problem with the paint. Mixing a little paint into the clay will act as a good binder (or else use a gum arabic). Once the lustre has been applied, fire the work, after which you'll find the resist material washes off, leaving the lustre decoration behind.

The tile in Fig. R21 was the test for some lustre-resist bowls. The lower right bowl shows the decoration using acrylic paint, then the application of the resin lustre by an airbrush. The difference between the top two bowls is that the glaze underneath the one on the right is all dark blue, while on the left it is blue and green. Gold lustre was applied first to the bowls, then mother-of-pearl on top. Note on the test tile how a mother-of-

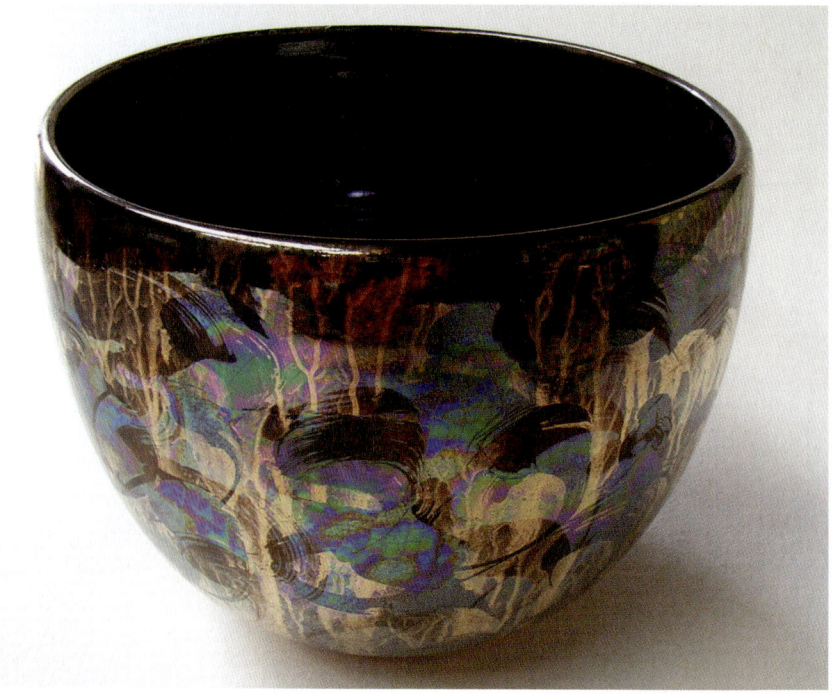

Fig. R22: Stoneware bowl with tenmoku glaze by Greg Daly. Paint resist decoration with thinned gold lustre fired on, then mother of pearl lustre over. Ht: 10cm (4in). *Photo by Greg Daly.*

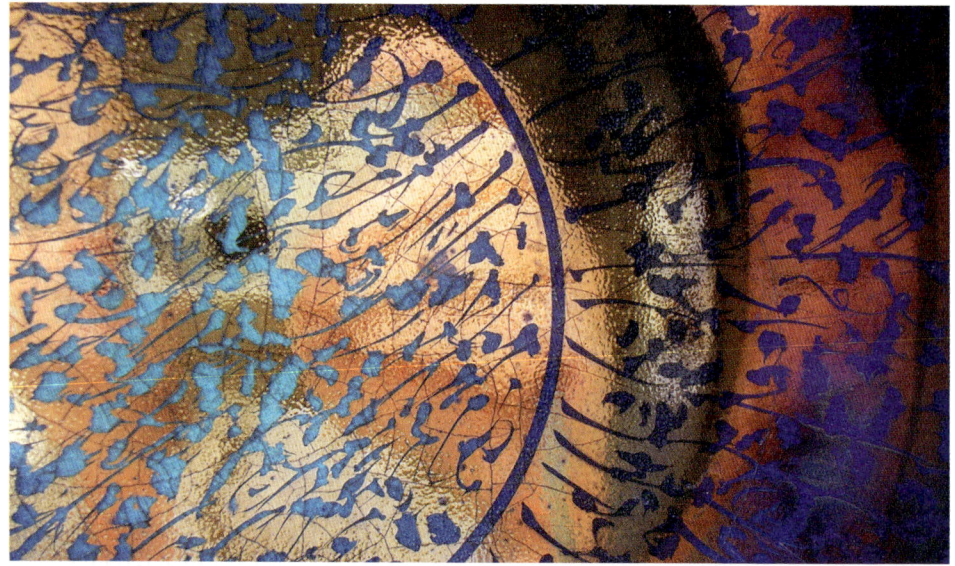

Fig. R23: Platter with resist decoration by Greg Daly. Resist decoration over copper-green and cobalt-blue glaze, with gold lustre airbrushed on and mother-of-pearl overlapping on the rim area. *Photo by Greg Daly.*

114

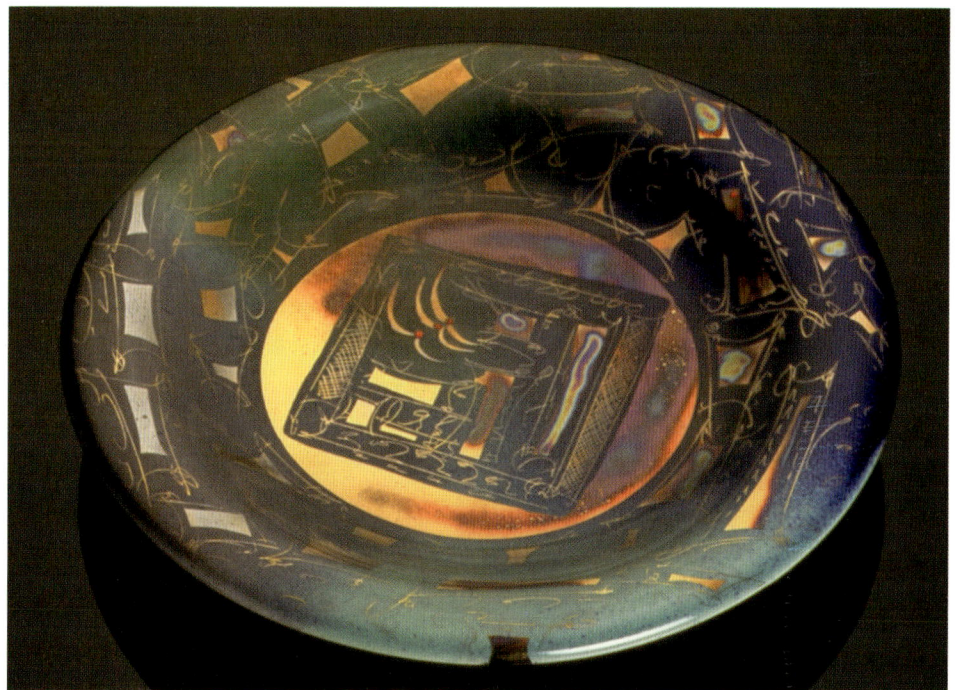

Fig. R24: Lustre resist-decorated stoneware bowl by Greg Daly. Clay painted on as a resist then sgraffito-decorated using a wooden tool. Gold lustre sprayed on in varying thicknesses, with mother-of-pearl to break up the gold. Dia: 48cm (19in.). *Photo by Greg Daly.*

pearl pattern can be created by the use of the airbrush.

You will need to test the resist material on your earthenware glaze, to see if and at what temperature the glaze softens. Then fire just under this temperature. Otherwise, with pigment lustres the resist can start to fuse to the surface of the glaze.

There is no reason why all lustre techniques can't be done in a single firing! I have had to do this at a few workshops where only one kiln was available. The results that came out from the firing were certainly worth working on and developing.

Stencilling is very similar to resist, but it is temporary; normally you remove the stencil as you go. Masking tape, Sellotape, contact or sticky-back plastic (plastic covering for books), paper and card cut-outs can all be used. You can have very exacting control with these materials. A pot can be taped up with a geometric pattern, and one lustre sprayed on. This is then fired before the next part of the pattern is applied. Numerous firings may be done to build up surface designs in this way (but refer to your test tiles of grids of lustres applied over each other). You can apply and fire resin lustres as many times as you like to achieve the effects you're after.

Alternatively, you may prefer the effects from the other tests you did – of lustre brushed over lustre and then fired once. In this case, you should leave the first lustre to dry completely, then use a paper or plastic stencil to cover those

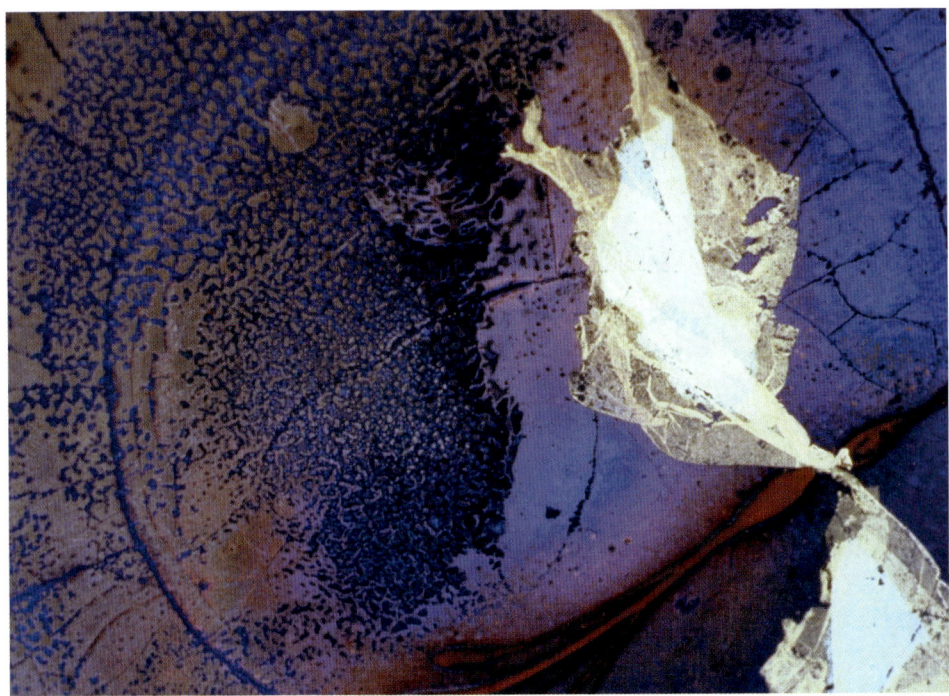

Fig. R25: Silicone furniture polish applied to areas before spraying on lustre. The siliconed surface creates a special effect, causing the lustre to form droplets or beads.

areas you want to mask, as tape can pull off parts of the lustre. Equally, the marks left by tape can lead to other effects to explore. Be careful to handle the piece carefully, as finger marks can easily be left in the resin.

The condition of the work's surface will also affect the application and result of the lustre, so try to avoid things like oily finger marks. Before applying the lustre, first wipe the surface with a thick oil like olive oil, so that when the lustre is sprayed on there is a different surface tension between the two oils, producing an uneven thickness and beading of the lustre which when fired will a give beading pattern and varied colours on the fired lustre surface. I also use a silicone furniture polish, lightly sprayed on and left to dry, to create similar effects.

Tony Laverick's response when asked what attracts him to lustre was:

That's a tough question when you have to put it into words! Maybe it's a bit of the magpie in me, but like lots of people I was always fascinated by the iridescence of a peacock feather or the effect of oil on water. I saw a fantastic piece by Zsolnay in the City of Stoke-on-Trent museum back in 1984, a particularly deep, iridescent green. I have since read that he became almost obsessed in his pursuit of the technique. His work was a big influence on my developing techniques, as was the work of Tiffany. I was interested in reproducing the effects and colours on ceramics that I had seen on glass.

116

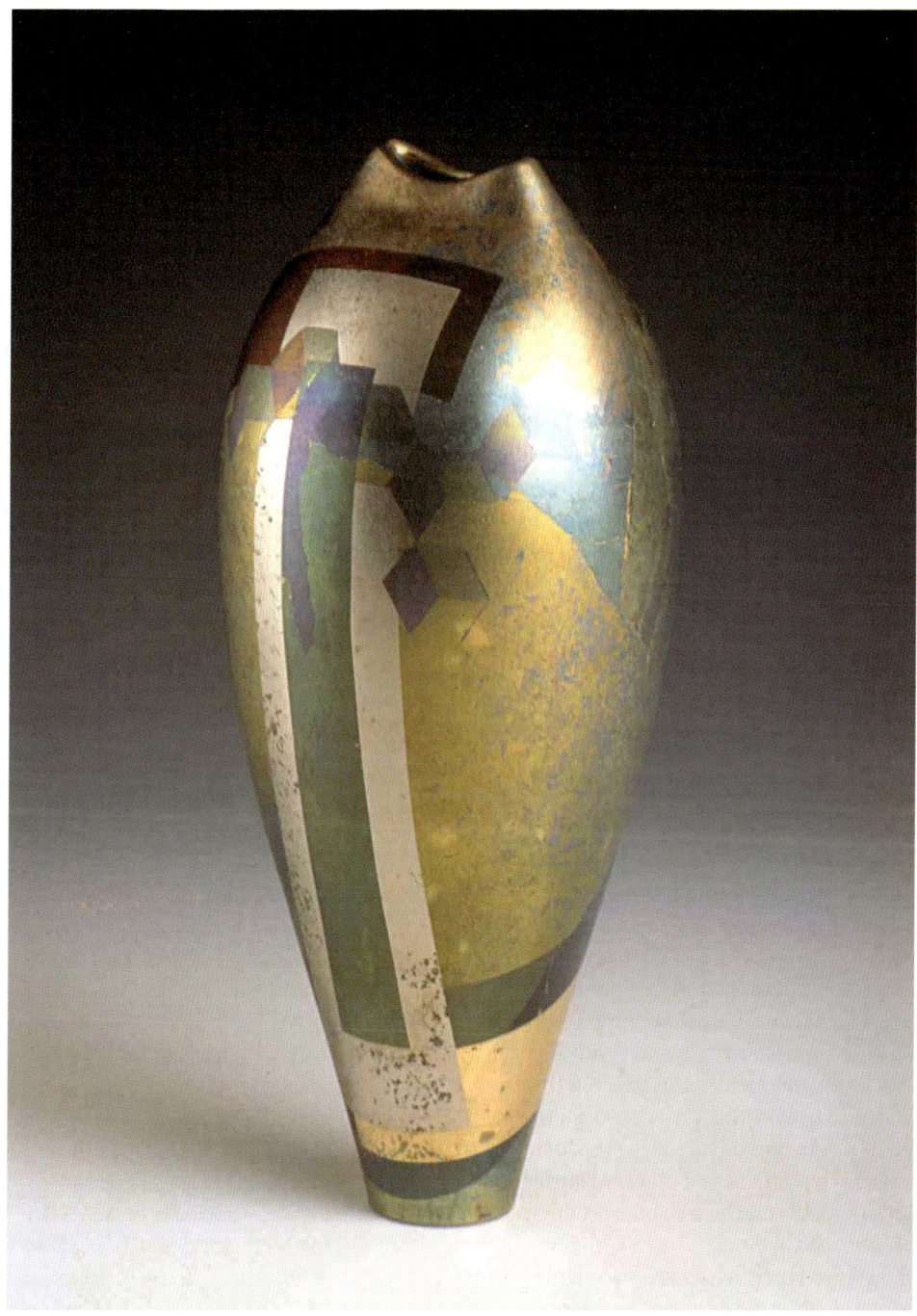

Fig. R26: Vase by Tony Laverick, 2005. Thrown porcelain, bisque-fired at 1280°C (2336°F). Several firings at low temperature using glaze and lustre. Ht: 30cm (12in.). *Photo courtesy of the artist.*

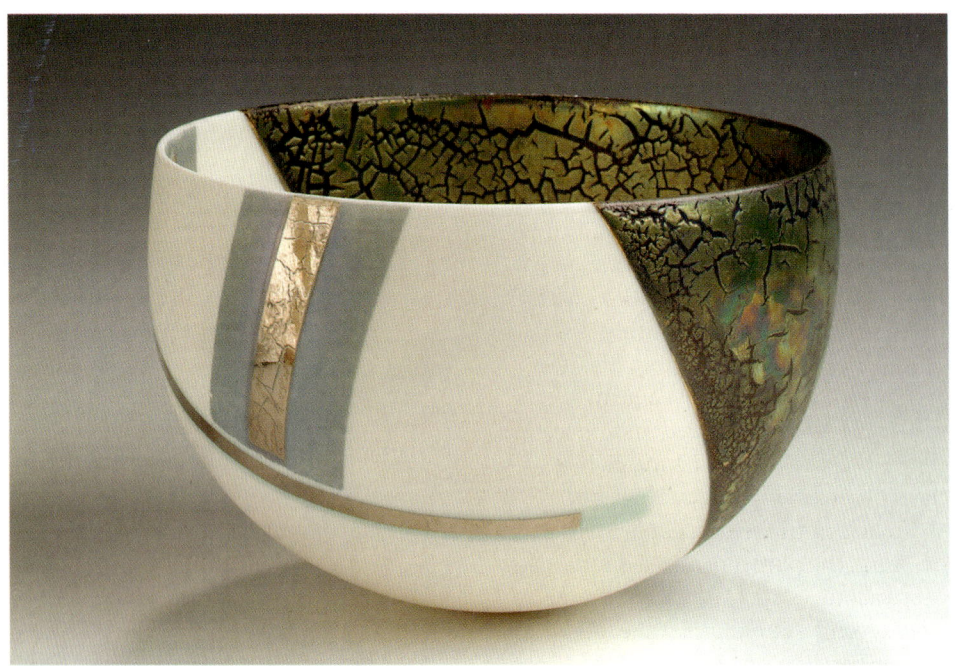

Fig. R27: Bowl by Tony Laverick, 2007. Thrown translucent porcelain, bisque-fired at 1280°C (2336°F). Several firings at low temperature using glaze and lustre. Dia: 30cm (12in). *Photo courtesy of the artist.*

In 20 years of being a full-time potter, I have used reduction lustres, commercial lustres, raku and various fuming techniques using tin chloride, strontium nitrate and metallic saturation glazes (manganese gold). All these techniques, and many others which I use, are, I think, just tools in the process of creating what I hope is a beautiful pot.

Firing

Firing of resin lustres is usually done in an electric kiln, but they can also be happily fired in a gas kiln. I have applied them to and fired them on sawdust blackware pots with good results. But remember that if the surface is satin or matt then the gold lustre will also be satin or matt. The surface character of the glaze will determine the lustre's character too. Appling a lustre to a high-gloss glaze, means the lustres will be shiny, brighter and more lustrous.

Rainbow effects from the mother-of-pearl mixes are also best on a shiny and highly lustrous surface. Application on satin and matt glazes will give a reduced lustre but with still interesting results. A point to watch when applying lustre to satin and matt surfaces is to have the lustre mix a little thicker for line work. If the mix is too thin, it can bleed on the edges of the decoration as the surface of a satin and matt glaze is finely textured and can be porous. Mary Rich uses satin glazes with her work applied with fine brushes (see Fig. R18, p110).

It is felt with resin lustres that a slow firing with the vents open for most of the firing is best. If fired too quickly during the first 400°C (752°F), the resin can bubble and lift, leaving dots of bare glaze; after this temperature is reached the rate of climb can be increased. With small pieces I fire the kiln in three to four hours. But with large platters of about 80–100cm (31–39in.) in diameter the firing is slow to stop the work from dunting (the pot tending crack under uneven heating or cooling). Having been fired to stoneware, the body is vitrified, and if the platter hasn't been evenly heated it will dunt.

To help with the heating (fired in a gas kiln), the platter is raised on three props about 10cm (4in.) above the kiln shelf (evenly spaced under the foot of the pot). Where the rim wall is a third of the diameter of the platter, the rim wall heats quicker as it has heat circulating around it. On the other hand it takes time for the heat to penetrate the base and shelf. Thus raising it on props and allowing heat to pass between the base and the shelf dramatically reduces the risk of dunting the platter. Even so, I still take eight to ten hours to reach 740°C (1360°F). So in answer to the question 'How fast can I fire?' I would answer: until you have a problem with the lustre surface or the pots dunting. On smaller work you can fire faster. But as a general rule, obviously the slower you fire, the safer for the work.

In a gas kiln you have natural venting up through the flue, but with an electric kiln you need to keep the top vent open for the whole firing. Some people leave

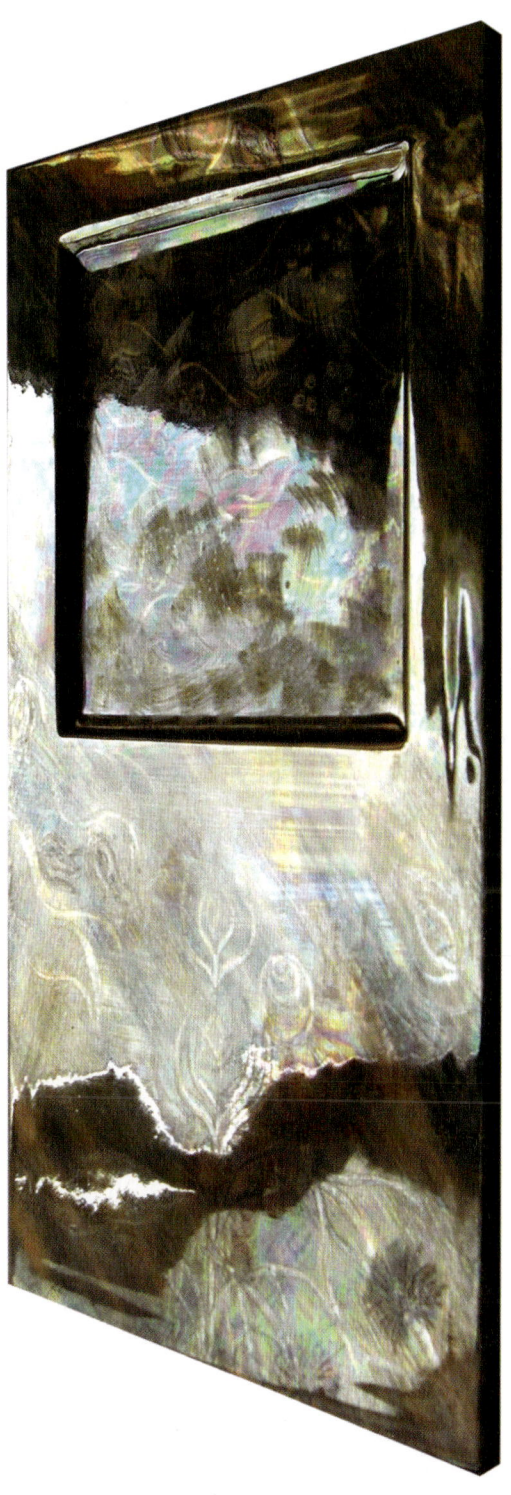

Fig. R28: Kamuran-Sevim Çizer, *Mirror Door*, 2010. Porcelain, resinate lustre 'door', 55 × 30cm (22 × 11¾in.). *Photo courtesy of the artist.*

the door open, but I feel this doesn't change the outcome of the lustre. If you have large work or open bowls or platters, the open door may lead to dunting as the work heats unevenly, so leave the front vent or spyhole open till 400°C (752°F). In any case this is a huge drain on energy and thus the economic viability of your kiln firings.

In a narrow kiln with two banks of elements I fire platters standing on their rims facing the elements, leaning against a brick in the centre. This way the platter is heated evenly with the radiant heat; this is a good solution to preventing dunting in platters.

I mentioned that I fire quickly, but as the work gets larger you do need to be moderate in heating. It isn't so much the speed as the evenness with which you heat the piece. I have mentioned how a large platter is fired. The mid-size range, especially with open bowls and platters, has a larger footprint on a shelf than a tall vase with a small base. The danger is in the 573°C (1063°F) change in silica from alpha to beta (this change has a linear expansion of 1% in the pot) so slow down around this temperature if possible. This I never worry about when glaze-firing, as the body hasn't vitrified and isn't fused as in a stoneware or porcelain body. Work that has been to stoneware temperatures has a high percentage of glass in the body (porcelain is transparent because of this glass). So in reheating a large pot for a lustre firing, even heating is important as the body will no longer have experienced the same thermal shock as a bisque body going to high temperature for the first time. My firing schedule in a programmable kiln is 140°C (252°F) per hour until 550°C (990°F), then 60°C (108°F) per hour until 600°C (1220°F), then 100°C (180°F) per hour until 740°C (1364°F).

You may need to vary the speed depending on your kiln and the density with which you have packed it. In a dense pack put cones in the centre middle and bottom middle where it could be cooler. This will give you feedback as to how evenly your kiln is firing and why some lustre may rub off easily. If this happens, then the pieces are underfired and need more heat to combine the lustre with the glaze. A general rule of thumb is that earthenware glazes will soften lower, below 740°C (1364°F), while stoneware glazes may need a higher temperature of another 20°C (36°F). But test them first – 740°C (1364°F) is a good temperature to begin with.

In summary, resin lustres are easy to use and fire. The mixing of lustres (even if commercially purchased) then their intermixing, as well as varying thickness of application, multiple firings and applications, and the underlying glaze colour and surfaces, will give you a wide spectrum of colours and finishes to work with which are easy to use. Resin lustre like all the different types, have their own character and create their own quality of unique surfaces and colours.

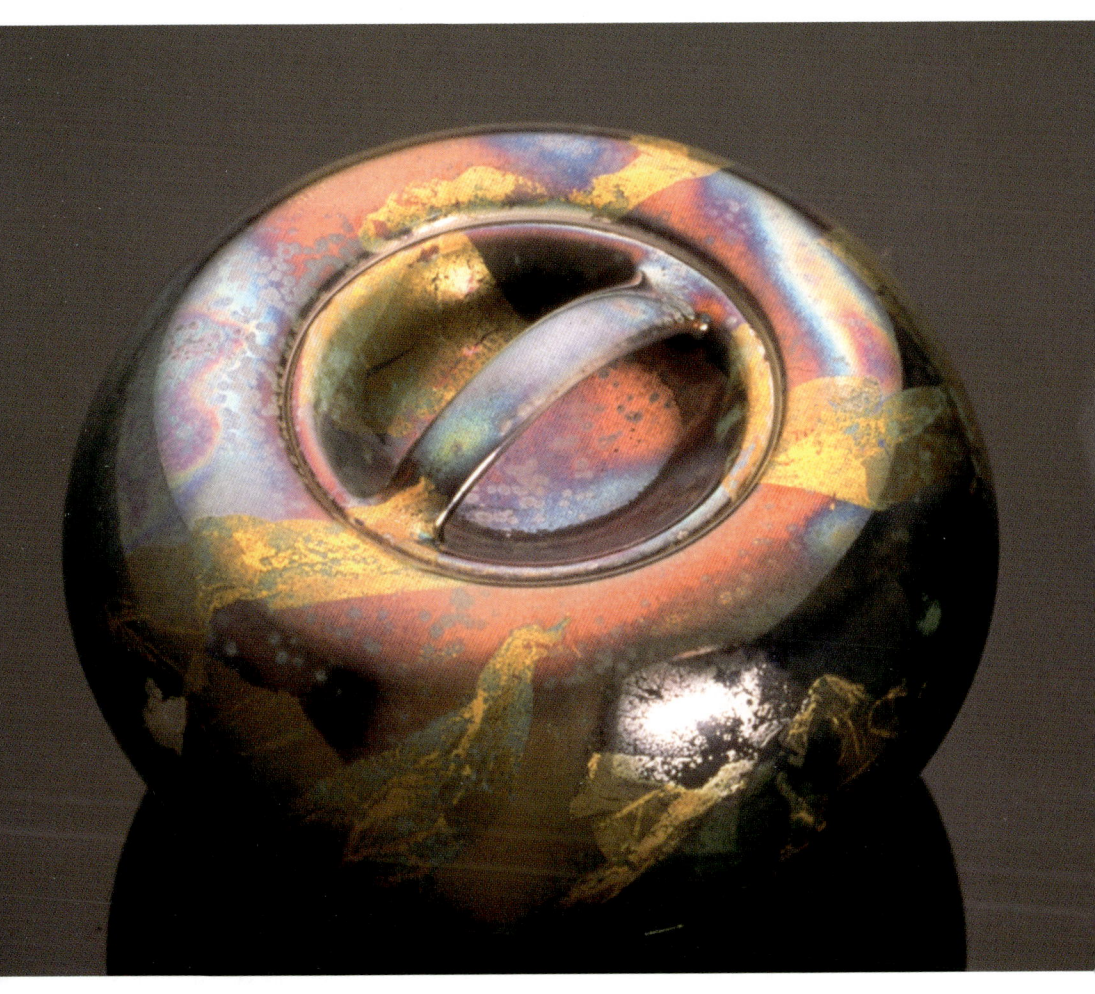

Fig. R29: Lustred lidded stoneware pot by Greg Daly, 1992. Gold and silver leaf with gold lustre airbrushed and bismuth/stannous lustre overlaid. Stoneware, green base glaze. Dia: 20cm (8in.). *Photo by Russel Baarder.*

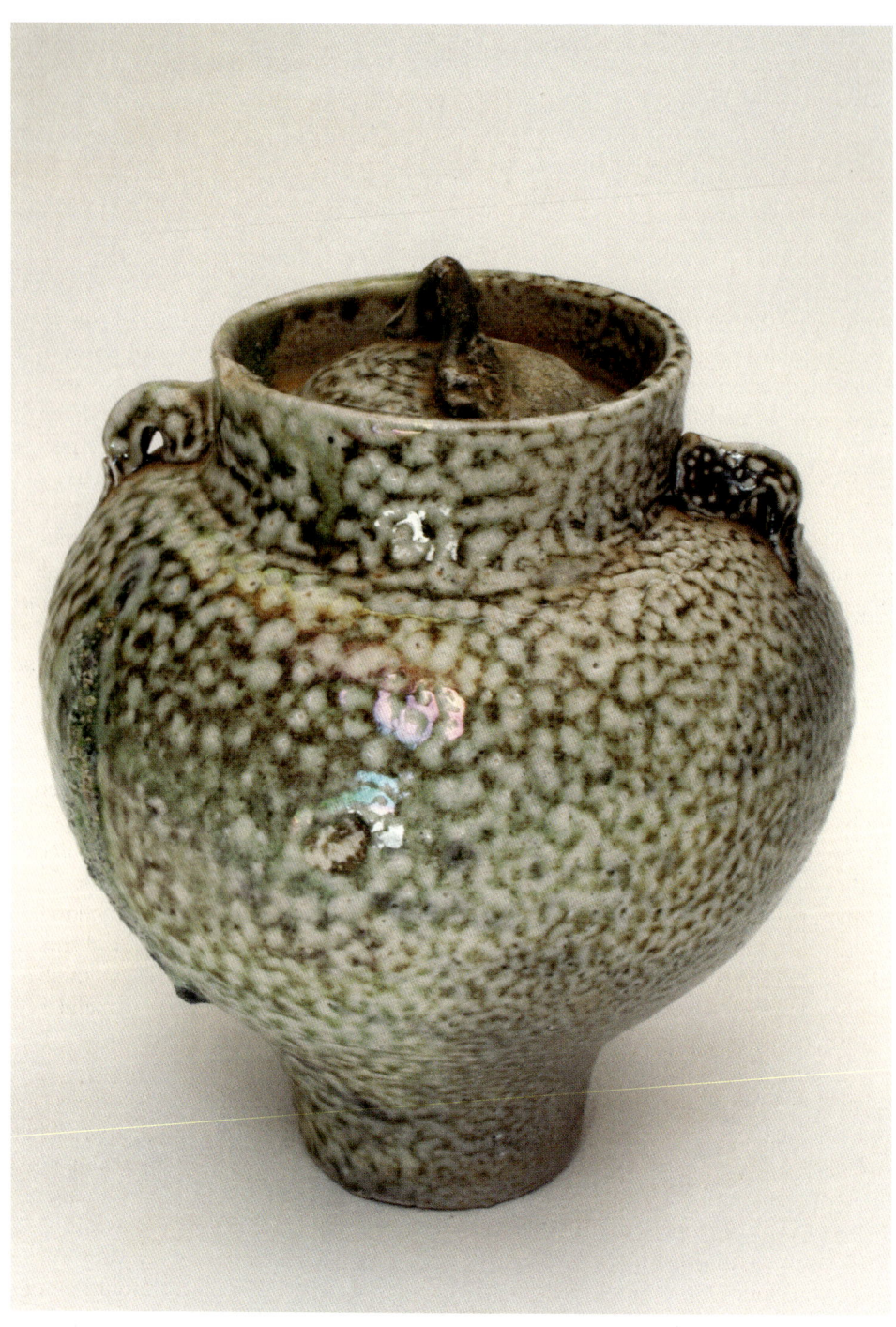

Fig. F1: Salt-glazed and fumed lidded pot by Janet Mansfield, 1985. Ht: 32cm (12½in.). *Photo by Greg Daly.*

Chapter 5

Fuming

Fuming is another lustre technique to add to those covered in previous chapters. It is a technique borrowed from glass, with Louis Tiffany glass standing out as an iconic example (see Fig. H15 on p.24). Many glass artists since have taken this technique and developed rich iridescent surfaces of patterns and colours. The underlying glass colour, or colours, is important to the final effect. The colours develop when chlorides are sprayed onto the hot glass, before it is put back in the glory hole. Silver chloride will respond to a reducing flame, while stannous chloride doesn't need the reduction. The process is as follows for blown glass: you blow the glass on the punt (a punt is a pipe for blowing glass, onto which the molten glass is first gathered and from which the basic form is then blown), putting it back into the glory hole each time to reheat the glass (a glory hole is a kiln used to reheat the glass between blowing the form and shaping it), then when it is shaped you spray the glass with a fuming agent and reintroduce it back into the glory hole again, sometimes with a reducing flame. Variations involve using coloured canes of glass to create colour which the fuming agent responds to, having a different colour for the light to reflect off. A predominantly reducing flame is used when fuming the glass.

Before going further into the technique of fuming, you need to aware of the dangers of handling and using these materials. They are both corrosive and poisonous. Protective gloves (both latex for handling the chemicals and leather for kiln work) are very important, as are proper masks with appropriate gas filters. The kiln gives off chlorine fumes during this process. Even inhaling small amounts will give you problems with your bronchial passages and lungs, and the vapour can damage mucous membranes. Chlorine is a dangerous material in gas form in the lungs and damage will occur with constant exposure. The reducing gas of a kiln is carbon monoxide, which is also dangerous but does not destroy your lungs. You will also need to protect your eyes from the corrosive vapour with an eye mask. Good air extraction from the kiln area is essential. As if this wasn't enough, the chemicals are soluble, poisonous and also corrosive to metal.

Fuming salts

There are different fuming approaches that can be used. In Singer and Singer's book *Industrial Ceramics* the technique described is to spray the ware as it is drawn when hot from a glaze kiln, around 200°C (392°F) with solutions of metal chlorides or nitrates. The solvent evaporates and the salt is decomposed, leaving a very thin deposit on the surface of the glaze. It is then refired in a decorating muffle kiln (see below). No mention of atmosphere in the kiln is made or temperatures given in the Singers' book, but a low red heat is needed, around 550°C (1002°F) – 650°C (1202°F). Glazes recommended most suitable are lead-based with a small zinc content.

The Singers suggest with these materials that certain colours are obtainable with the following materials:

Copper: red, violet and blue
Iron: blue, black and violet
Titanium: blue, cloudy white and violet
Molybdenum and vanadium compounds: bluish iridescence

More intense results can be obtained if silver is added to the above.

More reactive mixes suggested by Singer are:

Red: 88 parts stannous chloride, 7 parts strontium nitrate and 5 parts barium chloride
Opal: 90 parts stannous chloride and 10 parts bismuth nitrate
Blue: 80 parts stannous chloride, 5 parts strontium nitrate and 15 parts barium chloride.

These mixes are for spraying onto hot ware and then refiring them. The reference is to a muffle kiln, which is not to be found today.

A muffle kiln is a kiln chamber within a kiln, the principle behind which is that the fumes of the fuel should be kept from entering the chamber. Among the reasons why they were used in the past was that if the fuel was coal, or wood, or a combination of coal and gas, this would damage the ware, in particular in low-temperature enamel firings. Ware was packed in different-sized-and-shaped saggars to protect it from the fire and the impurities of the firing atmosphere.

One way to recreate the Singers' muffle-kiln technique is to fire your work in a saggar of your own. For this low-temperature firing, any clay will do. Seal the top with a kiln shelf and wadding, or make a lid for the saggar using a coarse raku or handbuilding body. The saggar should be at least two thirds bigger than the work or works you intend to fire. The saggar can be thrown or slab-built, or even simply a box made of kiln shelves (though make sure you seal it well). This can be placed into your gas or wood kiln. Electric kilns won't provide a good-enough seal, and continued use for fuming will be corrosive to an electric kiln and its elements. Therefore, I would not recommend their use for fuming.

In Fig. F2 there are nine tests using chlorides, nitrates and a sulphate. These were mixed using 4g salts per 50ml water. The mix was painted onto a preheated tile. As can be seen, the watery mixes did combine. Future tests would involve one mix per tile for a clear result rather than combining them (but this intermixing shows interesting combinations to try). Interesting information gathered on the reaction with other salts is worth retaining for further investigation.

In Fig. F2 the left tiles were fired to 700°C (1292°F) in an electric oxidizing firing, while the two tiles on the right were fired to the same temperature but were reduced at this temperature for 15 minutes. The two top base glazes are PG4 & PG1, while the lower ones are PG2 (pigment lustre glazes). Applying fuming salts to the fired glaze and then refiring will give you other results, but these will

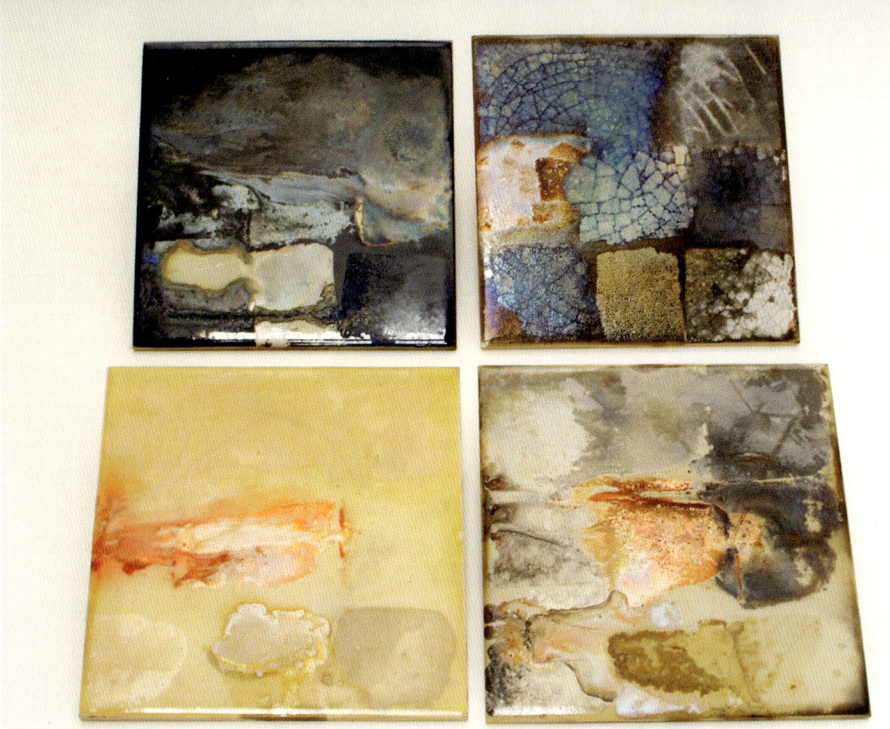

Fig. F2: Fuming salts test. Tiles on left (top and bottom) were oxidized, while tiles on the right were reduced.

Fuming salts test for Fig. F2

Stannous chloride 8g Strontium chloride 1.5g Barium chloride 0.5g	Stannous chloride 8g Strontium chloride 0.5g Barium chloride 1.5g	Stannous chloride 9g Bismuth nitrate 1g
Copper nitrate *	Iron chloride *	Molybdenum sulphate *
Stannous chloride *	Silver nitrate *	Lithium chloride *

* Each test was of 4g of material mixed with 50ml of water, keeping the solution concentration the same for comparison after the firing.

be quite different from introducing them into the kiln on a cooling cycle where actual fuming takes place.

Another technique used is to fire the work to top temperature (stoneware or earthenware) and on cooling introduce chlorides into the kiln at low red heat (600–700°C/1110–1290°F). Stannous, iron and titanium chlorides are three that are favoured, but silver chloride, barium and others can also be tested.

Examples of fuming technique can be seen on the work of **Janet Mansfield** (Figs. F1 and F3), as well as on the vases of John Dermer (Figs. F4 and F5). Both are salt-glaze firers (salt-firing is a fuming technique), but here a flux (sodium chloride) is thrown in at 1300°C (2372°F), causing the fumes to react with the silica and alumina of the body to create a glass. This fuming with metal-based salts takes place at a

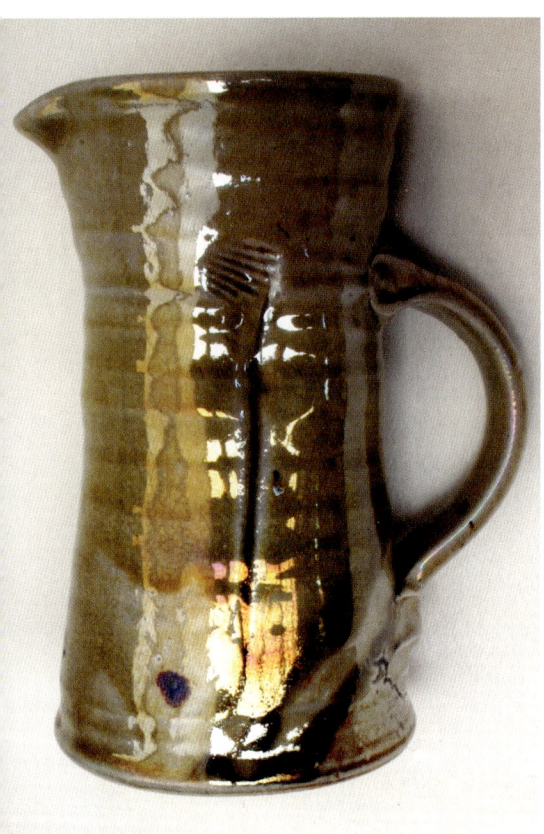

Fig. F3: Salt-fired and fumed jug by Janet Mansfield, 1987. Ht: 19cm (7½in.). *Photo by Greg Daly.*

lower temperature.

Janet uses stannous chloride, iron chloride and occasionally titanium chloride to fume her salt-glazed surfaces, introducing the chlorides in a just-red heat. This brings another dimension and some very subtle colours to the surface. As you move around the work, the light touches the iridescence on a shoulder, lid or belly of the pot then quietly disappears.

John Dermer only uses stannous chloride, and has found that temperatures around 650°C (1200°F) gave him his best results. John's background is from the Leach–Hamada movement, and he is conscious of pure and balanced line in an honest form. His first love for over 40 years has been salt-glazing. He feels that this process can produce magical, timeless pots whose whole process of making and firing cannot be hidden beneath an unctuous surface. John sees fuming as an added dimension to the work.

With some firings the fuming is spectacular, with an almost casual throw of stannous chloride into the firebox of the kiln. But the next firing may not produce such positive results. John comments: 'From one firing to the next, even when recording amount, and temperature, one doesn't always get it right,' John will throw 60g of stannous chloride into a 1cu. m kiln at 665°C (1230°F), through the salting ports in the firebox. He then opens the spyhole to get accross-flow of the vapours. The effect is either instant or not; he doesn't throw in any more if there is no result. A halogen torch shone into the kiln shows the effect from the fuming. Too much stannous chloride and a dull scum will occur, even though John will clean away the opaque scum from the surface to reveal the polished, fumed, lustred surface. He has found that given the same level of initial salting, whether the surface is matt or gloss can affect the amount of fuming taking place on the surface of the pots. Fuming adds a wonderful dimension to John's work, as can be seen in Figs. F4 and F5.

Fuming is a technique widely used in conjunction with raku firings. As with glass, you take the piece from the kiln, allowing the glaze to cool and solidify, then spray the surface with stannous chloride (or any of the mixes mentioned earlier), before refiring the piece, usually in a reduction atmosphere. One person who, instead of taking the pot from the kiln, leaves it in

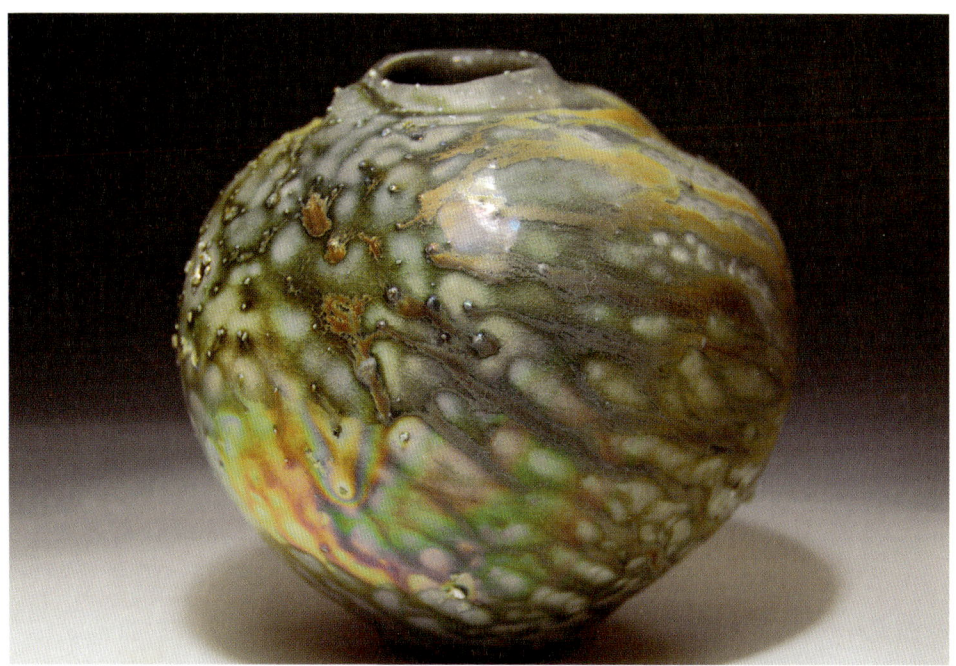

Fig. F4: Fumed, salt-glazed thrown vase by John Dermer, 2010. Ht: 33cm (13in.). *Photo by John Dermer.*

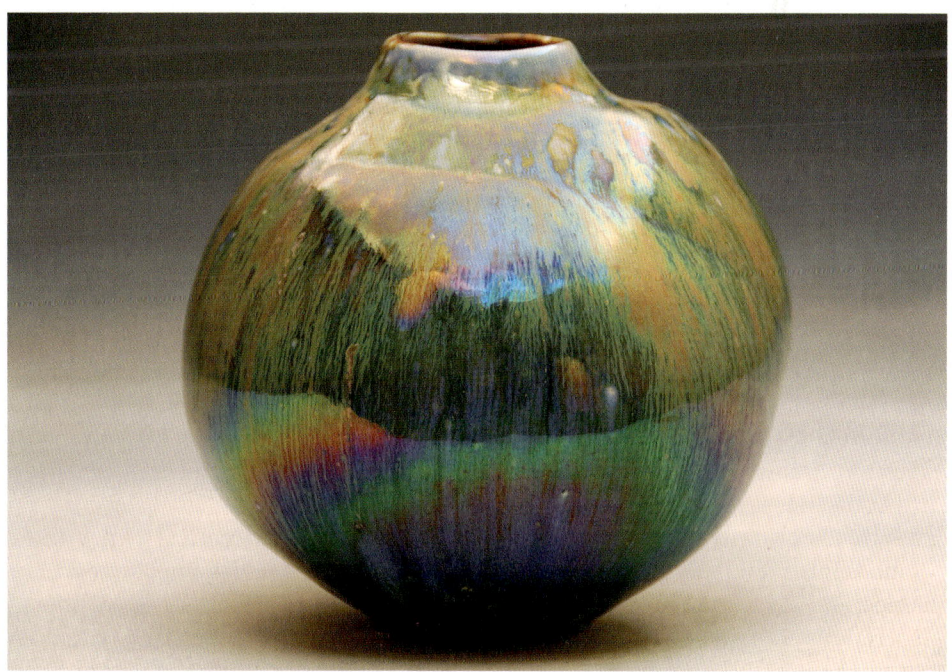

Fig. F5: Fumed, salt-glazed thrown vase by John Dermer, 2010. Ht: 28cm (11in.). *Photo by John Dermer.*

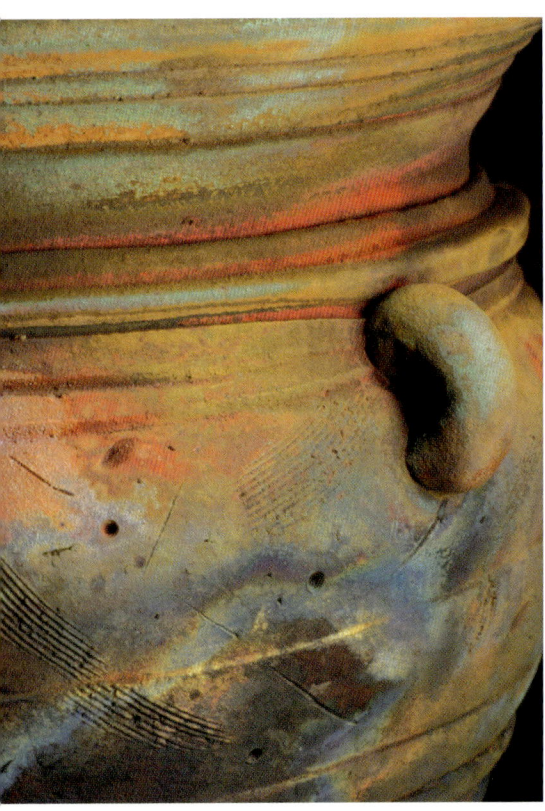

Fig. F6: Detail of fumed vessel by Jeff Mincham, 1989. Copper glaze with iron chloride and copper oxychloride. Ht: 40cm (15¾in.). *Photo by Grant Hancock.*

and fumes it with combustible material is **Jeff Mincham**. The glaze doesn't have to be glossy to fume: as with resin lustres, if applied to a satin or matt surface the fumed result will be likewise and will have a similar surface quality. Jeff uses a copper base glaze and fumes with iron chloride and copper chloride between 650 and 750°C (1202° and 1382°F).

Testing and firing

The fuming approach that I have always used in the past works well with both earthenware and stoneware.

However, in writing this book I decided to revisit this technique after many years, with interesting results. I began testing from scratch to relearn, and come to terms with, this technique. My approach was to pre-fire pieces of both earthenware and stoneware, with coloured and clear glazes, then in a small gas kiln fire them up to different temperatures starting from 800°C (1472°F), and with each successive firing dropping the starting temperature by 50°C (90°F) down to 400°C (752°F),before the stannous chloride is introduced and the kiln flue sealed. (Note: It is best not to fume in an electric kiln as the corrosive nature of the chemicals will in time damage the elements.)

The stannous chloride was introduced into the kiln via a spoon wired to a rod, and was tipped into a small ceramic dish that I had set up within easy reach inside the kiln for when the door was opened. The material can be introduced via the spy hole, too, but you may have to enlarge this to give easy access into the kiln. The salts can be wrapped up in paper like a cigar and thrown in through the spyhole, but this can also lead to bad placement. If you place the chlorides directly onto the shelf, they will impregnate the shelf, which can and will affect later firings, so use a broken shelf or tile. I have also found a piece of steel good for placing in the kiln for the chlorides.

I was puzzled by the tests as with my first three firings not much happened. The stannous chloride came from a newly opened jar that had been sealed but was 25 years old. I don't know if this was a problem or if the stannous chloride (which comes in different forms) was the wrong one. By luck I had ordered more, in this case a stannous chloride dehydrate,

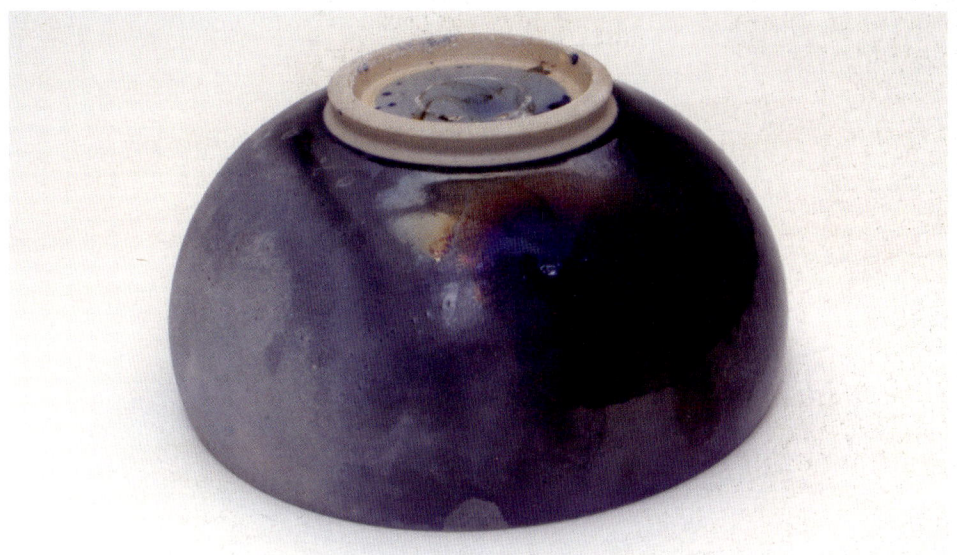

Fig. F7: Fumed bowl, over-fumed on the left side.

and this new batch really fumed. The result at 650°C (1202°F) was a white matt film on most of the pots, and tests with a trace of lustre on the edge facing away from where the stannous had been introduced (see Fig. F8).

The left side of Fig. F7 has a white fumed surface that was facing the fuming bowl, while away on the far right-hand side the fumed lustrous surface can be seen. From this information I cut back on the amount that was introduced. I had used 25g of stannous chloride in a 0.11m/¾cu. ft kiln – it was too much. During further test firings I lowered the amount and divided it between two separate fuming bowls placed on opposite sides of the kiln, one introduced 15 minutes after the other, and lowered the temperature to 550°F (1022°F). This gave

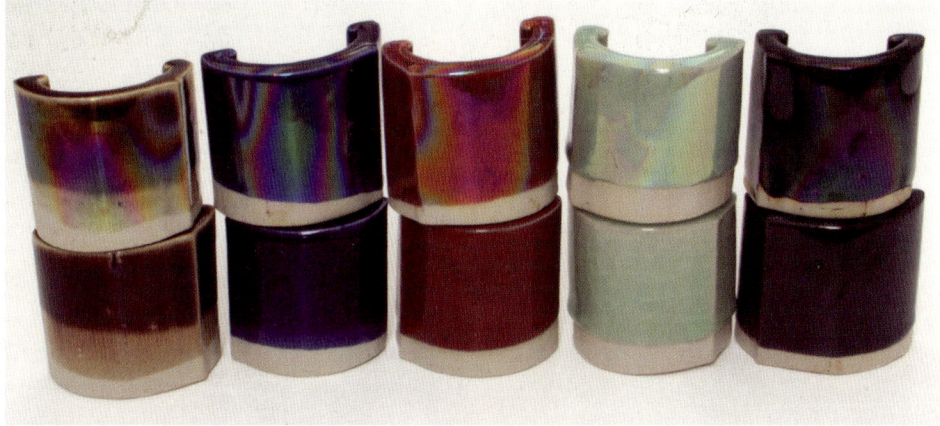

Fig. F8: Fumed stoneware glazes with stannous chloride. The top row has been fumed, the bottom layer has not.

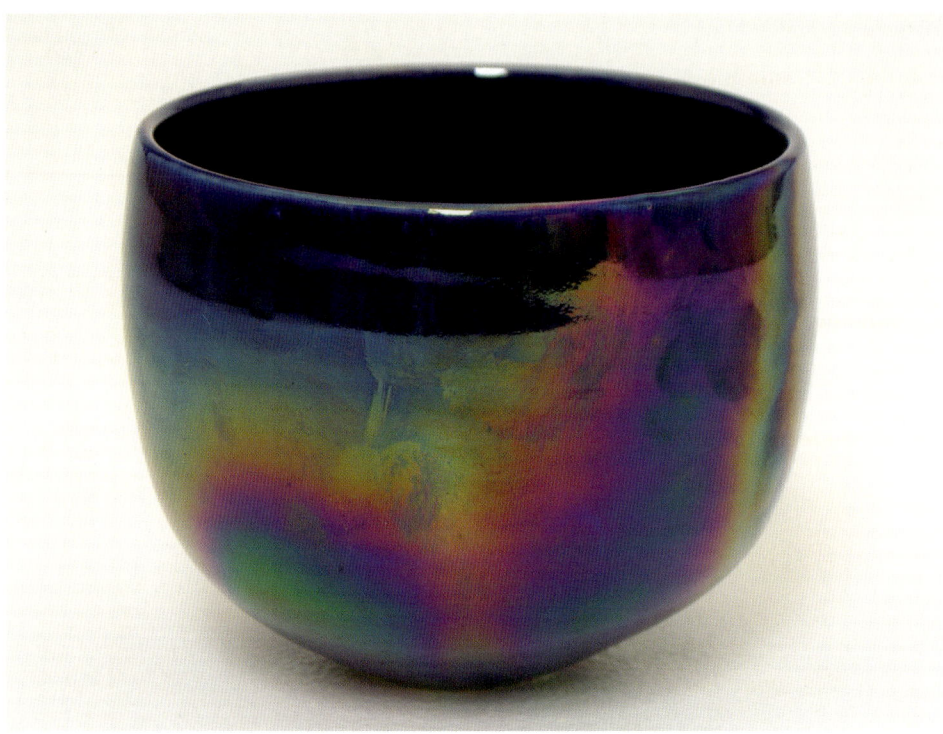

Fig. F9: Earthenware test bowl using cobalt glaze (PG4), fumed with stannous chloride at 550°C (1020°F). *Photo by Greg Daly.*

my best results. As you can see in Fig. F8 these tests show stoneware glazes fumed on top with an unfumed test underneath. The fuming firing went up to 600°C (1112°F) and cooled down to 550°C (1022°F) for fuming. This allows the heat to be more even throughout the kiln.

I have repeated this by fuming on the way down from full stoneware temperature and the results were the same. The blue glazes bowl (Fig. F9) is the earthenware glaze P4 from the chapter on pigment lustres. I did find that earthenware glazes with some lead content (15% upwards) in the form of lead bisilicate fumed better than those using pigment glaze PG2. But I was only testing using soft sodium borosilicate frit.

Testing with other frits may prove the opposite.

As can be seen in Fig. F10, I eventually arrived at the best method for packing a fuming firing. The bowl for the chlorides is placed under the ware so that the fumes rise up around the work. For better distribution of the chloride vapour, a shelf or metal plate placed at the bottom instead of the bowl allows you to spread out the chloride over a larger area, resulting in a better fuming. The use of wire mesh – in this case two layers of normal steel mesh (3–4mm gauge) wired together – instead of a shelf allows for even better fuming of the work. As the temperature is only raised to around 550–600°C (1022–

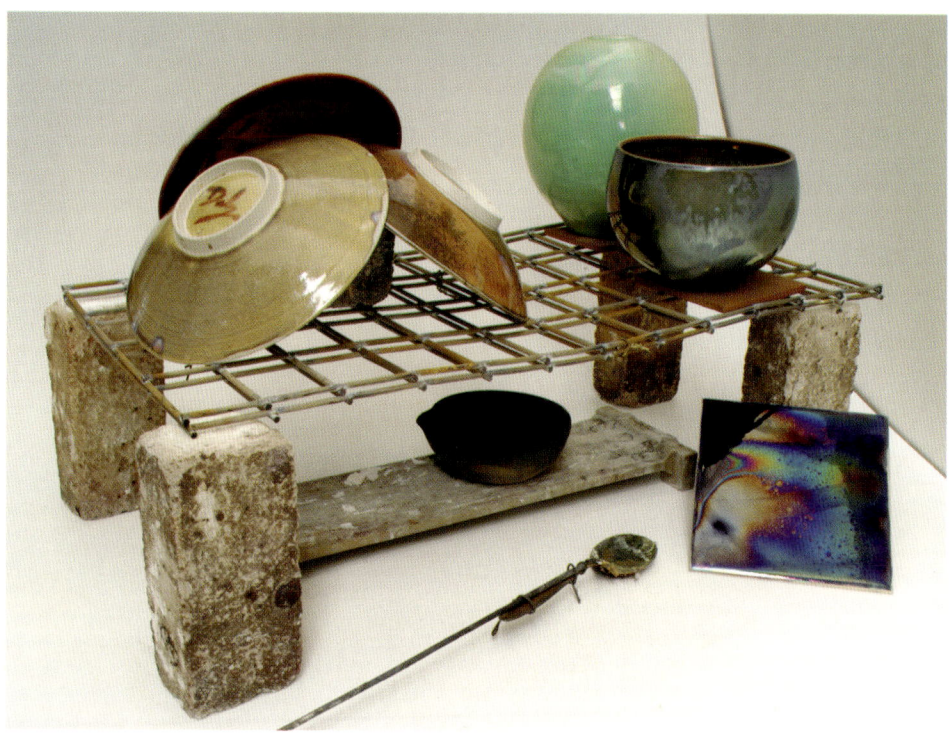

Fig. F10: Mock set-up of fuming kiln packing, showing how things are arranged inside a kiln. (Note: A bowl has been placed on the floor of the kiln to hold the fuming agent, as, if tipped directly onto a shelf, a percentage of the agent will penetrate the shelf and contaminate future firings.)

1112°F) metal can easily be used in the same way as with pigment lustres. The glaze doesn't soften enough to allow any fusing to the kiln shelf, so bowls and tiles can be placed upside down on the mesh or, as in Fig. F11, leant up against a prop. A vase can also be laid down on its side to encourage more fuming on one side than another.

It is important that the mesh is not too close to the fuming point, or matt areas will develop. I use a spoon wired onto a rod to introduce the chlorides, as I found I had more control of placement than when wrapping up the chlorides in paper and throwing them into the kiln. As with other lustre firings you have to go through your movements first mentally, before starting the kiln. Turn off the burners and close the damper. Then make sure you have easy access for placing the chlorides in the position you want, and consider how you are going to access the inside of the kiln to do this. Do all these actions before starting to fire, so that the process is already familiar when the time comes actually to fume the kiln. **Opening a kiln door at this temperature (around 550–600°C/1022–1112°f)) is quite safe if you take the proper safety precautions: face mask, fume mask, leather gloves and good protective clothing, wearing natural fibres like wool.** The kiln door doesn't need to open fully – this will expose you to unnecessary heat exposure and will

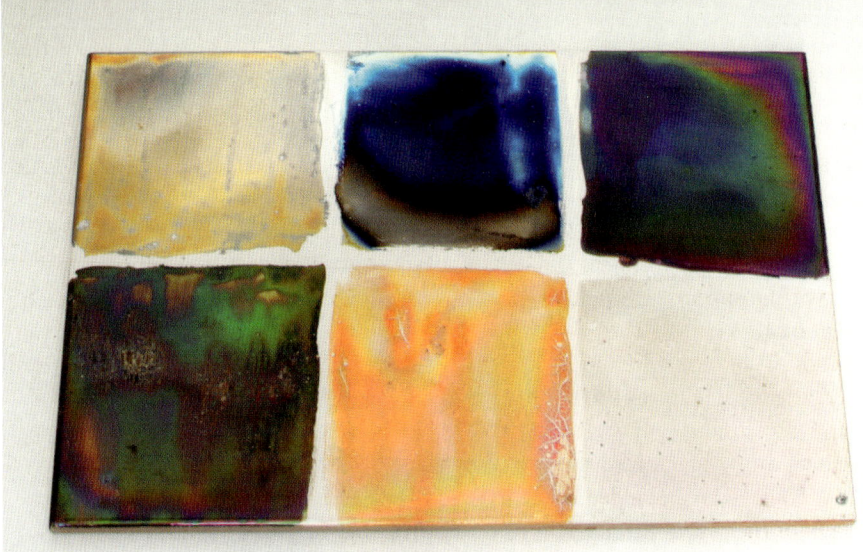

Fig. F11: Fumed resin lustres on a tin-glazed earthenware tile.

Fumed resin lustres on tile in Fig. F11

Uranium resin lustre	Platinum resin lustre (commercial)	Cobalt resin lustre
Gold lustre	Iron resin lustre	Bismuth resin lustre

most likely cause a pot to crack. Instead open it just wide enough to allow you to insert the spoon with the chloride. Once you have closed the door, white chlorine fumes will start to come out of any place they can – this can continue for 10 to 15 minutes, depending how much salt you have used, so move away.

I generally use one dessert spoon of chloride for a 3–4cu. ft kiln. Less is sometimes better if you want to create less dynamic surfaces. Variations can be experimented with – for example, the fuming bowl can be placed at the front of the kiln on the first shelf. Note that when fuming agent is placed into the kiln the damper should be left very slightly ajar so as to allow vapour flow across the pots, creating a pattern across the surface.

One other technique is to mix the chlorides in a water solution and spray the solution into the kiln via the spyhole. The mix turns to vapour immediately. **Please make sure you are wearing a proper mask, with a cartridge designed for vapour and eyewear.**

In the fuming firing I find it is best to fire higher by 100°C (180°F), as this makes sure there is heat throughout the kiln that reaches all the ware. A pyrometer which reads the temperature at its tip should be placed in an open space where heat can easily be measured, and not in the middle of the pack or lower down in the kiln. Fire high, turn off the burners and close the damper. Wait until the kiln has cooled to the temperature at which you are going to fume, then open the kiln slightly and (or through the spy hole) introduce the chlorides. Finally, close up the kiln and withdraw to an area out of range of any escaping gas.

You can draw a test ring to see how the fuming developed, and reheat the kiln if you want a second fuming. For added effect on the work, if the flue is left with a small opening when fuming takes place, the movement of the vapour through the kiln can give an added effect to the surface, though a larger amount of chloride may need to be added to compensate for the loss of fumes out of the flue. All these are variations that you can try. There are some people who like to reduce immediately after fuming, but with stannous chloride I find this isn't necessary: just close down the kiln and leave to cool. With silver chloride, however, post-reduction fuming does help, I find, to develop the lustre surface from the silver.

Fuming resin lustres

You can also fume resin lustres, creating an added surface result giving a rainbow of colours. First decorate the work with resin lustre then fire to 740°C (1364°F), then allow it to cool before fuming it with stannous chloride at 550°C (1022°F). Resin lustres such as gold, cobalt and platinum give the biggest reaction. The gold lustre produces varied colours, described variously as cantharides green, gold and blue. This in combination with various glazes leads to a large window for further development. The platinum surface turns an electric blue where the uranium lustre has taken on a silver tone, but there is no real reaction with the bismuth lustre.

Any resin lustre can be tried, as well as a further firing for pigment lustres that have already been fired. The lustre surface will not be lost if you refire them to a lower temperature; instead further enhancement of the surface will take place from the fuming.

Alan Watt takes a different approach to fuming, which for him takes place during the blackware firing itself. The mix of copper and borax is thrown into the flame path at the burner port. A percentage of the copper is volatilized and deposited on the surface of the unglazed work. Note that in the technique Alan describes there is no dark black smoke given off, as on reaching temperature the kiln is sealed completely, before oil is dripped into the kiln through a small pipe introduced through the wall at the base of the kiln. The rest of the

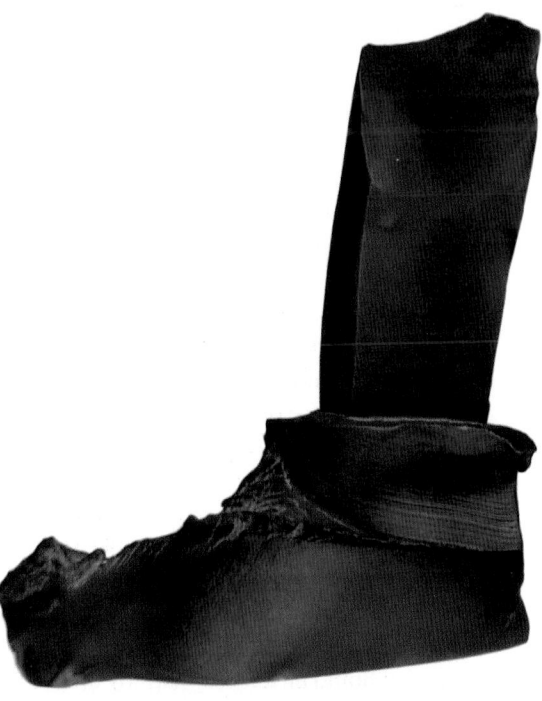

Fig. F12: *Heeled Blue Pinnacle* by Alan Watt, 2008. Fumed blackware with copper and borax.

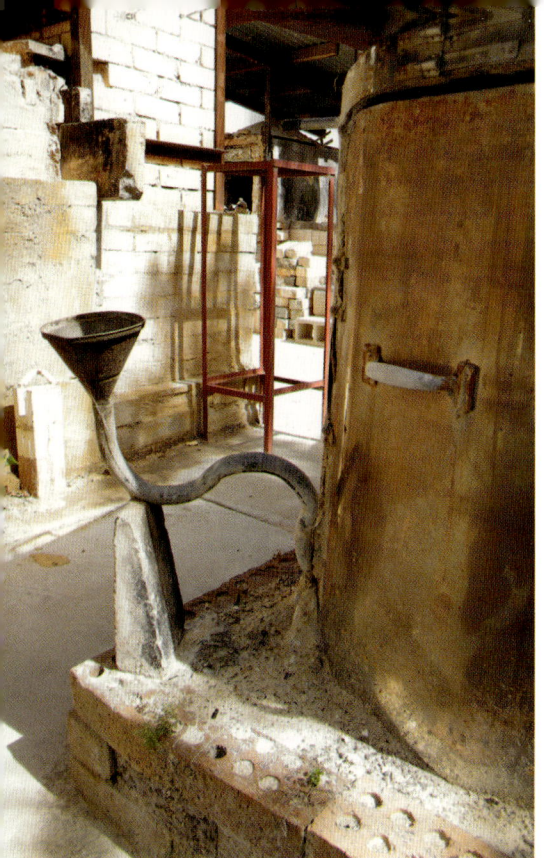

Fig. F13: Alan Watt's kiln, with an S-bend in the pipe to create an oil lock to stop air getting into the kiln. The burner port can be seen to the right of the pipe at the base and the oil-drum tap that drips oil into the funnel.

A separate outdoor kiln capable of being completely sealed is essential for this process. The floor will eventually be covered in a soda or copper glaze after repeated use.

The process is to stack the bisque works on shelves towards the back wall and at the end of the horizontal flame path which travels beneath the shelves (i.e. with the flames not quite touching the ware at the front of the packing), and fire up to about 700°C (1292°F). This is a simple updraught kiln with burners coming in at the base in the centre of the kiln. The kiln is also top-loading, with old shelves and bricks used to cover the top of the kiln (where the work is also packed in), and a flue opening left at the burner end, which is sealed when the oil is begun. A fibre or cast roof can be made for more permanent use.

Alan's kiln is rectangular in shape (two and a half bricks wide, three to four long, and six to seven high). The first shelf inside is raised off the floor by 15–18cm (5–6 in.). This gives space for the flame path and fuming agents. There is also a ramp leading from a shelf at a 45-degree angle, propped against the wall opposite the burner opening. This is there to help deflect the flame and heat upwards rather than it just hitting the wall.

At 700°C (1292°F) a dry mix of copper carbonate, borax and sodium bicarbonate in equal proportions is thinly spread along the length of a right-angle-folded cardboard strip, and introduced into the kiln through the burner port and alongside the flame path. The mix immediately bursts into a volatile gas carrying the 'fuming' components through the kiln. This is repeated at regular intervals until just under 1000°C (1832°F) is reached. The burner is

kiln is sealed over with slurry to stop any oxygen getting in. There is no set amount of oil, so keep dripping it in until the temperature has dropped below 600°C (1112°F). If a whiff of smoke escapes, the flue hole is covered with clay/sand slurry. You are aiming to have a totally sealed kiln on cooling.

Alan Watt writes of his work in a letter to me: 'The surface of the work seems to pick up the lustre better if it is smooth and of a fine body. Terra sigillata or burnished surfaces seem the best. The work should be bisqued to less than 1000°C (1832°F).'

then turned off and the same process is repeated as the kiln drops in temperature to 700°C (1292°F).

At this point a right-angled bent steel pipe is introduced at floor level beneath the main body of work, and every opening is sealed with a clay and sand mix in the ratio of 1:4. Then waste oil (used car oil) is slowly trickled into the pipe and feeds into the kiln, producing dense smoke (heavy reduction). It is best to have an S-bend smoke seal at the feeder end to prevent smoke escaping the feeder pipe (Fig. F15). To save having to constantly feed the oil at regular intervals by hand, a drum with a simple tap can provide a regulated stream of oil (about 2mm diameter) entering the kiln. It is important to be able to control the flow of oil: initially a higher flow then diminishing to just a trickle, you keep dripping oil in until the temperature has dropped below 600°C (1112°F). This can take approximately 3–4 hours for a small kiln.

If there are any small gaps in the kiln, these will be revealed by escaping smoke and should be immediately covered with a mixture of slurry made from clay and sand. Do this by painting over the gap with the fluid clay and sand mix. The carbonization of the kiln should continue until cool enough to prevent any re-oxidation occurring. Although Alan has attempted to exactly repeat the process on dozens of occasions, there have been times when little or no lustre results (See Fig. F12.) He has no idea why.

There is another variation on fuming the work. The fuming agent is placed into the kiln at the beginning of the firing, as the temperature increases the chloride fumes, and with the gas flow in the kiln the fumes are taken across and around the work. In Fig. F16 (p. 138) a vase has been fumed by placing a small amount of stannous chloride near its base – only a few grams are needed. The glaze LG7, first fired in a glaze firing, is then refired with a reducing cycle beginning at 730°C (1346°F) and dropping to 630°C (1166°F). As you can see, the stannous chloride has fumed and been taken by the flame/gas path across the vase, fuming and changing the glaze result.

Fuming is a technique that can be used to change both stoneware and earthenware glazes, including gloss, matt and unglazed surfaces, and to interact with and change lustre glazes and resin lustres. Pigment lustres can also be fumed: after your pigment lustre cycles you can fume the undecorated areas (where there is no pigment).

I have come to think of fuming as the cherry on the cake, the little bit extra that can be added to all firings, as demonstrated by Janet Mansfield and John Dermer's salt firings, where fuming takes place upon the cooling of the firing and not as a separate firing. All glaze firing can be fumed on the way down to achieve this form of lustre. A separate third firing just for fuming the work can also be arranged and stacked, to establish a control effect over and around the work.

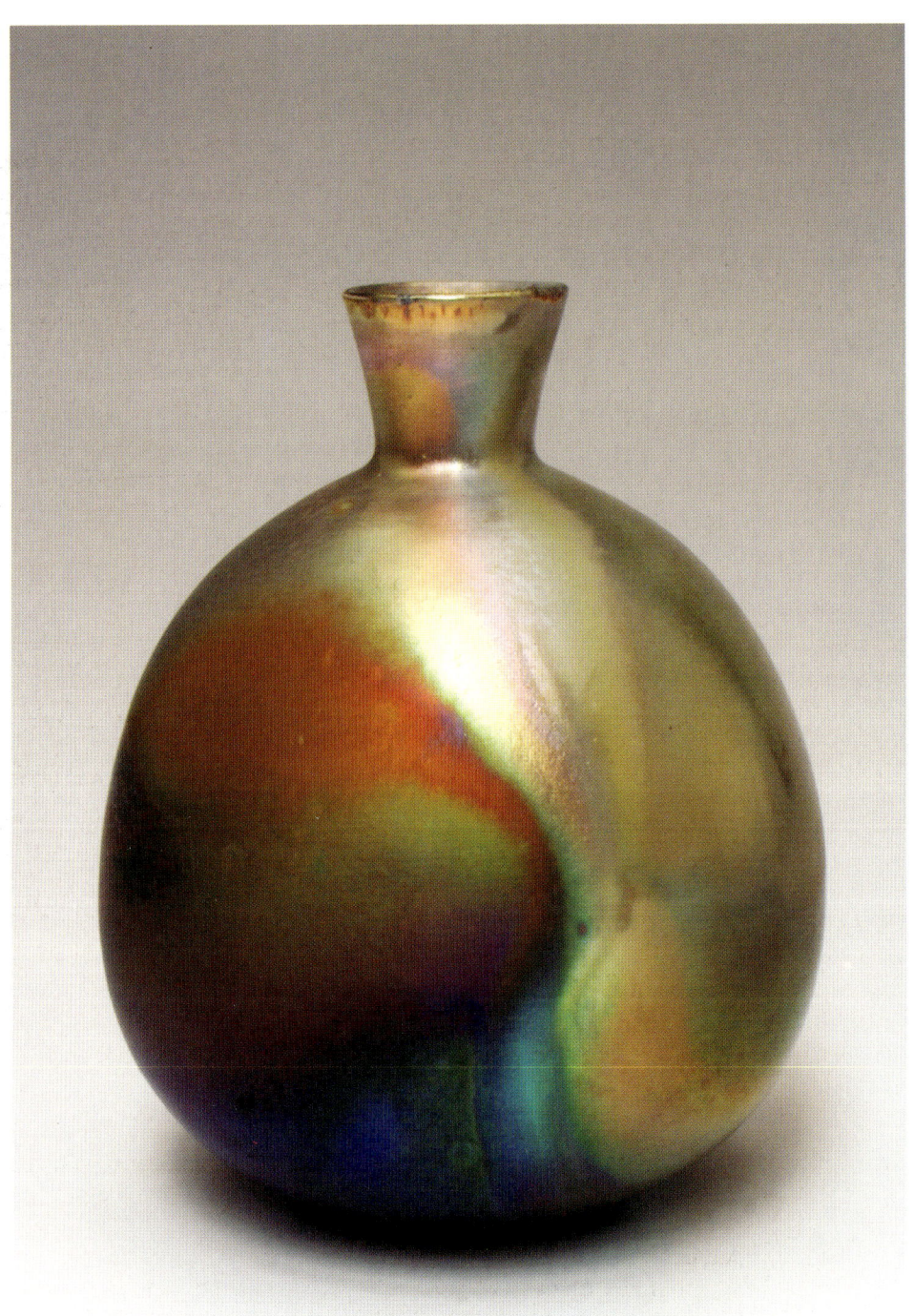

Fig. F14: Fumed lustre-glazed vase by Greg Daly. Lustre glaze LG7 fumed with stannous chloride. Ht: 24cm (9½in.). *Photo by Greg Daly.*

Bibliography

Caiger-Smith, Alan, *Tin-Glaze Pottery in Europe and the Islamic World: The Tradition of 1000 Years in Maiolica, Faience and Delftware*, Faber & Faber, 1973.

Caiger-Smith, Alan, *Lustre Pottery*, Faber & Faber, 1985.

Catleugh, Jon, *William DeMorgan Tiles*, Trefoil Books London, 1983.

Charleston, Robert. *World Ceramics*, Hamlyn, 1968.

Clement Massier: Master of Iridescense, Jason Jacque Gallery, New York, 2006.

Clinton, Margery, *Lustres*, Kangaroo Press, 1991.

Cooper, Emmanuel. *A History of World Pottery*, Batsford, London, 1988.

Csenkey, Eva, Gyugyi, Laslo and Harris, Eva, *Zsolnay: the Gyugi collection*, Helikon, 2006.

Csenkey, Eva and Steinert, Agota (editors), *Hungarian Ceramics from the Zsolnay Manufactory*, Yale University Press, New Haven, London 2002.

Cullen, W. Parmalee, *Ceramic Glazes*, Cahners Books, Boston, 1973.

Franchett, Louis, *Ceramic Decoration – Its Evolution and Its Application*, Washington Government Printing Office, 1910.

Lightbovn, Ronald and Caiger-Smith, Alan, *The Three Books of the Potters Art, Piccolpasso*, Scolar Press, London, 1980.

Lomax, Abraham, *Royal Lancastrian Pottery 1900–1938*, Lomax, Ainsworth House, Bolton, 1957.

Mason, Robert B. J., *Shine Like the Sun*, Mazda Publishers Inc., Royal Ontario Museum, 2004.

Nelson, Glen, *Ceramics – A Potter's Handbook*,1971, Holt, Rinehart, Winston, 1984.

Péres Camos, Josep et al., *La cerámica de refejo metálico en Manises*, 1850 –1960, Museo de Cerámica De Manises, Spain, 1998.

Ray, Anthony, *Spanish Pottery 1248–1898*, V & A Publications, 2000.

Rudolf Hainbach, *Pottery Decoration, A Description of The Principal*, Scott, Greenwood & Son, London, 1924.

Sanders, Herbert, *Glazes for special Effects*, Herbert Sanders Publishers/Watson-Gupthill Publications, New York, 1974.

Shaw, Kenneth. *Ceramic Colours and Pottery Decoration*, MacClaren & Sons, 1962.

Singer, Felix and Singer, Sonja, *Industrial Ceramics*, Chapman and Hall, 1963.

Spanish Pottery 1248–1898, by Anthony Ray

Stefanov and Batschwavov, *Ceramic Glazes/Keramik-Glasuren*, Bauverlag GmbH. Wiesbaden and Berlin, 1988.

Sutton Taylor Lustre, Catalogue, essay by Moira Vincentelli, Hart Gallery, 2009.

Watson, Oliver, *Ceramics from Islamic Lands*, Kuwait National Museum, Thames & Hudson, 2004.

Watson, Oliver, *Persian Lustreware*, Faber & Faber, 1985.

Articles

Ceramic Review – Numbers: 61, 82, 90

Colomban and Truong. 'Non-destructive Raman study of the glazing technique in lustre potteries and faience (9-14th centuries): silver ions, nanoclusters, microstructure and processing'. *Journal of Raman Spectroscopy*, 2004, 35–195/207.

Malins and Tonge. 'Reduction processes in the formation of lustre glazed ceramics' *Thermochimica acta*, 1999, 340/341.

Molera, Bayes, Roura, Crespo and Pradell. 'Key Parameters in the Production of Medival Lustre Colours and Shines' *American Ceramic Society Journal*. 90 7 2245/2254.

Molera, Mesquida, Perez-Arantegui, Pradell and Vendrell. 'Lustre Recipes from a Medieval Workshop in Paterna'. *Archaometry* 43–4, 2001.

Padeletti and Fermo. 'Italian Renaissance and Hispano-Moresque lustre-decorated majolicas: imitation cases of Hispano-Moresque style in central Italy'. *Applied Physics* A 77-125/133, 2003.

Pradell, Molera, Roque, Vendrell-Saz, Smith, Pantos and Crespo.'Ionic-Exchange Mechanism in the Formation of Medival Lustre Decoration' *American Ceramic Society Journal* 88 5 1281/1289.

Lustre-glazed vase with silver and copper decoration by Greg Daly, 2010. Ht: 28cm (11 in.), dia: 29cm (11¼ in.). *Photo by Stuart Hay.*

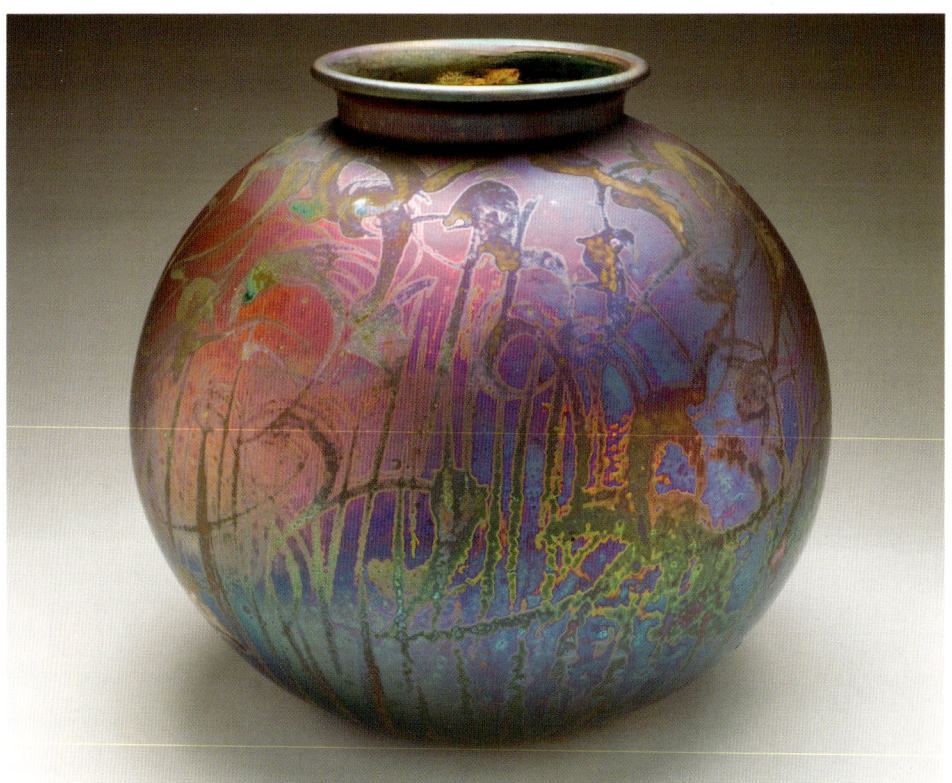

Chemical suppliers

Silver, bismuth and cobalt nitrates need to be sourced from chemical companies in your own country as chemicals such as silver nitrate cannot be posted in most countries. Google-searching for a silver nitrate supplier in your country is a good beginning or look in Yellow Pages or similar. Copper, iron sulfates can easily be obtained from garden centres. Resin (or Rosin) for resinate lustres can be purchased from art supply shops used for printing or music shops (rosin is used for violin bows). Most pottery suppliers don't carry these materials.

UK

Potterycrafts
Campbell Road
Stoke-on-Trent
Staffordshire ST4 4ET
Tel: +44 (0)1782 745000
Fax: +44 (0)1782 746000
www.potterycrafts.co.uk
Commercial (resin) lustres

ReAgent Chemical Services Ltd
18 Aston Fields Road
Whitehouse Industrial Estate
Runcorn, Cheshire
WA7 3DL
Tel: 0800 990 3258 (UK only)
www.reagent.co.uk/
Silver nitrate

The Potters Connection Limited
(online only)
(Stoke-on-Trent)
Tel: +44 (0)1782 598729
Fax: +44 (0)1782 765833
www.pottersconnection.co.uk/
Silver nitrate, bismuth nitrate.
commercial lustres

USA/CANADA

US Pigments
815 Schneider Drive
South Elgin
IL 60177
Tel: +1 (630) 893-9217
Fax: +1 (630) 339-2644
www.uspigment.com/
Bismuth nitrate, silver nitrate, silver chloride, stannous chloride, burnt umber, cobalt sulphate, copper sulphate, iron sulphate, potassium dichromate.

Laguna Clay (HQ)
14400 Lomitas Avenue
City of Industry, CA 91746
Toll-Free Tel: +1 (800) 4-LAGUNA
Local: +1 (626) 330-0631
Fax: +1 (626) 333-7694
www.lagunaclay.com
Commercial (resin) lustres, burnt umber

Salt Lake Metals
1115 East Brigadoon
Salt Lake City, UT 84117
www.saltlakemetals.com/Silver_Nitrate.htm
Tel: (801)265-8921
Silver nitrate, gold chloride

Del Amo Chemical Company
535 W. 152nd Street
Los Angeles,
California 90248
Phone: +1 310-532-9214
Fax: +1 310-719-1342
www.delamochemical.com
Bismuth nitrate, cobalt nitrate, silver
nitrate, silver chloride, stannous chloride

Coasty Resource Canada (online only)
130-8191 Westminster Highway
Unit 585
Richmond BCV6X 1A7
www.coasty.com
Bismuth oxide, stannous chloride,
gum rosin

AUSTRALIA

Gold Leaf Factory (online/phone only)
Phone: +61 39786 2247
Fax: +61 39785 1145
http://www.goldleaf.com.au/
Burnt sienna, colophony resin

Alpha Chemicals
18 Inman Rd
Cromer, NSW 2099
Tel: +61 (0)2 9982 4622
Fax: +61 (0)2 9982 4399
www.alphachem.com.au
Silver nitrate, bismuth nitrate
stannous chloride, cobalt nitrate

Walker Ceramics
Shop 2/21 Research Drive
Croydon South
Victoria 3136
Tel: +61 (0)3 876 16322
Fax: +61 (0)3 876 16344
www.walkerceramics.com.au/
Commercial (resin) lustres

Ace Chemicals
119a Mooringue Avenue
Camden Park SA 5038
Tel: +61 (0)8 8376 0844
Fax: +61 (0)8 8295 8563
www.acechem.com.au
Bismuth nitrate, silver nitrate, silver
chloride, cobalt nitrate, stannous chloride,
rochelle salt, eucalyptus oil, lavender oil, liver
of sulphur, gold chloride, iron chloride

HUNGARY

Budapest Keramia
1194, Budapest Fadrusz J. u.2.
Tel: +361358-14-10
Fax: +361358-14-09
www.bpkeramia.hu

Interkeram
Interkerám Ltd.
H-6000 Kecskemét
Parasztf iskola 12–16. Pf.: 197
Tel: +3676481-440/ 414-953
www.interkeram.hu

Orton cones

	Large					Small		
Cone No.	Bending temp. Heating rate 60°C/hr (108°F)		Bending temp. Heating rate 150°C/hr (270°F)		Cone No.	Bending temp. Heating rate 300°C/hr (540°F)	
	°C	°F	°C	°F		°C	°F
021	602	1116	614	1137	021	643	1189
020	625	1157	635	1175	020	666	1231
019	668	1234	683	1261	019	723	1333
018	696	1285	717	1323	018	752	1386
017	727	1341	747	1377	017	784	1443
016	764	1407	792	1458	016	825	1517
015	790	1454	804	1479	015	843	1549
014	834	1533	838	1540	014	870	1596
013	849	1560	852	1566	013	880	1615
012	866	1591	884	1623	012	900	1650
011	886	1627	895	1641	011	915	1680
010	887	1629	905	1661	010	919	1686
09	915	1679	923	1693	09	955	1751
08	945	1733	955	1751	08	983	1801
07	973	1783	984	1803	07	1008	1846
06	991	1816	999	1830	06	1023	1873
05	1031	1888	1046	1915	05	1062	1944
04	1050	1922	1060	1940	04	1098	2008
03	1086	1987	1101	2014	03	1131	2068
02	1101	2014	1120	2048	02	1148	2098
01	1117	2043	1137	2079	01	1178	2152
1	1136	2077	1154	2109	1	1179	2154
2	1142	2088	1162	2124	2	1179	2154
3	1152	2106	1168	2134	3	1196	2185
4	1168	2134	1186	2167	4	1209	2208
5	1177	2151	1196	2185	5	1221	2230
6	1201	2194	1222	2232	6	1255	2291
7	1215	2219	1240	2264	7	1264	2307
8	1236	2257	1263	2305	8	1300	2372
9	1260	2300	1280	2336	9	1317	2403
10	1285	2345	1305	2381	10	1330	2426
11	1294	2361	1315	2399	11	1336	2437
12	1306	2383	1326	2419	12	1355	2471
13	1321	2410	1346	2455			
14	1388	2530	1366	2491			

Temperature conversion chart

°C	°F	°C	°F	°C	°F	°C	°F
0	32	330	626	660	1220	990	1814
10	50	340	644	670	1238	1000	1832
20	68	350	662	680	1256	1010	1850
30	86	360	680	690	1274	1020	1868
40	104	370	698	700	1292	1030	1886
50	122	380	716	710	1310	1040	1904
60	140	390	734	720	1328	1050	1922
70	158	400	752	730	1346	1060	1940
80	176	410	770	740	1364	1070	1958
90	194	420	788	750	1382	1080	1976
100	212	430	806	760	1400	1090	1994
110	230	440	824	770	1418	1100	2012
120	248	450	842	780	1436	1110	2030
130	266	460	860	790	1454	1120	2048
140	284	470	878	800	1472	1130	2066
150	302	480	896	810	1490	1140	2084
160	320	490	914	820	1508	1150	2102
170	338	500	932	830	1526	1160	2120
180	356	510	950	840	1544	1170	2138
190	374	520	968	850	1562	1180	2156
200	392	530	986	860	1580	1190	2174
210	410	540	1004	870	1598	1200	2192
220	428	550	1022	880	1616	1210	2210
230	446	560	1040	890	1634	1220	2228
240	464	570	1058	900	1652	1230	2246
250	482	580	1076	910	1670	1240	2264
260	500	590	1094	920	1688	1250	2282
270	518	600	1112	930	1706	1260	2300
280	536	610	1130	940	1724	1270	2318
290	554	620	1148	950	1742	1280	2336
300	572	630	1166	960	1760	1290	2354
310	590	640	1184	970	1778	1300	2372
320	608	650	1202	980	1796	1310	2390

Analysis of frits used

Frit	Na_2O	K_2O	CaO	PbO	Al_2O_3	B_2O_3	SiO_2
Lead Bisilicate	0.97			64.92	2.02		32.10
Soft sodium borosilicate ferro frit 3110/ 4110 (depending on country)	15.31	2.54	6.13		4.20	2.68	69.15

Index

Abul'I Quasim 11, 14
alkaline glazes 31, 34,
Arabian/Persian Lustres 14, 29

Bamford, Rod 64, 66
Bennett, Catherine 80, 81
bismuth 43, 47, 95, 96, 101, 104
bismuth 66, 67, 69, 74, 75, 78, 81, 82
burnt umber 40, 42, 44

Caiger-Smith, Alan 13, 15, 27, 40, 42,
    44, 45, 54, 60
calcining 48, 49
Chiswell-Jones, Jonathan 9, 59,
chlorides 123-125
Cizer, Sevim 92, 119
Clinton, Margery 57
cobalt 95, 97
Conerry, Bob 39, 44, 57, 58
cones 51
copper 13, 40, 42-47, 49, 50, 66, 67,
    69, 75, 78, 81, 82

Daly, Greg 62, 93, 105, 114, 115, 121,
    136,
DeMorgan, William 12, 18, 20, 21
Dermer, John 126, 127
draw rings 29, 55, 61, 62,
durta 16

eucalyptus 98

Fatmid Dynasty 14
frits 31, 34, 36,
fuming 24, 123-135

gerstley borate 72
gold 95, 100, 102, 104, 108
Gubbio 16, 18, 20
gum arabic 41,

Hainbach, Rudolf 96, 101
Halmos, Ferenc 63, 86, 91
Hispano-Moresque 15

lavender oil 98
Laverick, Tony 116, 117, 118
lead glazes 31, 36, 95
line blend 31, 34,

Mansfield, Janet 122, 126
Massier, Clement 12, 18, 19, 20, 24, 92
Massier, Jerome 19
Mastro Giorgio 12, 17
Mincham, Jeff 128

Nanotechnolgy 13, 26

ochre 40. 44 47

Parmelee 97
Peascod, Alan 33, 103
Piccolpasso, Cipriano 12, 53,
pigment lustres 29, 38, 40-42, 51
Pilkington Lancastrian Pottery 18, 24,
    25
pyrometer 50, 51

reduction 21, 29, 34, 36, 47, 50, 56-
    62, 65, 72, 76, 84-92
resin/resinate lustres 25, 26, 95, 96,
    132
resist 113
Rich, Mary 109, 110, 118

Sicard, Jacques 12
silver 13, 30, 40, 42-47, 50, 66, 67,
    69, 74, 75, 78, 81, 82
Spanish lustre 14
stannous chloride 95, 104, 124-131,
stencilling 115

Swindell, Geoffery 94, 99, 100

Taylor, Sutton 27, 45, 54, 87
Tiffany, Louis 24

vinegar 41, 42, 48, 49

Watt, Alan 133, 134
Wedgwood 22
Wheeldon, John 111, 112,
Woods, Beatrice 89

Zsolnay 21, 22, 23, 117